HISTORY'S
WORST
DECISIONS

and the People Who Made Them

HISTORY'S WORST DECISIONS

and the People Who Made Them

Stephen Weir

METRO BOOKS

NEW YORK

For Jack, who was delivered just before this book

CONTENTS

INTRODUCTION

History is strewn with mistakes. Many of them were made by well-intentioned people who were bright, intelligent, and capable, but who just made the wrong decision. Many fall into the simplest category of error—they took Route A instead of Route B. And a lot of those decisions "seemed like a good idea at the time." However, there were also some monumentally stupid decisions made, and this book takes a journey through the sheer idiocy of humanity. These are not honest blunders but really, really dumb ones; not just poor choices but choices with very nasty implications for the rest of us. Inclusion in *History's Worst Decisions and the People Who Made Them* demands idiocy that exacted a very high price, in lives or livelihoods, or sometimes even the end of countries and dynasties.

A book such as this needs operating principles. It's too easy to blame sheer stupidity. No one that dumb really gets much chance to make dumb decisions that truly matter (royal families and heirs or heiresses excluded). Many are impelled by emotions outside their control to lose whatever sense they may once have had, and Pope Gregory the Great, in the late sixth century, kindly categorized these types of emotions as the Seven Deadly Sins, of which you will find many examples in the following pages. But it would be foolish to believe that only the wicked are stupid. So you will also find examples of each of the Cardinal Virtues of Faith, Hope, and Charity, impelling their followers to utmost folly.

From Adam and Eve deciding to go for the apple, to those Asian governments who until the end of 2004 decided that tsunamis, which have occurred regularly every hundred years or so, just weren't worth the extra expense of early warning sensors; from the Crusaders traveling thousands of medieval miles to join up with the army of a great Christian leader who didn't exist, to Gerald Ratner who destroyed his own company in a moment, we meet some of history's famous idiots, and a few more obscure ones besides.

Those readers who welcome the opportunity to relive the idiotic mistakes of the past may be interested in the Santayana Historical Re-Enactment Society, whose members actually re-enact great idiotic events of history in the hope that people will awake to the famous phrase of the man who inspired it, George Santayana: "Those who cannot remember the past are condemned to repeat it."

MOTIVATION

anger
charity
envy
faith
gluttony
greed
hope
lust
pride
sloth

IN THE BEGINNING: ADAM AND EVE

4004 BCE, Ussher–Lightfoot chronology

Main Culprits: Adam and Eve

Damage Done: Original sin

Why: The essential folly of humankind starts here with the original humans

Public Domain

Of Man's First Disobedience, and the Fruit
Of that Forbidden Tree whose mortal taste
Brought Death into the World, and all our woe,
With loss of Eden ...

John Milton, *Paradise Lost* i.1–4

Unto the woman He said, I will greatly multiply thy sorrow and thy conception; in sorrow thou shalt bring forth children; and thy desire shall be to thy husband, and he shall rule over thee. And unto Adam He said, Because thou hast hearkened unto the voice of thy wife, and hast eaten of the tree, of which I commanded thee, saying, Thou shalt not eat of it: cursed is the ground for thy sake; in sorrow shalt thou eat of it all the days of thy life; Thorns also and thistles shall it bring forth to thee; and thou shalt eat the herb of the field; In the sweat of thy face shalt thou eat bread, till thou return unto the ground; for out of it wast thou taken: for dust thou art, and unto dust shalt thou return.

Genesis 3:16–3:19, King James Bible

The original idiots, the ones responsible, purportedly, for all the idiocy that came after them, including those lambasted in these pages, were the two first humans: Adam and Eve. Many of the prime motivations that we shall see throughout this book come into play here: envy; gluttony; lust; greed for knowledge and whatever else lay beyond; certainly a strong element of faith that everything would be just fine, even if orders were disobeyed. Not for nothing is the story of Adam and Eve the elemental creation myth.

The essential parable of Adam and Eve—God creates Man, God creates Woman from Man, Man meets Woman, Evil makes Man want Woman, Man and Woman fall from Paradise—recurs in the creation myths of many religions and cultures in one form or another.

Oddly enough, scientists using DNA analysis have found that were indeed two individuals whom we can all consider to be our common ancestors. All women receive their mitochondrial DNA from their mothers, and it is possible, working back, to find a common female ancestor, an earth mother, who lived around 200,000 years ago, and is in essence, give or take a few generations, your 10,000-times great grandmother. Science knows her as "Mitochondrial Eve." Similar research using Y chromosomes places "Y-Chromosomal Adam" only around 90,000 years ago. Although not the first humans, like the Adam and Eve claimed by the Abrahamic religions, "Mitochondrial Eve" and "Y-Chromosomal Adam" are considered, as are their mythical counterparts, to be our common ancestors.

ALL ABOUT EVE

There is also a strong element of misogyny in the whole myth, which essentially blames Eve for the Fall. She is tempted by Satan in the form of a serpent, and talks Adam into trying the Forbidden Fruit. Adam— the good, if slightly naïve gardener who has been busy naming flora and fauna—suddenly realizes that he is naked, she is naked, and the good times are over (or just starting, depending on your point of view). Satan gets well and truly into the picture, the Bible, the Talmud, and the Koran get a proper villain, and there's always someone to blame for everything thereafter.

The story is fundamentally the same in all the Abrahamic religions: God created Adam, either from the earth or from clay (*Adam* in Arabic means "earthy" or "red"). Then Eve is formed from his body—*Eve* derives from the Hebrew *chayah* ("to live"). Different interpretations present the serpent as simply God's test of his new creations, or as Satan—a Fallen Angel angry at the appearance of this new creature and God's insistence that man is in his own image and must be bowed down to. Some sort of fruit is always part of the story, though the apple as such does not appear in the Book of Genesis.

Greek mythology presents a similar story, albeit in many different forms. Having charged Prometheus with the task of creating mankind, which he fashioned out of clay, Zeus subsequently punished him for stealing fire and giving it to the mortals. Prometheus was chained to a rock on a mountain and had his liver eaten by an eagle, only for it to heal overnight, before being eaten again the next day. Man's punishment, however, took the graceful but deadly form of Pandora, the first woman, who was created by Hephaestus at Zeus' command. Like Eve she introduces suffering into the human story, although this time the conduit is a jar containing all the evils of the world. Again, like Adam and Eve, she was unable to withstand temptation and opened the jar, unleashing every form of evil, with the exception of hopelessness which remained within. Again the mortal world is changed forever by the loss of Paradise.

ADAM AND EVE
A mural depicting the story of Adam and Eve on the side of a house in Ardez, Switzerland.

Many locations have been claimed for the Garden of Eden. The Bible gives only the description and the hint that it lies at the confluence of four rivers—the Tigris, Euphrates, Pison, and Gihon—though unfortunately, the latter two are no more to be found. The general area is typically thought to be somewhere in the Persian Gulf, or Anatolia in Turkey. Some have claimed that after the last Ice Age, as the waters rose, the Pison and Gihon, and the fertile lands they created, disappeared under the Persian Gulf, and it was the loss of this Paradise that resulted in the myth. Indeed, both the words *Eden* and *Adam* are suggested to mean, in a pre-Sumerian language, "fertile plain" and "settlement," suggesting clearly that it was the loss of the land, attributed to God's anger, that led to a literal expulsion from Eden; and moreover, the end of an easy life, resident on fertile land that provided ample wealth, and the transition to a more complicated and nomadic hunter-gatherer existence.

However, Elvy E. Callaway, of Bristol, Florida, claimed that humankind was created on the banks of Florida's Apalachicola River. Callaway studied the matter for 75 years and, as his proof, cites Genesis 2:10, which reads: "And a river went out of Eden to water the Garden; and from thence it was parted and became four heads." He maintained that the Apalachicola was the only four-headed river system in the world. He also equated the Bible's mention of the gopher-wood tree with *Torreya taxifolia*, an evergreen conifer that grows only in the Florida Panhandle; however, even those who take the Garden of Eden literally debate the meaning of the word "gopher" and the exact species that it relates to. And to undermine such lofty speculations further, no one who ever saw the Australian comedian Paul Hogan's comedy show can forget his brilliant proof that the Garden of Eden is actually to be found in Dubbo, New South Wales.

Wherever the Garden of Eden was, or was not, Adam and Eve were most certainly not allowed back in. Once cast out from Paradise, they did what most couples do in such dire circumstances and started a family—a dysfunctional one at that, with one of their sons, Cain, killing his brother Abel. And there is still the unexplained mystery of where their children's spouses came from. The consequences of original sin? Everything that follows. . .

AND A RIVER WENT OUT OF EDEN TO WATER THE GARDEN; AND FROM THENCE IT WAS PARTED AND BECAME FOUR HEADS.

GENESIS 2:10

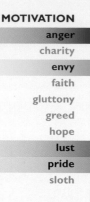

MOTIVATION

anger
charity
envy
faith
gluttony
greed
hope
lust
pride
sloth

MENELAUS AND HIS LOST WIFE
1190–1180 BCE

Main Culprit: Menelaus (c.1280–1150 BCE)

Damage Done: Destruction of the city of Troy; two-decade-long abandonment of Greek territory

Why: Chasing a lost wife halfway across the known world

So far there had been nothing worse than woman-stealing on both sides; but for what happened next the Greeks were seriously to blame; for it was the Greeks who were, in a military sense, the aggressors. Abducting young women, in their opinion, is not, indeed, a lawful act; but it is stupid after the event to make a fuss about avenging it. The only sensible thing is to take no notice; for it is obvious that no young woman allows herself to be abducted if she does not wish to be.

Herodotus, *The Histories*

Public Domain

The story of Helen of Troy, first related by the great Greek poet Homer in the *Iliad*, and still the subject of fanciful reinterpretation—now cinematic rather than bardic—was widely disbelieved for many centuries. Homer's version is full of copulating gods disguised as animals, and dubious beauty contests, but there is little question that the later Greek bards and historians were describing events that at least in part took place, as the archaeological evidence suggests.

Homer wrote the *Iliad* some five centuries after the events it describes. It would hardly be surprising if he appealed to contemporary sensibilities and introduced the gods into the story to spice it up a little. It would have been scarcely more of a stretch to accept that Helen was the daughter of Zeus than it is for us to accept Brad Pitt as Achilles.

The saga of the abduction of Helen and the subsequent Trojan Wars remains one of the finest examples of the dangers of lust. On the whole, history has shown it unwise to be a guest in a man's house and take his wife away with you. We add to this the categorical double idiocies of anger and envy, compounded when Menelaus insisted on old treaty rights and dragged his entire nation and those of his neighbors on the revenge mission that was the siege of Troy. It took many of them the best part of 20 years to wage war and get back home, and it actually killed most of them, leaving their homelands and families to rack and ruin—barely surviving, records suggest, raiding parties and perhaps some sort of natural disaster.

There have been attempts to explain the causes of the war—generally agreed as lasting ten years—as economic or political. Troy did indeed command the Dardanelles (the importance of which will be seen again on pages 116–19) from its hilltop, and was a reasonably rich trading city as an entry point for Black Sea. However, there is plenty of evidence that the Greeks didn't even know where it was—they were just following Helen's trail. And they certainly didn't gain much by hanging about for ten years and then burning the place to the ground. The reasons for the war remain a mystery, but the accounts, from Homer and others, suggest it deserves its place in these pages.

Certainly, plenty of important people in ancient history believed in the legend. Xerxes, Alexander the Great and Julius Caesar all reputedly visited the site of Troy to pay their respects to the great heroes and absorb some of their bravery. Perhaps because the war was fought for ideological reasons and not out of the more pragmatic desire for conquest or trade, the sheer bravery of the combatants has a resonance through the ages that far outweighs more tawdry conflicts.

It is indeed clear that the young nobleman Paris took Helen, the beautiful wife of Menelaus, away with him. His mother Hecuba, the queen of Troy, dreamed that she would give birth to a flaming torch, a dream which was interpreted by the seer Aesacus as a prophecy that the baby would destroy his own homeland. Following the birth of the child, Hecuba found herself unable to kill the baby herself, and King Priam asked his chief herdsman Agelaus to leave his son on a mountainside to die. Paris was, however, suckled by a she-bear and, upon finding the infant still alive nine days later, Agelaus relented and raised the child as his own.

HECUBA, THE QUEEN OF TROY, DREAMED THAT SHE WOULD GAVE BIRTH TO A FLAMING TORCH, A DREAM WHICH WAS INTERPRETED BY THE SEER AESACUS AS A PROPHECY THAT THE BABY WOULD DESTROY HIS OWN HOMELAND.

Paris grew up to become the most beautiful young man in antiquity and reclaimed his position in Troy. According to Homer, he was pulled into an argument between three goddesses over who was the most beautiful, and had to present a golden apple to the one he chose. Each offered him glittering prizes, but he picked Aphrodite, Goddess of Love, who bribed him with the greatest beauty of the age, Helen. The losers, though, were largely blamed for the disasters that followed.

Even if you don't buy the goddesses' revenge story, the idiocy displayed by Menelaus in chasing across the Aegean to a place the Greeks had never heard of takes some explaining. For one thing, Menelaus was clearly not an especially inspiring man. He only got his kingdom in the first place by marrying Helen, and barely managed to get the Greek fleet under way by persuading his brother Agamemnon, king of Mycenae and of all the Greeks, to sacrifice his own daughter Iphigeneia in order to appease the wrath of the goddess Artemis. Several kings feigned madness or pretended to be women to evade their obligations to his cause; and while the scribes wrote plenty about Agamemnon, about the brave Achilles, about the fair Helen, and about the peripatetic Odysseus, Menelaus, who just seems to have been "ticked off" that his wife had been stolen, inspired barely a word.

The tale of the war barely needs repeating. Menelaus finally set sail with his fleet of 1,000 ships and 100,000 men. They laid siege to Troy for ten mostly fruitless years. The *Iliad* recounts the battles, duels, feuds, interventions by the gods, treacheries, and bravery of those long years. Finally, the Greeks came up with the infamous Trojan Horse, withdrawing their fleet and apparently leaving an offering to the gods. Perhaps they'd poisoned the water too, because it is hard to see anyone falling for the trick, but the Greeks inside the Horse certainly brought the war to a swift conclusion, once the gullible Trojans had brought them within the city walls, torching the city, finding Helen, and then sailing for home. Military historians have rather prosaically suggested that in other wars a similar horse-shaped object was used as a superior battering ram to take down stubborn city gates, but as always, Homer spins a much better story.

THE TROJAN HORSE

Troy was destroyed and many Trojans died for Paris's vainglory. It took Menelaus and Odysseus almost as long to get back to Greece as it did to fight the war. This was fortunate for literature in that the jealousy of Menelaus inspired three major fixtures in the canon of literary masterpieces: the *Iliad*, the *Odyssey*, and Virgil's *Aeneid*. It also gave rise to numerous paintings, sculptures, novelizations, and films.

Helen had a lot to answer for. However, she was taken back by Menelaus, despite the fact that she had four children while in Troy and married Paris's brother after his death. Menelaus dealt harshly with the unfortunate man, and indeed, planned to kill Helen—but by the time they got back to Greece her charms had overwhelmed him again. Apparently they lived happily until Menelaus died of old age, upon which Megapenthes, his illegitimate son, seized the throne and exiled Helen. She sought refuge in Rhodes with Polyxo, purportedly a friend of hers, but also the widow of Tlepolemusa who had died on the first day of fighting on the Trojan beaches. In revenge for Helen's part in her husband's death, Polyxo ordered her maidens to dress as Furies, and they seized Helen and hanged her from a tree.

HELEN WAS TAKEN BACK BY MENELAUS, DESPITE THE FACT THAT SHE HAD FOUR CHILDREN WHILE IN TROY AND MARRIED PARIS'S BROTHER AFTER HIS DEATH.

Only 80 years after the war, it seems that the homelands of most of the Greeks who waged the war were overrun by Doric raiders. Not for the last time, it seems heading overseas for obscure reasons to take over a land you don't know much about is not good for those at home.

HISTORY OR MYTH

Archaeological investigations of the original site of Troy put the date of the war in the thirteenth or twelfth century BCE. It is more or less agreed that Troy was in what is now called Anatolia, south of Istanbul in present-day Turkey, somewhere near the town now known as Hisarlik. Troy seems to have been destroyed around 1180 BCE having stood for at least five centuries. It remained in the realm of myth until the German archaeologist Heinrich Schliemann found it in the late nineteenth century. In his memoirs, Schliemann wrote:

> As soon as I had learnt to speak, my father related to me the great deeds of the Homeric heroes. I loved these stories; they enchanted me and transported me with the highest enthusiasm. The first impressions which a child receives abide with him during his whole life; and, though it was my lot, at the age of fourteen, to be apprenticed in the warehouse of E. Ludwig Holtz in the small town of Fürstenberg in Mecklenburg, instead of following the scientific career for which I felt an extraordinary predisposition, I always retained the same love for the famous men of antiquity which I had conceived for them in my first childhood.

Schliemann left his apprenticeship for St. Petersburg, then traveled to California, becoming a merchant during the Gold Rush. He returned to Europe, making a small fortune as a trader during the Crimean War. Then, armed with millions, he followed his dream, and with the help of the British consul in Turkey and a new Greek wife, set about excavating a hilly area they believed to be the site of Troy. Three years later the excavations had produced more than 8,000 objects and what Schliemann at least felt to be proof that the Trojan War had really happened. Many since have disputed exactly what was found, but the city he excavated is referred to as Troy VII, the seventh major city on the site. It was burned to the ground, probably by Greek invaders.

The last word belongs to Lucian of Samosata, in his wry commentary on lust and where it leads:

> MENIPPUS But show me Helen; I can't pick her out on my own.
>
> HERMES   This skull is Helen.
>
> MENIPPUS Was it for this that the thousand ships were manned from all over Greece; for this so many Greeks and barbarians were killed and so many cities destroyed?

HERMES   Ah, but you never saw the woman alive, Menippus, or you yourself would have said that it was excusable that they "for a long time suffer hardship for a woman like this." [Iliad III, 157] For if one sees flowers that are dried up and faded, they do indeed appear ugly; but when they are in full bloom and color, they are supremely beautiful.

MENIPPUS Well, Hermes, what does surprise me is this; that the Achaeans didn't know what a short-lived thing they fought for, and how soon its beauty would fade.

HERMES   I have no time to moralize with you, Menippus. Choose a place to lie down in, wherever you like; I'm off now to fetch some more dead.

IMPORTANT CITIES OF THE ANCIENT AEGEAN

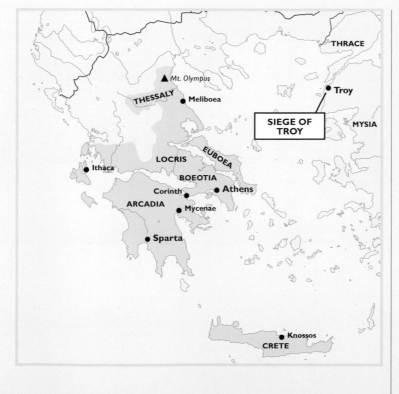

This map shows several of the more important locations in the Ancient Aegean at the time of the Trojan War. These include Mycenae, the seat of Agamemnon, King of all the Greeks; Sparta the city-state of Menelaus and Helen; and Ithaca, Odysseus's kingdom.

MOTIVATION

anger
charity
envy
faith
gluttony
greed
hope
lust
pride
sloth

HANNIBAL AND THE AVALANCHE

Spring, 218 BCE

Main Culprit: Hannibal (247–183 BCE)

Damage Done: Destruction of half his own army, ruining one of the great invasions of history

Why: An act of impetuousness, which caused an avalanche

The track, which led down the mountainside, was both narrow and steep, and since neither the men nor the animals could be sure of their footing on account of the snow, any who stepped wide of the path or stumbled overbalanced and fell down the precipices. These perils they could endure, because by this time they had become accustomed to such mischances, but at length they reached a place where the track was too narrow for the elephants or even the pack animals to pass. A previous landslide had already carried away some three hundred meters of the face of the mountain, while a recent one had made the situation still worse. At this point the soldiers once more lost their nerve and came close to despair.

Polybius, *The Histories*

Hannibal (247–182 BCE) really does this one all on his own—the hero of the hour, a great strategist, and at the same time the perpetrator of one of the most daring and dubious feats of military history, rooted in arrogance and impetuousness, which arguably cost him the one thing he desired more than anything else—the conquest of Rome.

Hannibal was born in 247 BCE in the middle of the Roman humiliation of his home state, Carthage, near present-day Tunis. A great trading and seafaring nation, the Romans had figured out how to take on the Carthaginians at sea and had thrown them out of their island provinces of Sicily, Corsica, and Sardinia. Aged ten, with this first Punic War not four years over and civil war raging in Carthage, young Hannibal was taken to Carthage's territories in Spain by his father, the Carthaginian general Hamilcar, who conquered new territories there, including what is now Cartagena. Hannibal grew up in Spain, marrying an Iberian princess, and the Romans believed that Hamilcar had instilled in his son a lifelong hatred of them. After his father's death, Hannibal's brother-in-law reigned peacefully over the new territories, until he was murdered and the 22-year-old Hannibal was subsequently elected commander of the Carthaginian army in Spain. He immediately switched back to his father's aggressive tactics and recklessly attacked and captured Salamanca, then laid siege to a major Roman town, Saguntum, moving his army rapidly across the whole Iberian peninsula. After Saguntum fell, the Romans, although occupied with other confrontations in their territories, had little choice but to declare hostilities. The second Punic War had begun.

HANNIBAL IN ITALY
One of four scenes in the 1508–13 fresco painted by Jacopo Ripanda in the Hannibal Hall of the Palazzo dei Conservatori, at the Musei Capitolini in Rome.

It was in Hannibal's nature to take the attack to the enemy, but the Romans knew there were only three possible ways onto the Italian mainland: they controlled all the sea routes; there was a long overland route; and there was an impossible route over the Alps. A Roman army was despatched to Marseille to head off the invaders. But in 218 BCE Hannibal set off from Cartagena and decided to go straight across the little-known mountainous region to conquer Rome with 50,000 troops, 9,000 horses and pack animals, and 37 elephants at his command.

The elephants were certainly a novelty in southern Europe and caused much panic among enemy soldiers, though some reports have it that they were equally terrifying to Hannibal's own horses. It was to become one of the most second-guessed troop movements in history. It was entirely in character that he had almost no idea of the route or what he would find along the way; even now, no one is entirely sure which of a number of routes he took. His impetuosity was both a wonderful triumph and the seed of his ultimate failure.

IT WAS ENTIRELY IN CHARACTER THAT HANNIBAL HAD ALMOST NO IDEA OF HIS ROUTE OR WHAT HE WOULD FIND ALONG THE WAY.

He made one fatal mistake along the way that cost him half his army, most of his animals, and left him unable to conquer the city of Rome. He never could press home his advantage. Instead, he laid waste to the Italian countryside for 15 years before being forced back to Africa to defend Carthage itself, where he was convincingly beaten by Scipio Africanus at the Battle of Zama. In the end he supposedly drank poison to avoid being captured by the Romans.

No one disputes his abilities as a general, and he certainly had surprise on his side. Unfortunately, he had less than half his army and only a handful of his vaunted elephants left by the time he got to Italy, although his army hadn't fought a major battle and it had been less than a month since it had left Spain. Hannibal had, inadvertently but personally, been responsible for most of those deaths himself. There were many things Hannibal, born in Africa and brought up in southern Spain, didn't know about the Alps—and one of them is that they are notorious for avalanches.

THE JOURNEY

The trip across the Pyrenees went relatively smoothly, but then the army faced the immensity of the River Rhône. Hannibal devised some form of buoyancy system for the elephants, probably formed from pigs' bladders, and built huge rafts to get the army across safely.

Further problems lay in wait, however, and a number of fierce Gallic tribes launched a wave of ambushes and assaults on the army, causing mounting casualties. Only clever tactics on Hannibal's part prevented the army from being wiped out by the Allobroges, a tribe that he had originally hoped would join his side. Already, things were not quite going as planned. Two days later they ran into another ambush. Hannibal protected what he considered to be his most important asset—the baggage train—simply by putting the infantry out in front, and lost many of his men as a consequence. However, that turned out to be the easy part.

It is interesting that our knowledge of Hannibal's exploits comes solely from his enemies, the Romans; specifically two historians, Livy and Polybius. For centuries afterwards the story of Hannibal was told—and perhaps exaggerated—to remind the Romans of how close they came to being defeated by a surprise attack, and what a valiant enemy they finally vanquished. Nonetheless, there is no reason to disbelieve the essence of the story, since Polybius's version came from the eyewitness accounts of one of Hannibal's own soldiers.

Problems began almost immediately as they attempted the descent of the Alps. With little knowledge of the paths across, and untrustworthy local guides, the army found going down much harder than going up. The terrain turned out to be a lethal mixture of mud with treacherous ice underneath, as the ground here never truly thaws. The horses and elephants in particular found the going hard and sank down into the ground. The following morning saw a disaster—an early autumn snowstorm laid a thick layer of snow on top of the treacherous ground. It proved impossible to move at all, and if this was the beginning of winter then serious problems lay ahead.

Hannibal was beside himself. Livy takes up the story:

> But even so he was no luckier; progress was impossible, for though there was good foothold in the quite shallow layer of soft fresh snow which had covered the old snow underneath, nevertheless as soon as it had been trampled and dispersed by the feet of all those men and animals, there was left to tread upon only the bare ice and liquid slush of melting snow underneath. The result was a horrible struggle, the ice affording no foothold in any case, and least of all on a steep slope; when a man tried by hands or knees to get on his feet again, even those useless supports slipped from under him and let him down; there were no stumps or roots anywhere to afford a purchase to either foot or hand; in short, there was nothing for it but to roll and slither on the smooth ice and melting snow.

According to the story, Hannibal was also famous for never allowing others to do what he could not or would not do himself. He was at the

THE TERRAIN TURNED OUT TO BE A LETHAL MIXTURE OF MUD WITH TREACHEROUS ICE UNDERNEATH, AS THE GROUND HERE NEVER TRULY THAWS.

back of the march when everything came to a complete stop. Desperate to capitalize on the element of surprise, and furious at the delay, he came to the front, marched down the mountain, walking cane in hand, and slammed it hard down into the drift to prove there was solid ground beneath and that everyone could pass safely if they just showed a little more determination.

There are more avalanches in the Alps than in any other part of the world. Of the nearly one million avalanches that take place every year, half happen in this small region. There are valleys where it is unsafe to do much more than whisper. In later centuries witches were burned for causing avalanches, and even now there are still enormous and deadly avalanches in the region that make international headlines. It doesn't take much to set off an Alpine avalanche and Hannibal's rashness was more than enough: it triggered an enormous slide. Many men and animals were buried; others fell off precipices trying to escape. It took four days for the rest of the army to dig themselves out and find a way of getting down the mountain. Fifteen days after charging into the Alps, less than half the original 50,000 men and only a handful of elephants and pack animals emerged.

UNDERMANNED BUT DETERMINED

Undeterred by his losses, Hannibal charged down into the Po plain with what was left of his army. He picked up a few fresh troops from a Gallic tribe, impressed by his appearance, took the Romans totally by surprise, and won two rapid battles against small and unprepared forces. A huge Roman army belatedly set out and met Hannibal's depleted force at the plain of Cannae. Hannibal fought one of the finest battles in military history and beat the Romans in a wonderful set piece maneuver. But he no longer had sufficient numbers to attack Rome itself, and he knew it. The few elephants left were little more than a novelty, and his troops were exhausted and too few in number. Hannibal had pulled off an amazing lightning assault, but at the cost of his campaign, when a slightly steadier hand might well have seen his army safely over the Alps.

After Cannae, the Romans took a new tack. They realized Hannibal was too smart for them in open battle. They also realized that he was cut off from his supply lines and could succeed only if he persuaded enough city-states and tribes to join him. He sent to Carthage for reinforcements and his brother Hasdrubal followed in his steps as far as Andalusia in Spain. Hasdrubal was the opposite of his older brother, particularly as a tactician. It took him several defeats and three years to fight his way out of Spain. He then proceeded to follow Hannibal's route, elephants and all, across the Alps. But perhaps because of his more cautious approach to life, he not only managed to get the entire force safely across, but added another 30,000 men from Gallic tribes which he successfully persuaded to join his cause. Unfortunately these forces never reached Hannibal. The Romans were ready and waiting, and destroyed Hasdrubal's army as soon as it entered Italy; while Hasdrubal's head was thrown into Hannibal's camp, just to underline the point.

HANNIBAL'S ROUTE FROM SPAIN TO ITALY

Hannibal's route out of Iberia took him and his army from Cartagena across the Pyrenees in 218 BCE. He then traversed the River Rhône, before being ambushed by several Gallic tribes along the route. The exact location of the crossing of the Alps is hotly disputed, but Hannibal fought and won subsequent battles on the plain of the River Po, and a major victory at Cannae. Despite these victories Hannibal's forces were never able to attempt an assault on Rome itself and a stalemate persisted where despite tactical victories Hannibal was unable to land the final blow. Significant reinforcements and supplies failed to emerge and Hannibal was finally forced to return to Carthage in 203 BCE.

That was Hannibal's last hope—his army was now too tired and too depleted. The Romans simply avoided open conflict, and for 10 years they let Hannibal wander around southern Italy, but never engaged him head-on. Then, the young Roman general Scipio Africanus simply took a reverse strategy; avoiding Hannibal entirely, he started to recapture the lost Spanish territories and finally moved over to Africa to launch an assault on Carthage itself. The Carthaginians recalled Hannibal, who had still never been beaten on European soil, and his bedraggled and tired army was routed by Scipio in northern Africa. The Romans imposed a harsh peace treaty and the Carthaginians were thrown out of Europe for good, never to return.

Hannibal returned to Carthage, fighting one more battle, a conclusive defeat at the Zama in 202 BCE, before spending the next 20 years trying to make alliances and send another army to attack Rome. But as before, his temper and lack of tact put off almost all his potential allies, and he failed to raise any sort of army. Hannibal posed probably the greatest single threat to the rise of the Roman Empire close to its beginning. It was not to be seriously challenged for another six centuries. Victory for the Carthaginians—essentially an African power—could have led to a very different world from the one the Romans did so much to shape. Arguably, Hannibal's moment of anger and impetuousness, his catastrophic mistake with Italy at his mercy, changed the whole shape of European civilization.

Hannibal's trek over the Alps continues to provoke awe and is one of the most famous verifiable incidents of ancient times. You can today follow Hannibal's route across the Alps—or at least one possible route, as there is a whole vitriolic literature arguing about which route he actually took.

The second Punic War is famous for Hannibal's exploits; however, few reflect on the fact that although spectacular, Hannibal's brave charge and moment of madness in all likelihood destroyed his campaign before it had really begun. The dogged tortoise Scipio Africanus ended up beating the hare-like Hannibal to the line. It says something about what appeals to us today that we remember the spectacular but short-lived achievements of the loser instead.

CLEOPATRA'S MEN

69–30 BCE

MOTIVATION

anger
charity
envy
faith
gluttony
greed
hope
lust
pride
sloth

Main Culprits: Cleopatra (69–30 BCE); Marc Antony (83–30 BCE)

Damage Done: Two empires lost, Ptolemaic and Roman

Why: A little too much lying down for the country

Age cannot wither her, nor custom stale
Her infinite variety: other women cloy
The appetites they feed, but she makes hungry
Where most she satisfies.

The barge she sat in, like a burnished throne, burn'd on the water; the poop was beaten gold, purple the sails, and so perfumed, that the winds were love-sick with them, the oars were silver, which to the tune of flutes kept stroke, and made the water which they beat to follow faster, as amorous of their strokes. For her own person, it beggar'd all description.

Shakespeare, *Antony and Cleopatra*

Isn't it odd that Cleopatra, the last of the Ptolemies, a legend far beyond her own short time, a feminist icon, and one of the first femmes fatales, should leave almost no images that we can positively identify as her own? She was a remarkable leader of the Egyptians, even though her attempts at strategic foreign policy seem to have been largely horizontal and ultimately disastrous. In all the 300 years of the Ptolemaic dynasty (they were Greeks from Macedonia), Cleopatra VII was the only one who actually bothered to learn to speak and read Egyptian. At her accession in 51 BCE, at age 17, she was not really expected to take power. In a matrilineal monarchy such as this, the female leader had to be married—no matter whether to her father, brother, or son—in order to appear to be in power, but normally the men were the real rulers. The young Cleopatra married her younger brother Ptolemy XIII, and the generals confidently expected their power to be secure. This proved to be far from the case, and within a few years Cleopatra was forced by her brother and his cronies to flee Egypt. Cleopatra may not have had the beauty of Helen of Troy, nor was she a tough warrior like the British queen of the Iceni Boudicca, but she was formidable, as her brother would discover.

© Everett Collection | Rex Features

CLEOPATRA
The 1963 poster art for the film Cleopatra. Starring Elizabeth Taylor, as well as Rex Harrison as Julius Caesar (left) and Richard Burton as Mark Antony (right).

The Egyptians were just hanging on to their independence at this time—a few decades before the birth of Christ, with Julius Caesar supreme in Rome, and the Roman Empire approaching its zenith from one end of the world—Britain—across the Middle East to Parthia. Egyptians had remained independent only by ingratiating themselves and paying due obeisance to Rome. Ptolemy, however, took this a step too far. The Roman general Pompey, fleeing Rome after losing the civil war to Julius Caesar, sought refuge in Alexandria. Ptolemy had him killed instead. Caesar, who had defeated Pompey, was in fact his son-in-law and considered this an affront to Roman dignity. He pushed himself into the internal affairs of Egypt, arriving in Alexandria and announcing his intention to determine whether Ptolemy or Cleopatra would rule.

As the story goes, Caesar was presented with a fine carpet that was unrolled to reveal the 21-year-old Cleopatra inside. Suffice to say she was rapidly returned to the throne. She spent the winter with Caesar on a two-month cruise up the Nile, where she was greeted by her subjects with the type of reverence they used to accord the Pharaohs of old. She also bore him a son, Caesarion. Cleopatra's plan was to gain power and save her ailing nation by forming a dynastic alliance with the powerful Romans. This time the plan failed. Once Caesar had returned to Rome, he took up again with his wife, and far from proclaiming Caesarion as the new emperor, adopted his great-nephew Octavian as the next ruler of Rome. Caesar was assassinated in 44 BCE, just when Cleopatra and her son were visiting Rome, perhaps hoping to persuade Caesar to change his mind; but her strategy was now fully worked out in Cleopatra's mind, and she wouldn't let the next opportunity slip through her fingers so easily. However, it is worth noting that she appears to have genuinely respected and cared for Caesar.

The problem, though, was who the next ruler might be. Caesar was replaced by a triumvirate: Octavian; Lepidus, an aging senator; and Marc Antony, a proud general whose oratory swayed the crowd against the assassins at Caesar's funeral (at least in Shakespeare's retelling). Meanwhile, Cleopatra returned to Egypt, had her brother killed, and married her son, ensuring her complete control of the state. She attempted to turn the country back from famine and plague and rebuild its forces, while waiting for the next leader to emerge in Rome. By 41 BCE that looked a lot like Marc Antony. Octavian was ill and Antony summoned Cleopatra to Tarsus for a conference. She arrived in as much style as perhaps has been mustered before or since, enough certainly to launch an abundance of movies. Antony, for all his generalship and oratory, was not a particularly bright man; he was known for his drinking, womanizing, and general vulgarity. He fell for Cleopatra's show-womanship absolutely.

Their relationship was immediate and intense, and soon resulted in twins. After a sojourn back in Rome to attend to a feud with Octavian (and his marriage to Octavia, Octavian's sister, in an attempt to patch it all up), Marc Antony set sail in 36 BCE, ostensibly to continue his war against the Parthians. In fact, he summoned Cleopatra immediately and from that point the two were doomed to a misbegotten relationship born of lust and greed. They could never realistically compete with the might

CLEOPATRA SPENT THE WINTER WITH CAESAR ON A TWO-MONTH CRUISE UP THE NILE, WHERE SHE WAS GREETED BY HER SUBJECTS WITH THE TYPE OF REVERENCE THEY USED TO ACCORD THE PHARAOHS OF OLD.

of the Roman Empire once Antony had left his real power base, and his betrayal of Octavian's sister meant that eventually something would have to be done.

At first, though, the liaison was remarkable—another child, a son, was born. With Egyptian funds and Antony's generalship, a large swathe of the Middle East was taken: Syria, Asia Minor, Cyprus, Armenia, and Crete were all awarded to the young children. Cleopatra herself was named Queen of Kings and Caesarion, her son with Caesar, pronounced heir to Rome instead of Octavian. Octavia was divorced, and the dawn of a Roman-Egyptian dynasty was declared, with Cleopatra as the new Isis.

CLEOPATRA HERSELF WAS NAMED QUEEN OF KINGS AND CAESARION, HER SON WITH CAESAR, PRONOUNCED HEIR TO ROME INSTEAD OF OCTAVIAN.

By 31 BCE Octavian had seen enough, and launched a fleet in the first attempt to subdue Antony and Cleopatra. Both showed up at the Battle of Actium, but Antony was so outnumbered that Cleopatra fled without him. By all accounts he deserted his own beaten forces and chased after her. Octavian then launched a full-scale assault on Egypt and within a year had captured Alexandria. Antony fell on his own sword to avoid capture, losing his life through his lust for power and his queen.

Cleopatra was made of sterner stuff, and she appears to have given it one more try with Octavian himself, suggesting an alliance under the normal terms. However, it was soon apparent that he had no intention of making any compact with the woman who had seduced his sister's husband. He wanted to bring her back to Rome in chains. The prospect of a grand procession, with the captive queen leading the array of plunder, burdened with chains and quite probably not surviving until the end of the parade, was not for Cleopatra. She had, in any case, in true Pharaonic style, built a mausoleum for herself after Actium, just in case Antony proved as useless at defending her on land as he was at sea. She locked herself away for three days until she was due to be taken to Rome, called for the now-emblematic figs and asp, and—possibly in the belief that the Egyptian religion guaranteed immortality following death by snakebite—died on August 12, 30 BCE Her dynasty ended with her. Octavian, soon to become the emperor Augustus, had little Caesarion strangled and Antony's children sent to Octavia in Rome, where all but one girl soon disappeared. Egypt now fell under the direct control of Rome.

Regardless of whether her theology was correct or not, Cleopatra did succeed in attaining some form of immortality: from Plutarch to Shakespeare; Shaw to Elizabeth Taylor; and from Cleopatra's Needles on the Victoria Embankment in London and Central Park in New York (both presented in the nineteenth century and actually dating from well before her reign) to the myriad Cleopatra-related items selling on eBay at any given moment.

The cost of her mistake was her dynasty, and indeed, the independence of Egypt for many centuries to come. Not without reason was she known as the last of the pharaohs. Perhaps somewhere she smiled as General Nasser won his victories in the cause of Egyptian independence during the Suez crisis many centuries later.

MOTIVATION
anger
charity
envy
faith
gluttony
greed
hope
lust
pride
sloth

NERO AND THE BURNING OF ROME

July 19, 64 CE

Main Culprit: The Emperor Nero (37–68 CE)

Damage Done: Burning down his own city

Why: To make room for his own new palace

For six days and seven nights destruction raged, while the people were driven for shelter to monuments and tombs. At that time, besides an immense number of dwellings, the houses of leaders of old were burned, still adorned with trophies of victory, and the temples of the gods vowed and dedicated by the kings and later in the Punic and Gallic wars, and whatever else interesting and noteworthy had survived from antiquity. Viewing the conflagration from the tower of Maecenas, and exulting, as he said, "with the beauty of the flames," he sang the whole time the "Sack of Ilium," in his regular stage costume. Furthermore, to gain from this calamity too the spoil and booty possible, while promising the removal of the debris and dead bodies free of cost, he allowed no-one to approach the ruins of his own property; and from the contributions which he not only received, but even demanded, he nearly bankrupted the provinces and exhausted the resources of individuals.

Suetonius, *The Lives of the Caesars*

The emperor Nero ruled Rome from 54 to 68 CE when he committed suicide, bringing to an end his rule and the dynasty founded by the emperor Augustus. He had become emperor at the age of 16, supposedly when his mother Agrippina poisoned the emperor Claudius, having first persuaded him to make young Nero heir to the throne. He was born in 37 CE, four years after the crucifixion of Christ, and exiled in the Pontian Islands during the fierce reign of Caligula. In 49 CE the great poet and tragedian Seneca was appointed Nero's tutor, and in 53 CE he married Octavia, the daughter of Claudius.

He lived during the beginning of turmoil within the Roman world, which at that point seemed to be at the height of its power. It encompassed more than 60 million people, a fifth of the world population, in 40 provinces. But Christianity, still an incipient and secret religious sect, was beginning to make inroads. The word of Jesus was spread throughout the empire by the Apostles. Paul visited Rome in 60 CE, and the Christians would play a significant role in the final phase of Nero's rule. The empire, however, continued to expand. Under Claudius, Britain was secured and gains were made in Thrace and North Africa.

History best remembers Nero from the reports of the historian Tacitus, who memorably depicted him as merrily playing his lyre while Rome burned below his window. Tacitus blamed Nero squarely for having caused the fire in the first place, out of his greedy desire to build a fine new palace for himself on the site of the city. If this is indeed true—and despite all the attempts through the centuries to come up with alternative explanations, Nero still stands as the most likely suspect—he deserves his place in this book, for not only did he clear the way for his own real-estate project; he destroyed most of his city.

NERO
Marble bust of Nero Claudius Caesar Augustus Germanicus (37–68 CE). Roman Emperor from 54 to 68 CE.

Famous fires usually have famous and sometimes controversial causes: the Great Fire of London has its monument in Pudding Lane; and only in the last few years has Mrs O'Leary's cow been publicly pardoned for the Great Chicago Fire of 1871. The conflagration that destroyed much of Rome is little different. In recent years attempts have been made to discredit Tacitus's theories, some by recreating the fire in controlled environments, others by claiming that Christians were trying to bring about the teachings of the book of Revelation by torching the Seven Hills. But there is plenty in Nero's character to suggest that he was capable of doing anything to get what he wanted.

NERO'S INTERESTS AND EXCESSES

Nero had a formidable interest in the arts, and was particularly obsessed with the aesthetic achievements of the Greeks. He loved writing poetry, acting, and dancing, and even went on tours of the empire, less to conquer than to perform. He was similarly fascinated by civil engineering and architecture. He introduced Greek games and arts contests to the Romans, and hired the famous lyre player Terpnus to tutor him. The instrument described by Tacitus was almost certainly a lyre, by the way, and definitely not a fiddle.

Unfortunately, Nero also inherited some of the less attractive traits of his predecessors, especially Caligula. He had some interesting sexual proclivities; according to historian Dio Cassius, these included "fastening young boys and girls to stakes, and then, after putting on the hide of a wild beast, attacking them and satisfying his brutal lust under the appearance of devouring parts of their bodies." His mother Agrippina was clearly in charge; she had arranged his accession in the first place and in all probability had Claudius murdered. On coins Nero and his mother were depicted face to face, with Agrippina's name on the back, indicating that she was the more important. But within a couple of years Nero had thrown her out of the palace. When she started to favor his brother Britannicus, Nero had him murdered, followed by Agrippina herself when she criticized his new mistress, Poppaea Sabina. Nero responded angrily, according to the historian Suetonius, with various attempts on his mother's life, three by poison and one by rigging the ceiling to cave in while she lay in bed. Even a collapsible boat was built, which was meant to sink in the Bay of Naples. But Agrippina managed to swim ashore and only the boat was lost. Exasperated, Nero sent an assassin who clubbed and stabbed her to death in 59 CE.

Poppaea, the wife of his best friend, was apparently behind some of Nero's worst excesses. Soon paranoia and terror reigned—by the year 62 CE Nero banished and then executed his wife Octavia; Seneca and other trusted advisors were killed; and anyone standing in the way of his will was summarily dealt with. In light of the subsequent fight with the Senate and Nero's rash actions relating to the fire, his temper and lack of control suggest that the end would have justified almost any means for Nero.

Nero had devised a grand scheme, along the lines of his interest in Greek architecture, to rebuild Rome, or more specifically an elaborate series of palaces, villas, and pavilions. The Senate was appalled and refused to cooperate with the type of demolition he sought.

It seemed a coincidence to few when fire broke out on the night of July 19, 64 CE, in shops lining the chariot stadium, the Circus Maximus. It was midsummer, and Nero was conveniently out of town in the coastal resort of Antium. Many eyewitnesses reported seeing the arson in progress. As Suetonius relates:

> Nero sent out by different ways men feigning to be drunk, or engaged in some kind of mischief, and at first had a few fires kindled quietly and in different quarters. . . This state of things lasted not one day, but several days and nights running. . . For the soldiers (including the night watch) with a keen eye for plunder, instead of quenching the conflagration, kindled it the more. . . A sudden wind caught the fire and swept it over what remained. As a result nobody troubled longer about goods or homes, but all the survivors, from a place of safety, gazed on what appeared to be many islands and cities in flames. No longer was there any grief for private loss; public lamentation swallowed up this . . . as men reminded each other how once before the bulk of the city had been even thus laid desolate by the Gauls. As with so much else in his Empire, Nero had lost control of his own land-clearing project. Greedy soldiers and the weather destroyed two thirds of his own city and killed untold numbers of his subjects.

Recent studies cast doubt on the verdict of ancient historians, citing prejudice, the possibility of accidental fires, and suggestions that Christians or other malcontents had started the fire. But it's hard to deny the vision that has come down to us through history of Nero atop the remains of his own palace, singing (according to Dio Cassius) and playing the lyre (according to Tacitus), overlooking the burning city with equanimity, before realizing the damage he had caused.

The disaster which the city then underwent had no parallel save in the Gallic invasion. The whole Palatine Hill, the theater of Taurus, and nearly two thirds of the rest of the city were burned. Countless people perished. According to Dio Cassius the rebuilding started immediately afterwards: "Nero now began to collect vast sums both from individuals and nations, sometimes using downright compulsion, with the conflagration as his excuse."

Not surprisingly, the citizens of both the city and the empire were less than impressed. For the urbanites, their emperor had burned down their city and their homes and was now extorting money from them to build his dream mansion, his "Golden House" (Domus Aurea). Realizing the problems this might create, Nero looked for scapegoats and conveniently found them in the underground Christian movement—which was in any case less than popular with most Romans, as Christian disapproval of Roman pagan rituals caused much disdain. Tacitus called the Christians "depraved" and Suetonius proclaimed them to be "of a new and mischievous religious belief." In any case, many were brutally murdered, burned, or torn apart by wild beasts. Rumor had it that Nero lit fires at his garden parties with the carcasses of the dead. It is even believed that the Apostles Paul and Peter died in this persecution.

NERO'S END Nero's power never recovered from the fire. The damage was immense and the burden on the populace, more to build his Golden House than to rebuild their houses, was enormous. Sedition galloped across the empire—there were revolts in Britain, Spain and Judaea—and within the Senate. Senators had seen their own houses destroyed too. There were plots to replace Nero, and two uprisings were ruthlessly crushed. Finally enough was enough. According to Suetonius, Nero killed himself as an assassination squad was coming to get him, uttering his last words: "What an artist the world is losing in me."

He did leave an extraordinary monument, however, as one of the Domus Aurea's most visible features was the Colossus Neronis, a huge bronze statue of Nero in imitation of the Colossus of Rhodes, one of the Seven Wonders of the Ancient World. The colossus was affixed with the heads of several emperors before Hadrian moved it to outside the Amphitheatrum Flavium. This building eventually took the name Colosseum in the Middle Ages, after the statue.

ERIK THE RED'S DREAM ISLAND: THE FIRST REAL-ESTATE SCAM

982–985

MOTIVATION

anger
charity
envy
faith
gluttony
greed
hope
lust
pride
sloth

Main Culprit: Erik the Red (950–1003CE)

Damage Done: Brought hundreds of people with him to an uninhabitable land

Why: It was the only place that would take him

Now, afterwards, during the summer, he proceeded to Iceland, and came to Breidafjordr (Broadfirth). This winter he was with Ingolf, at Holmlatr (Island-Litter). During the spring, Thorgest and he fought, and Eirik met with defeat. After that they were reconciled. In the summer Eirik went to live in the land which he had discovered, and which he called Greenland, "Because," said he, "men will desire much the more to go there if the land has a good name."

The Saga of Erik the Red

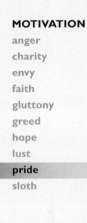

It is generally assumed that the European colonization of the world, especially of North America, was an uninterrupted rhythm of arrival, destruction of the native population, and integration. That was not always the case. The largest island in the world, Greenland, proved too much for its first colonists, who made a blunder of colossal proportions when they set foot on its icy shore. Although Greenland had no trees, the settlers arrogantly decided to create a regular settlement. They ultimately failed, and literally disappeared.

The Vikings began voyages of exploration from their native Norway in the eighth century. They were tough, cruel fighters, but also traders, and probably ranged as far as the Arab world. They established trading posts from Dublin to Kiev and undoubtedly reached the North American continent, definitely Newfoundland but perhaps much further into what is now the United States. They also developed several concepts of considerable importance for the growth of Western civilization, trial by jury and parliamentary rule among them. The Icelandic National Assembly, the Althing, established in 930, is the oldest assembly of its kind in Europe. Viking explorers had taken Iceland in 870 and established firm rule within those 60 years, declaring independence from Norway. Many dissidents and outlaws from Viking rule made their way to the new land, and one of these was Erik the Red.

ERIK'S REPUTATION HAS COME DOWN THROUGH HISTORY AS AN INTREPID AND FAMOUS EXPLORER, BUT IN TRUTH HE WAS LITTLE MORE THAN AN OUTLAW ON THE RUN.

Erik's reputation has come down through history as an intrepid and famous explorer, but in truth he was little more than an outlaw on the run. He had been forced to leave Norway in 980 with his father after committing a murder, but lasted only two years in Iceland before being summoned to the Althing to answer charges of another killing. He was banished for three years, but had nowhere to go, as he was a wanted man in Norway; so he sailed west.

He came upon a land covered mostly in ice with some low-lying green pastures. He spent three years exploring the island and decided to make it his domain, despite the inhospitality of the climate, even for Norsemen, and the fact that no trees could grow there. Nevertheless, Erik set up a colony on the southern coastline, and in what may well have been the first real-estate scam, named it "Greenland" to attract settlers. On his return to Iceland he managed to get twenty-five ships full of would-be settlers to come with him. The only human inhabitants of Greenland were Inuits, essentially nomadic hunters, as permanent settlement wasn't really an option. They were less than friendly, but kept mostly out of the way. Erik was undaunted, and set up an eastern settlement, using driftwood to build the houses. Fourteen of the twenty-five ships survived the perilous journey, and a later fleet set up a western settlement, some 400 miles (248 km) away.

The idea was apparently to live by trading. Traces of as many as 400 farms have been found, but the land was simply too poor for subsistence farming. Erik sent his son Leif to establish trading routes. Leif came back instead with a quite different import—a wife from Norway, and a priest. Christianity had reached the Viking lands and Leif had converted. Erik, a devout follower of Thor, went further west and became almost without question the first European to set foot on North America, finding what he called Vinland—a land with grape vines, salmon, cattle, and with day and night of more or less equal length, well south of Erik's settlement on Greenland.

THE VOYAGES OF ERIK THE RED AND OTHER VIKINGS

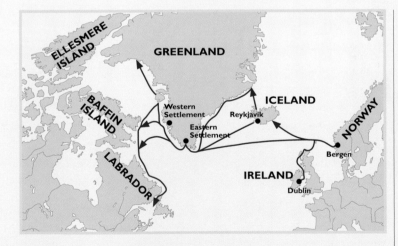

While Viking voyages spread far wider, this map illustrates the westward expansion that took place throughout the ninth, tenth, and early eleventh centuries. Iceland is thought to have been reached around 870, about 30 years after Dublin was founded by Vikings in 841. Further exploration took place with the voyages of Erik the Red to Greenland in 982, and later his son Leif Erikson first to what is probably now Baffin Island, then to Labrador.

Erik died around 1002, leaving those who had followed him in their bleak landscape reduced to foraging for driftwood for housing and fuel. They weren't able to make the voyage to Vinland because they no longer had enough wood for ships, and even journeys to Norway became few and far between, and the western settlement was wiped out by an Inuit raid. The Norse Empire had become Christian, and news of the Greenland outpost had reached the pope in Rome, who sent out an unfortunate to be his bishop there. The bishop was apparently instrumental in persuading the surviving locals that they were not really able to make it as an independent state any more, and in 1261 the assembly, such as it was, became one of the few in the history of the world to surrender its sovereignty voluntarily. The Norsemen of Greenland submitted themselves to the Norwegian crown, presumably in the hope that they would be sent aid.

However, none was forthcoming, no subsequent bishop was sent, and gradually, contact was lost. By 1409 a voyager found the eastern settlement deserted. Some claim that the Mandan Indians, contacted by explorer Pierre de la Verendyre in the upper Missouri valley in 1738, were white and European in conduct, but even if this is true they are more likely to be descendants of Leif's than the Greenlanders.

THE DEATH OF THE COLONY

Nobody really knows what happened to the unfortunate denizens of Erik's settlement. Carbon dating on bones from old churchyards unveiled a dramatic change in their diet; once the boats stopped coming, they started to eat mostly fish, like the Inuit. It also uncovered signs of malnutrition, suggesting that the Greenlanders literally starved. Oddly, this scientific breakthrough was possible because of the lack of wood; without coffins, dead Greenlanders were simply wrapped in blankets and preserved in the permafrost. Scientists have even been able to identify the bones of the one bishop who came to Greenland, as his diet was mostly Norwegian and more meat-based before his ill-fated posting. The diet changed over the 400 years of occupation from the 80:20 ratio of meat to fish to a 20:80 ratio. Without the nutrition from whales and walruses that the Inuit used to supplement their fish diet, it simply was not enough.

It was remarkable that the outpost lasted as long as it did in the conditions—as many as 5,000 settlers lived there at its peak. In 1721, a mercantile-clerical expedition was sent to look for Europeans on Greenland. Norway had by then become affiliated with Denmark, and the Danes assumed control over the island, or what there was of it. Today, Greenland still has only 50,000 or so residents; it achieved self-governance in 1979, a full 718 years after giving it up.

MOTIVATION
anger
charity
envy
faith
gluttony
greed
hope
lust
pride
sloth

POPE SYLVESTER II AND THE END OF THE WORLD

December 31, 999

Main Culprits: The faithful

Damage Done: Unknown number of deaths before the "end" came

Why: Mass panic, superstition, and fear of the unknown

It's the end of the world as we know it (and I feel fine).

R.E.M.

The real end of the world is the destruction of the spirit; the other kind depends on the significant attempt to see whether after such a destruction the world can go on.

Karl Kraus, *Beim Wort Genommen*

It doesn't say much for the second millennium that it was bookended by two outbreaks of mass idiocy on a global scale. Climbing mountaintops to await the end of the world was perhaps more understandable, given the extent of knowledge in the year 999, than cashing in frantically because the ATMs of the world were going to swallow your savings a thousand years later. There were plenty of outbreaks of foolhardiness over the course of the thousand years in between, especially belief in the evil of minorities and willingness to go along with their persecution, from the Jews in Nazi Germany to the witch hunts of early modern Europe and their more modern equivalent in McCarthyite America. But the apocalyptic panic that overwhelms otherwise sensible people is of a special quality.

The tenth century has been called the Century of Lead and Iron. The Saracens, the Spanish Moors, the Vikings, the Bulgars, and the Magyar horsemen all invaded Europe. The Chinese invented gunpowder.

Dhaka, now the capital of Bangladesh, was founded. The Hutu arrived in today's Rwanda, soon outnumbering the neighboring Tutsi; though they would wait until nearly the next millennium before trying to wipe them out. In Rome, rival popes imprisoned, starved, mutilated, and assassinated each other. Erik the Red probably became the first "white man" to reach the North American continent. In Ethelred the English had a king so feeble he was nicknamed "the Unready." Recurrent famines caused starvation in region after region, resulting in widespread cannibalism. These famines in turn were followed by outbreaks of disease caused by people eating infected grain.

Thus, in the year 999, an epidemic of terror of the end of the world spread among the masses. It hardly took the wandering monks and mendicants to suggest that the one-thousandth anniversary of the birth of Christ might have some mystical significance in a world as brutal as that.

POPE SYLVESTER II
A nineteenth-century engraving of the French Pope Sylvester II—also known as Gerbert.

The tenth century was not a particularly bright time in the history of the papacy. One thousand years after the reign of St. Peter, a succession of popes was brutally murdered and deposed, and the church endured 50 years of what was known as the pornocracy or "Reign of the Harlots,"

© The Art Archive | Private Collection | Gianni Dagli Orti

during which strong women dominated the papacy. By the end of the century the Holy Roman emperors, originally supposed to be appointed by the popes, had more or less turned the tables and taken over control of who became pope. Benedict V lasted only a month in 964 before having the papal scepter broken over him and being carted off to spend the rest of his life in a monastery. Benedict VI was strangled in 974 after the death of his mentor, Holy Roman Emperor Otto. Gregory V ascended to the papacy in 996, under the aegis of Otto III, and was the first German pope, but as such had to contend with an antipope put up by local Roman nobles. The unfortunate man was pursued and captured by papal and imperial troops, had his ears, nose, and tongue cut off, and was then sent to a monastery, where strangely enough he outlived the next five popes. Gregory didn't quite make it to the millennium either, dying in rather mysterious, though not entirely unexpected circumstances on February 6, 999.

So it fell to a new pope to usher the Christian Church through the dark days at the end of the millennium. The only success the papacy had enjoyed in the previous century was spreading the word to Iceland, to the deep discomfiture of Erik the Red. Otto III's choice for pope was odd, perhaps, and guaranteed to panic an anxious set of believers.

THE EVE OF THE NEW MILLENNIUM

On the last day of 999, in Rome, a mass of weeping worshippers waited for the dreaded Day of Wrath. Many poor entered the church of St. Peter's in sackcloth and ashes, having spent months doing penance and mortifying the flesh. Their fears were only heightened as they looked at the new pope celebrating the mass. He was Sylvester II, also known as Gerbert d'Aurillac, the first French pope. To say that the masses were waiting for horns to appear on his head would be a vast understatement.

Gerbert was born in the Auvergne region of France around 950. At 13 he went to the monastery of St. Gerald, where he was discovered by a rich, traveling count from Barcelona, who arranged to take him to Spain for education when he was 17. Spain at that time was on the border of the Christian and Muslim empires. Gerbert spent some time in Barcelona, but more in Andalusia, in Seville and in Cordoba, whose largest library contained 4,000 volumes—four times the size of any collection in the Christian world. There the young Gerbert learned mathematics; the Arabs had invented astronomy, the concept of the number zero, their own alphabet, and much else. Later Gerbert was to devise a type of steam organ and make use of the abacus. In 969 he was taken to Rome, at a time of relative peace within the papacy, and impressed both the pope and the emperor Otto II, who hired him as tutor for his son. It was therefore no surprise when Otto III came to power that Gerbert was rapidly elevated to positions of ecclesiastical eminence, notably the archbishoprics of Rheims and then Ravenna. When Gregory suddenly died, the emperor had little hesitation in naming Gerbert as pope. He took the name Sylvester in honour of the fourth-century Sylvester I, a close associate of Constantine the Great.

However, it was by no means straightforward to introduce a man of such unorthodox learning into an office more focused on simple survival than on teachings, either religious or scientific. Rumors abounded about Gerbert: that he had won the papacy by playing dice with the Devil, and would deliver Christianity to Satan at the stroke of midnight; that he had stolen a book of spells from an Arab philosopher in Spain and had escaped by sorcery; that he was in league with a rather unlikely female demon called Meridiana; and that he had invented and built a bronze head that had prophesied that the Devil would come back for him were he ever to preach in Jerusalem.

RUMORS ABOUNDED THAT GERBERT HAD WON THE PAPACY BY PLAYING DICE WITH THE DEVIL, AND WOULD DELIVER CHRISTIANITY TO SATAN AT THE STROKE OF MIDNIGHT

In the end, the last mass, of course, passed peacefully though anxiously, and a celebratory *Te Deum* was sung in St. Peter's, while many rather sheepishly came down from mountaintops or wherever else they had decided to view the impending End of the World, much as others were to use their ATM cards successfully a thousand years later. Gerbert, however, made the mistake of taking mass in the church of St. Mary in Jerusalem, in Rome, and promptly fell ill. He did not help his reputation by reputedly having his hands and tongue cut off in penitence and asking his cardinals to cut him up and scatter his bones across the city. Instead, he was placed in a tomb with a rather strange inscription that gave rise to a long-lived legend that his bones would rattle to presage the death of a pope.

POPE ALEXANDER III AND THE SEARCH FOR PRESTER JOHN

1165–1492

MOTIVATION
anger
charity
envy
faith
gluttony
greed
hope
lust
pride
sloth

Main Culprit: Pope Alexander III (d.1181)

Damage Done: An entire crusade failed to meet a non-existent army

Why: For more than three centuries, the Christian world of the West believed in a parallel, more glorious one in the East

Public Domain

This Emperor Prester John is Christian, and a great part of his country also. But yet, they have not all the articles of our faith as we have. They believe well in the Father, in the Son, and in the Holy Ghost. And they be full devout and right true one to another.

This Emperor Prester John when he goeth into battle against any other lord, he hath no banners borne before him; but he hath three crosses of gold, fine, great, and high, full of precious stones, and every of those crosses be set in a chariot, full richly arrayed. And for to keep every cross, be ordained 10,000 men of arms and more than 100,000 men on foot, in manner as men would keep a standard in our countries, when that we be in land of war. And this number of folk is without the principal host and without wings ordained for the battle. And when he hath no war, but rideth with a privy meinie, then he hath borne before him but one cross of tree, without painting and without gold or silver or precious stones, in remembrance that Jesus Christ suffered death upon a cross of tree.

Sir John de Mandeville, *Travels*

If urban myths existed in medieval Europe, Prester John would have won any poll going as the most widely believed. Urban myths don't matter all that much, as long as you don't believe in them. But sending several thousand warriors off across the known world in the expectation that someone who doesn't exist will join forces with you has to qualify for this book through the sheer irrationality of faith.

MAN OR MYTH?

As with most legends, a lot of truth—or truths, as Prester John remained a presence in European life for a number of centuries—lay behind the myth. Even now, it is hard to decipher exactly what was going on. The essence of the Prester John myth was created in 1165 when a letter arrived with the Byzantine emperor, with a copy to the pope and the Holy Roman emperor, from a great king in the East—somewhere in Asia—named Prester (or Presbyter) John. He was a Christian king who ruled over a vast and perfect Christian empire, dedicated to the defeat of Muslims and offering assistance with the ongoing Crusades. In fact, the Second Crusade had not long finished, and had gone very badly for the Christians. In need of a shot in the arm, a verification of faith, the letter was well timed indeed.

The name was already familiar in the courts of Europe, but until the letter arrived no one had really believed in him. Crusader Otto of Freising had reported news in 1144 of this great king, descended from one of the three Magi, who ruled over a wealthy and powerful kingdom, who had laid waste the armies of Medea, Persia, and Assyria, and who had sent an army to help the crusaders but had been turned back by the floodwaters of the Tigris. The letter confirmed what Otto had reported, though embellished by many fantastic tales of wealth, and placing Prester John in "the kingdom of the Three Indias," a kingdom that stretched, so he said, from the Tower of Babel to the Rising of the Sun. The Second Crusade had been a total disaster, and the non-appearance of help for the hapless French and German crusaders who had been badly beaten by the Seljuk Turks, and had failed even to take Damascus as a consolation, was a convenient excuse for the embarrassed Christians.

The legend soon took hold. In 1177 Pope Alexander III sent his personal physician, Master Philip, to Prester John with a reply urging his help. Master Philip made it to Palestine, but was never heard of again. Travelers, though, began to report that they themselves had been in

Prester John's kingdom and confirmed everything the letter said, with a few embellishments of their own. Giovanni Capini reported Prester John's army as soldiers made out of copper who were filled with fire and exploded when they reached enemy lines. Copies of the letter, each adding extra features, circulated for more than 100 years—the fountain of youth lay in Prester John's kingdom; giant women on horseback laid waste to the enemy; seven-horned bulls roamed the land. In the fourteenth century, John de Mandeville, a British adventurer, wrote the most fantastic account of all.

There were at least grains of truth to the story. St. Thomas, one of the Apostles, most definitely carried the word of Jesus to southern India. There is still a strong Christian sect in his name in Kerala, replete with a golden cross in honor of St. Thomas. The Nestorian Church spread from there through some of Asia also, although by 1100 many had converted to the Muslim religion. Much of the embellishment in the letters corresponds precisely with reports of the battles of Alexander the Great in other chronicles—the Amazon women, the soldiers who burn, a magical salamander—so there is no doubt that these aspects of the Prester John myth were lifted from that source. And around the end of the twelfth century, not long after the time of the original letters, the army of Genghis Khan was indeed vanquishing Muslim armies in Central Asia; although of course, the Christian part was just wishful thinking.

By around 1400, though, enough real explorers, Marco Polo among them, had penetrated deep enough into Asia and returned safely without finding Prester John to make it pretty clear that there was no great Christian kingdom there. Undaunted, the true believers simply said they had made a mistake; by Asia they meant Abyssinia, the kingdom of Ethiopia in East Africa. Again there was no doubt that Christianity had spread that far; indeed, Rastafarians are essentially descendants of a group that had been converted by Coptic missionaries coming south from Egypt around the year 400. And in 1488 a prince from Benin visited the Portuguese court and reported a great and powerful

POPE ALEXANDER III
A fresco of the coronation of Pope Alexander III in 1159 by Spinello Aretino, 1407.

king of the Mossi, which was interpreted as meaning the Kingdom of Moses. This set off all the rumor mills again, and was enough for the Portuguese explorers who rounded Africa to be on the lookout, and for maps of Africa at the time to begin to show the land of Prester John in the approximate area of Ethiopia. The legend, regardless of the fact that Prester John would by now have been close to 500 years old, lived on until the discovery of the Americas and the search for El Dorado killed off Prester John for good.

But none of this would really qualify for inclusion, any more so than belief in alien abductions would today, unless real damage results. It seems likely that the original letter was written by the Holy Roman Emperor Frederick Barbarossa as a deliberate attempt to destabilize the papacy. If there was a perfect Christian kingdom elsewhere, then it clearly wasn't in Rome. Barbarossa definitely had met Otto.

In the historical novel *Baudolino* by Umberto Eco, the whole myth is put together by an adventurer, Maudlin, who Barbarossa had sent to study with Otto. Eco's book mixes fact with fiction and the quest for Prester John with the quest for the Holy Grail, but people really did believe in all this, and sent thousands of men to futile deaths in crusade after crusade in the certain expectation that they would be met in the Holy Land by Prester John and his magical army to capture Jerusalem once and for all.

IT SEEMS LIKELY THAT THE ORIGINAL LETTER WAS WRITTEN BY THE HOLY ROMAN EMPEROR FREDERICK BARBAROSSA AS A DELIBERATE ATTEMPT TO DESTABILISE THE PAPACY.

GEORGE PODIEBRAD, THE LAST BOHEMIAN, AND WORLD PEACE

1458–1471

MOTIVATION

anger

charity

envy

faith

gluttony

greed

hope

lust

pride

sloth

Main Culprit: George Podiebrad (Jirí of Podebrady) (1420–1471)

Damage Done: For all his efforts, the last true Bohemian to lead his country for five centuries

Why: Attempting to create a union for trans-European peace guaranteed his fate

The first documented plan for a European confederation, responding to the desire to establish lasting peace between the nations of Europe, was proposed in 1463 to Louis XI by the King of Bohemia, George Podiebrad; it consisted of creating a political assembly, a court of justice, a combined army and a federal budget.

European Commission Roundtable, 2004

The tag "Bohemian" has long been separated from the country that gave birth to the word. Probably originating from the arrival of Catholic refugees from Bohemia in France early in the fifteenth century, the term was intermingled with the advent of gypsies around the same time, and eventually, the nomadic and dissolute life of the gypsies was called "Bohemian," a name that has lasted for many centuries. Shakespeare bizarrely gave Bohemia a coastline in *The Winter's Tale*. Thackeray and Walter Scott both used "Bohemian" to mean a wanderer with no country. *La Bohème*, in the 1890s, positioned Bohemians in the Latin Quarter of Paris. In the 1950s we find Norman Podhoretz condemning Jack Kerouac, the Beats, and specifically what he saw as their suburban, alienated followers as "Know-Nothing Bohemians."

Meanwhile, Bohemia, though liberated from many centuries of foreign rule, is subsumed within the Czech Republic. But there was once a country of Bohemia that ever so briefly had a king and its place in history, including *History's Worst Decisions*.

Public Domain

GEORGE PODIEBRAD
A mural by Alphonse Mucha (1860–1939) showing Cardinal Fantin demanding that the Hussite king George Podiebrad should submit to the authority of the pope in Rome.

Many leaders lost their kingdoms through the abuses of power catalogued throughout this volume, but George Podiebrad lost Bohemia for the crime of fostering a hope for the peaceful future of mankind. Almost forgotten today, he can be found as a footnote in the annals of Czech history, and in the origins of the United Nations as one of the first to come up with a charter for cooperation between nations leading to world peace, an idea that to this very day remains controversial. Ironically, the first manifestation of his dream died hundreds of years later, as the Nazis invaded his homeland in 1938, ending 20 years of self-rule that was the first moment of Bohemian independence since his death in 1471.

If this suggestion seems too outrageous to be true, it is worth noting that in 2003, in a major speech to the Council of Europe, the Danish Minister for Foreign Affairs commenced by crediting George Podiebrad with the first concept for a United Europe, while the historian Robert Frank puts Podiebrad in league with Kant and Mazzini among the progenitors of European unity. But none of these very recent paeans of praise document what befell George and his kingdom, as a result of his scheme. It has taken history more than 500 years to acknowledge his role, let alone the fate that befell his country.

Podiebrad came to power during a strange and tumultuous time for Europe. The Black Death had decimated much of the population in the fourteenth century. The Papal Schism of 1378 had driven the papacy from Rome to Avignon, reducing its power and putting it, in the minds of many, under undue influence from the French king. The Ottoman Empire was beginning to threaten from the East. It hadn't been that long before that Mongols had swept into Europe, specifically Hungary (the Magyars), and removed that part of what had briefly been a significant Bohemian kingdom under the banner of the Holy Roman Empire. While German influence, specifically that of merchants trading under the banner of the Hanseatic League, was creating economic and political pressure to the north.

The focal city of Bohemia, Prague, had seen golden days under Emperor Charles IV, but the dynasty that had ruled before had died out; Charles was from the House of Luxemburg, and on arrival in Prague could not speak a word of Czech. In 1348 he founded one of the first European universities, as well as building much of what still makes Prague one of the most elegant and beloved cities in the world. However, he still wasn't seen as Czech, and after his death, revolt started to foment among the Czech nobility, given voice by the beginnings of one of the great uprisings of the Middle Ages.

One of the first students at the university, and from 1408 its rector, was the priest Jan Hus. Influenced by the Lollard heresy in England, he preached against papal indulgences and the power of the papacy. He was excommunicated and burned at the stake in 1415, but not before he had laid roots for what became the Reformation 100 years later, and initiated discontent and nationalist pride in Bohemia itself.

JAN HUS

Charles's successors proved unable to keep the nobles in check. The Hussites themselves split into two factions, and it was George Podiebrad, one of the nobles from the more moderate of the factions, the Utraquists, who was elected King of Bohemia by the Czech Diet in 1458. Even if you count the earlier Przemyslid dynasty as Czech—descended from the Good King Wenceslas remembered in the

Christmas hymn—George was the first Bohemian king for centuries. He was also to be the last.

The son of an influential noble family; at 14 George had distinguished himself in the Battle of Lipany as a prominent nationalist against Austrian and Hungarian forces. Upon his election to the throne he was faced with immediate problems—the Turks had recaptured Constantinople in 1453 and were a fierce threat on one side; while the new pope, now back in Rome, refused to recognize his rule because he was a member of the Hussite heresy, and he was excommunicated. The Polish Jagiellon dynasty, with the support of many Catholics, had also tried to seize the throne before George's election, which was itself seen as an act of defiance. A holy war was declared against him.

At the same time, he inherited the mantle of Hus and issued a nationalist manifesto "Call To Arms in Defense of the Truth." The printing press, invented in 1454, was already leading to the availability of literature in the Czech language. His manifesto read in part, "Having in mind above all God's glory and the preservation of his holy truth and the calming of this Czech land, we understand that the pope, who should protect and defend that holy truth to his death, to the contrary wants to destroy that holy truth and moreover to destroy, wipe out, and utterly suppress the Czech language, merely to preserve his pride, his avarice, and the rest of his vices . . . he inflames and incites all the nations and languages of the surrounding lands against us." This was remarkable not just for its risky condemnation of the pope, but for its protonationalism in defining the Czechs by their language and its awareness of the power of the unity of nations.

"THE POPE, WHO SHOULD PROTECT AND DEFEND THAT HOLY TRUTH TO HIS DEATH, TO THE CONTRARY WANTS TO DESTROY THAT HOLY TRUTH AND MOREOVER TO DESTROY, WIPE OUT, AND UTTERLY SUPPRESS THE CZECH LANGUAGE"

In 1463 George attempted to find at least one ally by marrying his daughter Catherine to the Hungarian king Matthias Corvinus. Catherine, unfortunately, died the next year, and Corvinus soon declared himself an ally of the Bohemian Catholic nobles in support of the pope, who declared George officially deposed.

Perhaps more out of desperation than anything else, George came up with his grand concept. Conceivably it was a last-ditch attempt to save his country. Certainly it was one born more from hope than anything else, and its audacity sealed his country's fate. He sent his brother-in-law on a tour—seen by some as a pilgrimage—memorialized in a journal as a remarkable diplomatic mission and adventure.

On November 25, 1465, Leon de Rosmital, a Czech lord, left Prague "to visit all the Christian kingdoms as well as all religious and civil principalities on German and Roman soil and particularly the Holy Sepulchre and the tomb of the beloved apostle John." A great, and very pious lord? Admittedly, but he adds that he wishes this voyage "to bring profits and advantages for his own life," and that he wishes to benefit from it "in the exertion of military art" and "in the study of the practices of various countries."

THE BORDERS OF BOHEMIA IN THE CONTEXT OF MODERN EUROPE

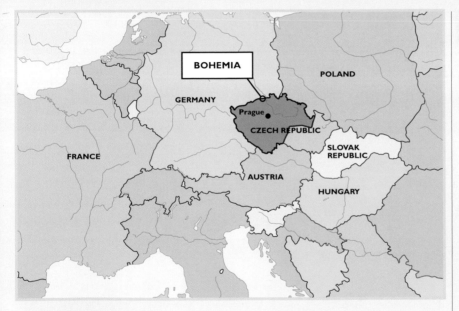

The extent of the State of Bohemia during the reign of George Podiebrad, overlaying a map of modern Europe. It encompassed parts of what is now south-east Germany and the western two-thirds of the Czech Republic.

These official motivations hid a secret diplomatic mission. He left as an ambassador of the king of Bohemia in order to convince kings and princes that he would visit to adhere to a great project, a European federation, independent of the pope and the Germanic emperor. The king of France, Louis XI, was seduced by the idea, which placed France at the head of this organization. In order to convince the other sovereigns, George Podiebrad offered to help them fight the Turkish advance into the Christian world by mobilizing this federation. Moreover, he proposed a permanent council charged with regulating the mutual litigations of the princes. Leon de Rosmital met, in addition to Louis XI, the duke of Burgundy, Philippe the Good; the king of England, Edward IV; the king of Castille, Henri IV; the king of Portugal, Alfonso V; and the king of Aragon, John II. Each of his hosts treated him well, inviting him to dinners, balls, tournaments and bullfights—but none of them took the invitation seriously. Pope Pius II was furious and redoubled his efforts to overthrow a leader who was not only a religious heretic, but whose suggestions of European unity he took as being less threatening to the Turks than to the papacy itself.

PIUS DECLARED A CRUSADE AGAINST PODIEBRAD AND THE CZECHS. MATTHIAS CORVINUS, GEORGE'S ERSTWHILE SON-IN-LAW, WAS DECLARED KING OF BOHEMIA BY THE POPE AND INVADED.

Pius declared a crusade against Podiebrad and the Czechs. Matthias Corvinus, George's erstwhile son-in-law, was declared king of Bohemia by the pope and invaded. George won a famous battle in 1468, but the Hungarians took much of the east of the country.

George, exhausted from battling on all fronts, died on March 22, 1471. His attempts at securing European unity died with him. There was no dynasty—this was an elected kingship, not a hereditary one—and this beleaguered nation could find no one within its own ranks to defend it. The members of the Diet gave themselves up first to the Polish kings, hoping for protection from the Hungarians, and 20 years later to the Hapsburgs, who, within two years, had removed them and the Czechs from power until the end of World War I. George's plan had so isolated his country and terrified his neighbors that the combination of religious heresy and political nonconformity that he represented was enough to persuade the surrounding nations that his ideas and his nation should be silenced forever.

The Prague Spring of 1968, the Velvet Revolution of 1989, and the subsequent ascension to power of playwright Vaclav Havel, perhaps gave belated recognition to the hope represented by George Podiebrad, even though his plans resulted in the long suppression of his country.

MOCTEZUMA AND THE RETURNING GOD

November 1519

MOTIVATION
anger
charity
envy
faith
gluttony
greed
hope
lust
pride
sloth

Main Culprit: Moctezuma (Montezuma) II (1466–1520)

Damage Done: Gave away his entire civilization

Why: Mistaking a Spanish conquistador for the return of the god Quetzalcoatl, Moctezuma welcomed the conquerors into his city with open arms

O our lord, thou hast suffered fatigue, thou hast endured weariness, thou hast come to arrive on earth. Thou hast come to govern thy city of Mexico, thou hast come to descend upon my mat, upon thy seat which for a time I have guarded for thee . . . I do not merely dream that I see thee, that I look into thy face . . . The rulers departed maintained that thou wouldst come to visit to thy city, that thou wouldst descend.

Emperor Moctezuma II to Hernando Cortés

Of all the gods in the Mesoamerican pantheon, the great god Quetzalcoatl was by far the most important; he was the creator of Heaven and Earth. Literally the name means "Plumed Serpent," but he could take many forms, including the human form of the high priest Topiltzin. The legend was that many centuries ago, in anger at the behavior of the Toltec peoples, Quetzalcoatl had taken off on the Eastern Sea for the Land of the Red on a raft of serpents, vowing one day, as gods are prone to do, to return and take power. Legend goes on to say that he had made his exit in the guise of Topiltzin, a fair man with a beard. (It is possible that this rather odd depiction was caused by the unexpected appearance of the Irish priest St. Brendan on the coast.) In any event, the ground was laid for what is perhaps the most extraordinary feat of misjudgment in these pages, the greeting of a marauding conqueror by one of the most powerful men in the world, not as an annoying insect to be crushed, but as a god. It led to the subsequent downfall of an entire civilization. Moctezuma II (also known as Montezuma), Emperor of the Mexica (cultural descendants of the Aztecs, but actually a different tribe), ruler of Tenochtitlán, in an act of faith, greeted the conquistador Hernando Cortés as the returning Quetzalcoatl. On this mistake turned the fate not just of the Mexican empire but of a whole continent.

GOLDEN OPPORTUNITY

It hadn't taken long from the time of Columbus's accidental discovery of the New World for the Spanish Empire to set up a base for exploration, discovery, and plunder. They chose Cuba as that staging post, a short hop to Florida and not so far across the Gulf of Mexico (known to the Mexica, logically, as the Eastern Sea) to Yucatán. Two expeditions had made some progress—some friendly contact, and some pitched battles with the Maya—enough to make it clear that the locals had no knowledge of gunpowder and that most of the artifacts the Spanish found or were offered were made of gold. The second expedition also found signs of human sacrifice and cannibalism. They discovered that the coastal tribes lived under the control of the Mexica in a giant inland city—and would be willing to ally with anyone who might free them of that yoke. The prospects were therefore exciting indeed—the chance for glorious imperial conquest; the opportunity to convert the heathen; and plenty of gold for the taking. So Hernando Cortés, not the wild barbarian that history suggests but a highly literate lawyer, student of law and Latin at the University of Salamanca, from a noble but illegitimate and poor branch of a leading Castilian family—and by now a magistrate in Santiago, the Spanish capital of Cuba—led the third expedition from Cuba in 1519. Unlike the two previous expeditions, he had with him not only heavy artillery, but horses and dogs. He also possessed an advantage over the empire of the Mexica that he could not possibly have foreseen.

History depicts the Spaniards as having wiped out the Aztec civilization. Moctezuma II and his predecessors had expanded their kingdom southward over the centuries and established the Mexica as the most powerful group in the region. They built their capital, Tenochtitlán, on a rocky island in the middle of the Lake of Mexico. They ruled neighboring tribes, including the remnants of the Mayan civilization and the Toltecs, and dominated at least 30 tribes. They had established themselves around the 1420s in a bloody series of struggles with the Tepaneca, and Moctezuma II was the ninth emperor to control the region, extracting mostly tributes in kind that helped to make for an immensely rich capital city. The Mexica worshipped a god of war, but combined this with the remnants of the Aztec belief system, including the legend of Quetzalcoatl as creator of the world. It made for a formidable and much feared combination.

Tenochtitlán itself—now Mexico City—was by the time of the Spaniards' arrival perhaps grander than any European city, with a system of canals that reminded the Spaniards of Venice. The Mexica were extremely skilled in design and sculpture, metalwork, woodwork, and mosaics. They had complex ball games and grand pageants of music and dance. They also, perhaps most devastatingly, had a very hospitable demeanor. They had a wonderful and beautiful city, but failed to make key technological advancements; they had not invented the wheel or gunpowder, and had no knowledge of seafaring. Moctezuma's costly leap of faith would probably not have occurred if they had.

There is no doubt that the Mexica were aware of strange happenings on the coast from the beginning of the century. As a civilization, they

MOCTEZUMA II
An 1892 color lithograph of a 1519 illustration entitled *Entrance of Cortez in Mexico*, depicting the first meeting of Hernando Cortés and Moctezuma II.

WORD SPREAD OF THE
FAIR-HAIRED, BEARDED
MEN WITH THEIR
STRANGE ANIMALS AND
FIERCE WEAPONRY
THAT MOVED OVER THE
GROUND SO EASILY.
THE MORE MOCTEZUMA
HEARD, THE MORE
NERVOUS HE BECAME.
THE PRIESTS HAD
PREDICTED THE RETURN
OF QUETZALCOATL
FROM ACROSS THE
EASTERN SEA THAT
VERY YEAR.

appear to have had very little contact with the outside world and very little curiosity about it. Word spread of the fair-haired, bearded men with their strange animals and fierce weaponry that moved over the ground so easily. The more Moctezuma heard, the more nervous he became. The priests had predicted the return of Quetzalcoatl from across the Eastern Sea that very year. The new arrivals fitted the descriptions all too vividly. For all his power and pomp and ceremony, these belief systems and superstitions apparently weighed heavily on Moctezuma. Even without his superior weaponry, Cortés had essentially already beaten the enormous empire of the Mexica as his small expeditionary force of 400 or 500 made their way across the mountains to the famed Tenochtitlán. Emissaries from the two sides had met in the mountains and exchanged gifts—garments for the Spaniards that turned out to be fashioned for a returning god—while those returning to Tenochtitlán were apparently anointed with fresh sacrificial blood, their reward for having met with the god.

In November 1519 Cortés walked onto the southern causeway linking the mainland with the capital. Moctezuma descended from his jewel-encrusted litter and greeted Cortés with the most ironic speech ever given to an opposing army in history; a speech which is quoted in the epigraph to this chapter.

After that, it was all over; there really wasn't any fighting. Moctezuma had essentially handed the kingdom over to the newcomer. Within three days he was a prisoner in his own palace. After two months Moctezuma had formally accepted vassalage to Charles V, king of Spain. By all accounts Cortés and Moctezuma got along famously over the succeeding months and even discussed alliances and the potential conquest of China. But by April 1520 word got back to Cuba of the improbable success of the expedition, beyond not only their wildest dreams, but also well beyond any orders that had been given. A force was sent, led by the deputy governor, to demand the renewed fealty of Cortés. He left the city to meet and ultimately defeat the Spanish troops; but while he was away his deputy Pedro de Alvarado, rather more skeptical of the whole surrender, took the opportunity to butcher the assembled ranks of Mexica nobility at a fiesta, sparking an insurrection and siege. Moctezuma was killed on the roof of his palace by his own people while trying to quell the fighting. Cortés returned to a bloodbath. By the time he retook the city a year later, many thousands of Mexica had died and the ruin of a great empire was complete. An entire civilization had surrendered itself to a conqueror on the strength of an inherited belief, and the once-feared Moctezuma had become the stuff of history.

MOTIVATION
anger
charity
envy
faith
gluttony
greed
hope
lust
pride
sloth

JOHAN DE WITT, NEW AMSTERDAM, AND PULAU RUN: THE WORST DEAL EVER MADE

1667

Main Culprit: Johan de Witt (1623–1672)

Damage Done: Dutch history was forever transformed by swapping Manhattan Island for a small Spice Island

Why: The Dutch monopoly on nutmeg turned out not to be worth the price of what became the greatest city on earth

Who were the Dutch and English to trade islands that didn't belong to them in the first place?

A native of the island of Run, quoted in the *New Yorker*

Nutmeg—Convicts and sailors sometimes have recourse to nutmeg. About a tablespoon is swallowed with water. Results are vaguely similar to marijuana with side effects of headache and nausea. Death would probably supervene before addiction if such addiction is possible. I have only taken nutmeg once.

William Burroughs, appendix to *The Naked Lunch*

In earlier times, the great empires of the world would trade territories. Whoever had lost the most recent war would give up pieces on the world chessboard and maybe get something smaller in return. By convention, the winner got to pick; but the first choice is not always the best. In a slice of error from history caused by greed and pride, and, it must be said, some bad luck, the Dutch managed to hand over what was to become the world's most valuable real estate in exchange for what is now a very poor, small island in the far-off reaches of Indonesia. Such is the story of Manhattan and Pulau Run.

THE SPICE RACE

Among the early prizes of colonialism were spices; these were such extraordinary supplements to European foodstuffs that they were the most valuable commodities in the world. Nutmeg was perhaps the most precious of all, both as a hallucinogen and an aphrodisiac, even as a cure for the plague. The fall of Constantinople in 1453, however, had closed the overland route to the spices and the race to find a seaborne passage began, da Gama in one direction, Columbus in another. Vasco da Gama (who was actually trying to find the kingdom of Prester John) reached Southeast Asia and returned laden with spices in 1499, while the expedition of Albuquerque brought the Portuguese the port of Malacca in 1511. Two small Portuguese galleons sailed on through the Indonesian archipelago and reached Banda, the main island in the Moluccas, soon known as the Spice Islands. For 60 years the Portuguese held sway in the region, but after Sir Francis Drake's expedition of 1574, mercantile exploration from Britain took off, with Queen Elizabeth signing the East India Company's charter in 1600.

The Dutch were also exploring—Jacob van Neck had returned to Amsterdam with a cargo that quadrupled his investors' capital; but more by luck than judgment, a small British pinnace with a crew of ten had been pushed by a storm towards the smallest of the Bandas, Pulau Run, which turned out to be one of the greatest sources of nutmeg. The Dutch, meanwhile, much better organized than the British, had almost entirely displaced the Portuguese by 1609, and after a run-in with local cannibals, built a fort on one of the Bandas. Only Pulau Run remained a British possession, indeed one of the first of the nascent British Empire. James I was rather bizarrely known as King of England, Scotland, Ireland, France, Puloway, and Puloroon.

Meanwhile, a separate but related competition saw British and Dutch explorers trying to find passages to the Spice Islands by way of the still unexplored North American continent. The Dutch hired the British explorer Henry Hudson for the task. Having failed to find the Northwest Passage, he sailed south from Newfoundland, past Cape Cod, and stumbled upon Long Island, and then a small, apparently fertile island at the mouth of what is now known as the Hudson River. Hudson was to be killed in a mutiny on his next trip, but the Dutch took a liking to the island he had found, and established a small colony at its southern tip of the island, building an exact duplicate of their fort on the Bandas. In 1626 Peter Minuit purchased the rest of the island from the locals for 60 guilders, and "Fort Nieuw Amsterdam" was born.

THE PURCHASE OF MANHATTAN
Peter Minuit Buying Manhattan from the Natives, 1626, Edwin Willard Deming (1862–1942).

THE COLONY OF NIEUW AMSTERDAM WAS NOT ESPECIALLY SUCCESSFUL THOUGH, AND ALTHOUGH THE DUTCH HAD SET UP SOME TRADING COLONIES ALONG THE HUDSON RIVER, THEY MADE LITTLE USE OF THEIR FOOTHOLD.

Hostilities between the two nations continued during the seventeenth century, mostly as minor skirmishes. At one point, when the British left Pulau Run unmanned, the Dutch commander Coen snuck ashore and had all the nutmeg trees cut down. Nutmeg was being sold by now in Europe at something like a 6,000 percent markup. The Dutch policy at this time was to replace the native population with settlers and create a monopoly. Three naval wars broke out between the powers during this period, ostensibly over European matters but actually in part over trade routes. The colony of Nieuw Amsterdam was not especially successful though, and although the Dutch had some trading colonies along the Hudson River, they made little use of their foothold. During the second war, while they made headway in Europe—burning the British fleet in the Thames—they lost Nieuw Amsterdam to a British force in 1664.

When it came to a settlement—the Treaty of Breda in 1667—Johan de Witt, the ruler of Holland and the United Provinces, negotiated what appeared to be a favorable agreement. The British were not enamored of their new island, and offered to trade it for the Dutch sugar holdings in Surinam, but were refused. Finally they agreed to keep to what was to become Manhattan in return for ceding the, by now nutmeg-free, island of Pulau Run, so that the Dutch could at least feel they had a monopoly, and both sides were satisfied.

Nutmeg proved easy to grow and when the British invaded the Bandas during the Napoleonic Wars they took the opportunity to replant it across the empire. Then the volcano of Gunung Api destroyed much of the crop, before nutmeg's use in oils was replaced by chemicals. To this day people are trying to grow nutmeg in quantity, and claim it is purchased by Coca-Cola—but it was still a poor trade.

Pulau Run—now part of Indonesia—gained independence from the Dutch after World War II. The Bandas were used as a penal colony, which was overrun by the Japanese, and the capital was nearly leveled by American bombing. Pulau Run has 1,200 inhabitants, no fresh water, and the remains of a Dutch nutmeg factory. Manhattan is, well, Manhattan. Could Johan de Witt have known? No. But Dutch greed was largely responsible for the unfulfilled promise of the Spice Islands; the Dutch East India Company was dissolved in 1800, millions of guilders in debt due, in part, to history's worst trade.

THE LOCATIONS OF MANHATTAN AND PULAU RUN

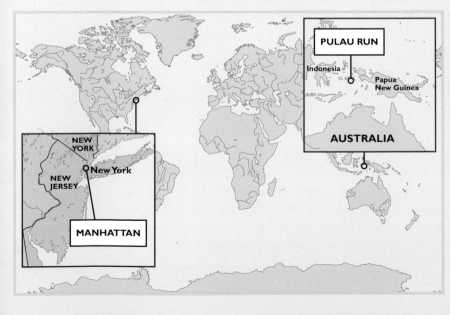

While the location of Manhattan on the East Coast of the USA is known to billions around the world, Pulau Run is a tiny island that few have even heard of. Part of the Indonesian Banda Islands it lies in the Banda Sea that separates the Indonesian island of Celebes to the west from Papua New Guinea to the east and Timor to the south.

MOTIVATION

anger
charity
envy
faith
gluttony
greed
hope
lust
pride
sloth

LORD NORTH AND GEORGE III'S TEA PARTY

December 16, 1773

Main Culprit: Lord Frederick North (1732–1792)

Damage Done: The loss of Britain's American colonies

Why: Trying to steal from the settlers

Once vigorous measures appear to be the only means left to bringing the Americans to a due submission to the mother country, the colonies will submit.

King George III

FAREWELL the Tea-board with your gaudy attire,
Ye cups and ye saucers that I did admire;
To my cream pot and tongs I now bid adieu;
That pleasure's all fled that I once found in you.
Farewell pretty chest that so lately did shine,
With hyson and congo and best double fine;
Many a sweet moment by you I have sat,
Hearing girls and old maids to tattle and chat;
And the spruce coxcomb laugh at nothing at all,
Only some silly work that might happen to fall.
No more shall my teapot so generous be
In filling the cups with this pernicious tea,
For I'll fill it with water and drink out the same,
Before I'll lose LIBERTY that dearest name,
Because I am taught (and believe it is fact)
That our ruins is aimed at in the late act,
Of imposing a duty on all foreign teas,
Which detestable stuff we can quit when we please
LIBERTY'S the Goddess that I do adore,
And I'll maintain her right until my last hour,
Before she shall part I will die in the cause,
For I'll never be govern'd by tyranny's laws.

Anon. "A Lady's Adieu to her Tea Table"

The East India Company is a frequent presence in these pages. Time and again it appears as a significant player at moments of folly, normally requiring a government bail-out of one sort or another. The year 1773 in England is a case in point. The company had stockpiles of tea and nowhere to sell it. Prime Minister Lord North, in a prime example of idiocy caused in part by greed but more so by arrogance, thought it would be a capital idea to undercut the merchants of the American colonies and allow the company to export and sell direct. It wasn't the first time, and certainly not the last, that companies called in political favors to salvage their own disasters (see the chapter on Enron for a contemporary example). But in this case, the consequences were extreme indeed, igniting the rebellion that led to the loss of the American colonies, the Revolutionary War, and a huge hole in the British Empire.

The Tea Party itself was essentially an act of mercantile rebellion against iniquitous taxes from London. The idiocy of George III and his ministers, most notably Lord North, essentially came down to a misunderstanding of the American colony and how it differed from the other British colonies that then existed. This wasn't India or some other settlement where British rule depended on force or uneasily sat alongside native government. The Americans had established a free colony and by the late eighteenth century were not prepared to be treated like vassals. It seems that George had no idea at all of this—he lost control of the colony with the greatest potential of all.

TEA AND TAXES

In 1766 the reign of the new King George III, who had ascended to the throne in 1760, began to be plagued by financial problems. His first minister Pitt the Elder lost control of financial affairs and under intense pressure was forced to reduce the Land Tax by 25 percent. Charles Townshend, Pitt's chancellor of the exchequer, had been instrumental in helping himself and his friends by reducing the tax, but resolved to make up the shortfall by taxing commerce out of the American colonies, introducing taxes not only on tea but on other staples such as glass, paper, even silk handkerchiefs, but easing taxation on British exports bound for the colonies:

> "An act for granting certain duties in the British colonies and plantations in America; for allowing a drawback of the duties of

customs upon the exportation, from this kingdom of coffee and cocoa nuts of the produce of the said colonies or plantations; for discontinuing the drawbacks payable on china earthenware exported to America; and for more effectually preventing the clandestine running of goods in the colonies and plantations.

WHEREAS it is expedient that a revenue should be raised in your Majesty's dominions in America, for making a more certain and adequate provision for defraying the charge of the administration of justice, and the support of civil government, in such provinces where it shall be found necessary; and towards further defraying the expenses of defending, protecting, and securing, the said dominions."

Charles Townshend, Tea Act, 1767

The English of all people should have known that you may be able to get away with taxing all kinds of things, but you can't mess about with the morning "cuppa."

John Hancock had been arrested and charged in 1768 with smuggling. This followed two Stamp Acts in the mid-1760s that had caused much uproar among the merchants of the states. Hancock organized a boycott of China tea coming in from the East India Company, a boycott especially interesting historically because it relied on women. Tea was widely replaced by coffee and infusions of local berries. The response was the Tea Act, felt to be clever in that it would reduce the price of tea to the end consumer by cutting out the middlemen completely and bypass the boycott. It completely misfired. All over the colony, the East India Company found ports closed to its tea ships. In Boston, however, the port remained open, and on December 16, 1773, 150 men, known as the Sons of Liberty, under the leadership of Samuel Adams and cheered on by a crowd of some 5,000, boarded three incoming ships,

THE BOSTON TEA PARTY
American revolutionaries dressed as Native Americans dump tea from a British ship into Boston Harbor.

broke open 342 tea chests, and hurled them into the harbor. Similar acts of rebellion broke out around the colony as word spread. Action from the now prime minister Lord North and George III was immediate, albeit futile: in four acts of 1774, the Coercive Acts, Massachusetts was to be severely punished for its crimes and for refusing to pay for the damaged property. Far from gaining greater representation, self-government was summarily reduced. The port was closed and armed reinforcements sent in. Within two years the colonies were at war, the Declaration of Independence had been signed, and the Americas were lost to Britain. Soon the British would face a series of other blows—the fear engendered by revolution across the Channel, the downfall of the French monarchy, and the aggrandizement of Napoleon. No serious effort would ever be made to recapture the colonies. Even now many British don't treat their former colonial subjects with quite the respect they deserve, and tea is most certainly not America's drink; indeed, it even gets iced.

WITHIN TWO YEARS THE COLONIES WERE AT WAR, THE DECLARATION OF INDEPENDENCE HAD BEEN SIGNED, AND THE AMERICAS WERE LOST TO BRITAIN.

Many historians sometimes downplay the obvious, including the personal motivations of people at the time. Of course it wasn't about tea, they opine, that was just an excuse. But sometimes the obvious explanation can be the right one. There was only a minimal interest in rebellion and independence at the accession of George III. The Sons of Liberty were seen at the time as a rather dangerous terrorist organization, as no doubt any group of people taking direct action against taxes would also be seen today. There was no historical inevitability about losing the American colonies at that point. The 13 colonies were far from secure; the French and the Spaniards were also claiming parts of the continent and significant threats to the safety of the colonies lay to the north and south. British military protection was not entirely a bad thing. Benjamin Franklin, of all people, was horrified by the Boston Tea Party and offered to compensate the British government out of his own pocket.

Sometimes it really is one stupid move that goes too far. Townshend's acts, followed by the Coercive Acts led Britain into a war that could have been avoided, and one for which Lord North was held largely responsible. He suffered the ignominy of becoming the first prime minister to be forced out of office by a vote of no confidence and he resigned in 1782. Ironically, Wroxton Abbey, North's family home, is now a school for Americans in England.

MOTIVATION

anger
charity
envy
faith
gluttony
greed
hope
lust
pride
sloth

NAPOLEON, THE MARCH TO RUSSIA, AND FRANKENSTEIN

June 1812 – June 1816

Main Culprit: Napoleon Bonaparte (1769–1821)

Damage Done: Destruction of the French army

Why: Overwhelming self-confidence betrayed by a strange encounter with a story

The idea so possessed my mind, that a thrill of fear ran through me, and I wished to exchange the ghastly image of my fancy for the realities around. I see them still: the very room, the dark parquet, the closed shutters, with the moonlight struggling through, and the sense I had that the glassy lake and white high Alps were beyond. I could not so easily get rid of my hideous phantom; still it haunted me. I must try to think of something else. I recurred to my ghost story—my tiresome unlucky ghost story! O! if I could only contrive one which would frighten my reader as I myself had been frightened that night! Swift as light and as cheering was the idea that broke in upon me. "I have found it! What terrified me will terrify others; and I need only describe the specter which had haunted my midnight pillow." On the morrow I announced that I had thought of a story. I began that day with the words, It was on a dreary night of November, making only a transcript of the grim terrors of my waking dream.

Mary Shelley, Preface to *Frankenstein*

Do you think I have come all this way just to conquer these huts?

Napoleon, July 1812, in Vitebsk

The appearance of Napoleon Bonaparte in this book should come as no surprise. His invasion of Russia in 1812 was not a good idea, and there are a number of theories as to what went wrong and why, ranging from simple megalomania to painful kidney stones to heroic Russian resistance, which to be truthful rather wisely consisted mostly of retreating faster than Napoleon could advance. Unquestionably, as he pushed further into Russia and into trouble, Napoleon made a number of uncharacteristic errors of judgment that resulted in eventual disaster—but it is not enough simply that he made mistakes. Many histories see the turning point not as the retreat from Moscow, nor the Battle of Borodino, but an apparent and seemingly inexplicable change of mind in the city of Vitebsk in what is now Belarus, which seems to have been caused by uncontrollable anger at a strange turn of events.

NAPOLEON
Jacques-Louis David's, *Napoleon Crossing the St. Bernard Pass* (1800–1801).

Four years after the fateful events of Vitebsk, with Napoleon defeated at Waterloo and in exile on Elba, it was fashionable again for the intellectuals of England to wander the byways of Europe. On the night of June 16, 1816, in the middle of a mighty storm in Geneva, Lord Byron was regaling his guests with ghost stories. One of the guests, Mary Shelley, was to leave with the idea for her novel, *Frankenstein*. The genesis of which links Napoleon to one of the great blunders of history.

It isn't quite fair to assume that the whole enterprise of the Long March to Russia was as stupid as it subsequently appeared to be, or as pointless. Tsar Alexander posed a genuine threat to the French Empire. Napoleon's armies had destroyed the armies of Europe stacked against him almost without fail. His enormous arrogance was not without justification. Hegel, in 1806, proclaimed Napoleon "the Emperor, the soul of the world. It is a marvellous feeling to see such a man who, concentrated here, on a single point, sitting on his horse, extends himself over the world and dominates it all." He controlled all of Western Europe, from the Portuguese border to the edge of the Ottoman Empire. He had soundly defeated the Austrians at Austerlitz in 1805, the Prussians at Jena in 1806, and the Russians at Friedland in 1807. As a result, he had control over what is now Poland, large parts of Austria and Prussia, and his empire stretched to the Elbe. He had faced and seen the weakness and poor leadership of the Russian army. He correctly deduced that the English would be diverted by the American War of Independence. But Russia had made peace with the Turks to the south and appeared ready to go head-to-head with Napoleon, though she could muster an army of only a quarter of a million against the combined French and client states' force of over 680,000 men. If anyone thought invading Russia was a bad idea, they probably deduced it would be a worse idea to say so.

After the march to Moscow began, Napoleon's troops found the going tough, and supply wagons failed to keep up, where a smaller, more dedicated army may have fared better. After the last of the cattle had been slaughtered there was nothing to eat. The Russians were leaving behind them little but scorched earth. Hunger, dysentery, diphtheria and typhus killed 60,000 of Napoleon's troops before a shot was fired. Horses with little to graze on died by the thousands, and Napoleon was losing 5,000 to 6,000 men a day to sickness and desertion.

On July 29, Napoleon and his army staggered into Vitebsk, after a minor skirmish with the Russian rearguard. Vitebsk was a ghost town. Napoleon was advised that he would soon have no cavalry left. He held a council, and his three top-ranking subordinates urged a halt. Napoleon agreed, saying that they were not going to repeat the folly of Charles XII of Sweden in 1708 by forging on ahead of his baggage train. But by the following day he had changed his mind. There are a number of contemporary reports suggesting psychological imbalance and strange behavior. Some thought he did not want to admit folly or show weakness. One writer recorded the following discussion:

A NUMBER OF CONTEMPORARY REPORTS SUGGEST NAPOLEON SUFFERED FROM PSYCHOLOGICAL IMBALANCE.

> GENERAL   There is the necessity of organizing liberated Lithuania, of setting up hospitals and supply depots, of establishing a central point for recuperation, defence, and subsequent departure on a line of operation which is growing longer and longer every day—shouldn't all this make us decide to stop here on the border of old Russia?

> NAPOLEON Do you think I have come all this way just to conquer these huts?

> 28 July, 1812

Napoleon accused his top subordinates of being too soft. He claimed to be eager to meet Tsar Alexander in battle, considered then the only way to achieve a victory, and he believed that such a battle would come either at Smolensk or at Moscow, places that he believed Alexander would not be willing to abandon.

NAPOLEON'S ADVANCE AND RETREAT FROM MOSCOW

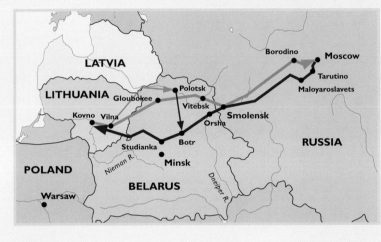

Having crossed the Nieman at Kovno on June 24, 1812, Napoleon's army separated at Vilna with Marshall Oudinot's much smaller northern force heading towards St. Petersburg, but being stalled at Polotsk in August, shortly after Napoleon had called a pause to the advance at Vitebsk.

Upon the resumption of the march Russian forces continued to withdraw in the face of the French, while fighting notable battles at Smolensk and Borodino. Moscow was abandoned before Napoleon entered the city on September 14 and occupied it for just over a month, before his untenable position forced him to leave.

Russian forces harried the retreating French army, and clashes at Tarutino and Maloyaroslavets forced their route further north. By the time the French recrossed the Nieman barely 10,000 men of the original 680,000-strong army remained.

There is plenty of evidence to confirm that Napoleon had seemed willing to stop, even to winter, at Vitebsk, call for reinforcements and replenish supplies. While the entire battle plan, like most of Napoleon's, had been based on surprise and speed, both were now lost, and even he seemed to accept that Vitebsk would be a good base. He had been promising his troops a rest at Vitebsk. Admittedly, the Russians had left much of the city deserted and in ruins so that Napoleon would find little food there, but even so, leaving was inadvisable. Yet Napoleon forced the army to march on to almost inevitable disaster, the retreating Russian army fooling him even beyond the gates of Moscow. Indeed, the 15 days in Vitebsk not only did little to provide rest and food for his own forces, they allowed the Russian general Barclay enough time to fall back and meet another Russian division to prepare for the clash at Borodino. The mistake was irretrievable: barely 10,000 of Napoleon's men made it back after he left Moscow in October. French casualties are estimated at between 400,000 and 550,000 men and 175,000 horses. Napoleon abandoned this sorry rabble as they crossed the Nieman River and went back to Paris. Within a month, the Prussians and Austrians had pushed French troops back over the Elbe and the Napoleonic Empire was at an end.

THERE IS A LITTLE-
KNOWN AND
REMARKABLE
EXPLANATION FOR
NAPOLEON'S DECISION
TO LEAVE VITEBSK.

There is a little-known and remarkable explanation for Napoleon's decision to leave Vitebsk. Intelligence officers had brought Napoleon a box full of papers they had found. It appeared to have considerable military significance—papers relating to an Englishman aboard a Russian ship and the activities of French royalists. The letters were mostly in English, and four officers with language skills were summoned to translate and read the papers aloud to the emperor. For ten evenings they read to Napoleon; apparently it was soon clear that there was no intelligence utility to the papers, but they seemed to weave a strange magnetic spell over the emperor and he frequently interrupted the story to make comments and thank Providence for giving him the papers. On the tenth evening, Napoleon suddenly lost his temper and ordered the papers burned. The translators feared for their lives, given the fearsome temper of the emperor, but were so intrigued that they disobeyed orders, read the rest of the papers, and kept them. The French army was on the road to Moscow and ruin within two days. This whole story could of course be a myth, but there is no question that the translators were there, although one was killed at Borodino, and they subsequently wrote about the story once the war was over. Their reports survived and subsequently they recognized elements of what they read in Mary Shelley's novel *Frankenstein*.

Conceivably, the Frankenstein connection was invented by Shelley. There is no doubt that many were fascinated by Napoleon's dynamism and sudden demise. However, no report explains Napoleon's sudden anger at the story to us. So let us at least speculate that the allegory of the fall of a man who sought to conquer nature and the world—it is not hard to draw the connection with Napoleon—proved too much for the fragile psyche of the emperor.

THE WAR OFFICE VERSUS THE LADY WITH THE LAMP: DISEASE IN THE CRIMEA

June 1854 – January 1856

MOTIVATION

anger

charity

envy

faith

gluttony

greed

hope

lust

pride

sloth

Main Culprits: Dr. Sir John Hall (1795–1866), Sir Benjamin Hawes (1770–1860)

Damage Done: 30,000 died from disease in the British Army during the Crimean War

Why: Total lack of interest from the War Office in the barbarous conditions of their troops

I stand at the altar of the murdered men, and, while I live, I fight their cause.

Florence Nightingale

Cannon to right of them,
Cannon to left of them,
Cannon in front of them
Volley'd and thunder'd;
Storm'd at with shot and shell,
Boldly they rode and well,
Into the jaws of Death,
Into the mouth of Hell
Rode the six hundred.

Alfred Lord Tennyson

The Crimean War usually summons thoughts of Tennyson's *Charge of the Light Brigade*, but this entry does not commemorate that. The Charge of the Light Brigade was caused by an honest mistake and probably exacted no more casualties than many similar military misadventures. It may not even have a place in the history books were it not for the stunningly memorable poetry of Lord Tennyson. One other famous personage arose from the Crimean War, though. The carnage, not from the fighting but from disease, caused by the sloth of the authorities whose ignorance was only matched by their lack of interest in the men they sent to their deaths, brought her to the fore. She fought to prevent further tragedy, and that puts the Crimean War and those in charge of the British Army in the record.

A force of 94,000 British Army soldiers embarked for the East in 1854. The British were seeking, with their allies the French, to control Russian ambitions in the Balkans, given the imminent breakup of the Ottoman Empire in the region. The British were anxious about Russian expansionism in many areas, especially any threat they might pose to India, part of the anxiety that led to the Indian Mutiny (see the next chapter). Theoretically, the British and French were fighting over the custody of the holy places in Jerusalem, but that was a convenient excuse for controlling the Russian threat. In 1783 the Russians seized the Crimea, a peninsula on the north shore of the Black Sea, now part of Ukraine, from the ailing Turks. In 1853 they used the Crimean ports as a base for launching an attack on the Turks and invading the Balkans. They sank the Turkish fleet at Sinope and launched a land grab. The British and French determined to stop them and set sail for the Crimea. In the meantime, the British in particular were doing much the same thing as the Russians, seizing small strategic parts of the Ottoman Empire in Egypt, Aden, and the Sudan. But the ability of the Russians to reach the Mediterranean through their control of the Black Sea, and essentially find an easier route into Persia, Afghanistan, and India, could not be countenanced.

LADY WITH THE LAMP
Florence Nightingale (1820–1910) depicted nursing during the Crimean War.

© Bettmann | Corbis

The British Army had not seen much action since it had routed Napoleon with the help of the Prussians at the Battle of Waterloo, and lost the

United States forever in the War of 1812. The British navy was close to its famed position of "ruling the waves." Britain had avoided the revolutions of 1848 and, apart from skirmishes in the empire, the army had not really performed for the best part of half a century. Nor had it ever fought in a region like the Crimea. Learning little or nothing from what had befallen Napoleon in Russia — and caring less — a good number of army personnel and politicians in London did not even know where the Crimea was, let alone what the conditions would be like; the men they sent were woefully unprepared. Later reports found administrative confusion, laziness, timidity, callousness, and stupidity, with massive shortages of food, clothing, animal fodder, and shelter. Essentially, the High Command had no idea at all how to conduct the campaign. Of the 94,000 men who embarked, 2,660 were killed in action. Casualties from disease and illness were nearly 30,000 in the British ranks. The French, Turkish, and Russian casualties from the fighting were higher, but it was this death or disabling from disease of 30 percent of the army that finally hit home and led to major changes in the army administration. In 1856 a Board of Review determined, in true military fashion, that all this was very regrettable but just part of the cost of war. "Nobody was to blame," it concluded. The government and the public were anxious to agree — but not without exception.

OF THE 94,000 MEN WHO EMBARKED, 2,660 WERE KILLED IN ACTION. CASUALTIES FROM DISEASE AND ILLNESS WERE NEARLY 30,000 IN THE BRITISH RANKS.

Florence Nightingale is deservedly one of the most famous women of the nineteenth century. She has been the subject of many hagiographies over the years, the "Lady with the Lamp" living on as one of the icons of British history. But later research has shown her to have been opportunistic, ruthless, power grabbing, publicity-hungry, and, all in all, a much less likeable person and a much more determined political campaigner than has widely been realized. Fortunately for generations of soldiers, it was these qualities that led to reform in the years following the war, rather than the wonderful nurse wandering around the wards at Scutari.

Nursing was, in the nineteenth century, still a very religious vocation without a great deal of skill involved. On a trip to Egypt, the young Florence had what she described as a series of encounters with God, who instructed her to be a nurse. But she was horrified in her training. Her letters describe high-minded spirituality and stupid nursing routines. She demanded that nurses in her command should actually help patients physically and morally, rather than worshipping while patients died in their own filth. In the eyes of the British High Command this was a dangerously revolutionary doctrine. Oddly enough, many years later it was exactly what detractors accused Mother Theresa of doing.

The other true hero of the war was W. H. Russell. It wasn't as if allowing troops to die of disease was new; what was new was that everyone knew about it for the first time, and that the medical knowledge and means to do something about it existed. Cholera, typhus, and complete lack of sanitation, as well as inadequate supplies for the winter, were rife, after the Battle of Balaclava in particular. He excoriated the High Command: "Are there no devoted women amongst us, able and willing to go forth to minister to the sick and suffering soldiers of the East in the hospitals of Scutari? Are none of the daughters of England, at this extreme hour of need, ready for such a work of mercy?" (*The Times*, September 15 and 22, 1854).

The Royal Navy had by 1800 discovered the cause of scurvy and, by radically changing its methods and routines, and the diet of the seamen, had more or less eradicated it. The army was just not interested. Russell was one of the first-ever war correspondents. He sent back despatches to *The Times* of London describing in detail not just the details of battles, but the horrific sanitary conditions and the dreadful death rate. The impact at the breakfast tables of 1854 London must have been similar to that of the first images of napalm-burned Vietnamese children. For Florence Nightingale, engaged in running a sanitarium on Harley Street in London, her time had come. Using her considerable skills in propaganda and determination, she took over the various volunteer efforts that sprang up.

The army brass were willing to allow her to go to Turkey but no further, and wanted the whole mission to be under the aegis of the Church. They disliked interference, but while they may have beaten the Russians, they were no match for Florence Nightingale.

Strangely enough, it doesn't appear that she was a particularly good nurse or administrator. Her letters are all about power and control—she took on and defeated everyone, from religious leaders to the British ambassador in Constantinople and even her own nurses (especially

"ARE THERE NO DEVOTED WOMEN AMONGST US, ABLE AND WILLING TO GO FORTH TO MINISTER TO THE SICK AND SUFFERING SOLDIERS? ARE NONE OF THE DAUGHTERS OF ENGLAND, AT THIS EXTREME HOUR OF NEED, READY FOR SUCH A WORK OF MERCY?"
W. H. RUSSELL, *THE TIMES*

the Irish Catholic ones, whom she loathed, and who were less than happy with her regime). Her goal was to get herself into the heat of the action and do things her way, whether the military liked it or not. With strong newspaper support from *The Times* and careful manipulation of politicians and society at home, she succeeded in her power grab. And without question, during her three visits to the Crimean war zone the death rate did drop dramatically in British war hospitals, fatalities from typhus alone falling from 46 to 2 percent.

Her real war, against the benighted High Command, had only just begun. She was determined to be the avenging angel: "I stand at the altar of the murdered men, and, while I live, I fight their cause," she wrote on her return in 1856. She refused to accept the "no blame" verdict of the first enquiry, and with support from Prime Minister Palmerston, and even with the support of Queen Victoria following a royal audience, she set her sights at demolishing those responsible: namely, Sir Benjamin Hawes, permanent secretary to the War Office and Sir John Hall, the army chief medical officer in the Crimea.

THE BIRTH OF AN ACTIVIST

In the end, the War Office more or less held together and most of her recommendations were turned down, but there were some real reforms: a new awareness of the need to improve sanitation in barracks and in hospitals, and a new permanent army hospital. The guilty men were never brought to the kind of justice they probably deserved, but the ignorance that led to losing more troops to disease than to enemy action was thoroughly and forever quashed.

Unfortunately, Florence Nightingale's medical beliefs soon lost touch with reality. She felt, for example, that quarantine was useless and ineffective, and was deeply suspicious of vaccination. But her place in history is assured, and ensures that the deaths of the thousands in the Crimean War were not entirely in vain.

MOTIVATION

anger
charity
envy
faith
gluttony
greed
hope
lust
pride
sloth

THE WAR OFFICE VERSUS THE INDIAN ARMY: MUTINY AND BEEF FAT

May 10, 1857 – September 1858

Main Culprit: Major General George Anson (1797–1857)

Damage Done: 11,000 British soldiers and many thousands of Indians killed

Why: Fuel for the fires of discontent: the new rifle cartridge was covered in grease from sacred animals

The double doors at the end of the courtyard were flung open again and the ladies ordered out. But they refused to move and tightened their grips on the verandah pillars and on each others' arms and waists, trying to keep from crushing their weeping children underfoot ... the Sepoys declared it impossible to separate them or drag them out of the building and backed out of the yard ... Now the jemadar (senior Indian officer) ordered his men to stand outside the doors and windows on one side ... at a signal from the jemadar, his men thrust the barrels of their muskets through the window shutters along the one wall ... Twenty Sepoys aimed their muskets into this wave of bodies and opened fire at point blank range. The first volley pared some of the foremost layer of women and children away, and may have wounded a few beyond. The Sepoys backed away from the smoking windows and a second squad moved in to take their places. From behind a pillar Mrs Jacobi suddenly lunged forward and knocked one of them down with one blow ... his comrades came to his rescue. First they hung her daughter Lucy on a hook by her chin and then silenced her mother by cutting her throat.

Eyewitness report quoted by Andrew Ward from
Our Bones Are Scattered

It is a truism that history is written by the victors, and another, perhaps less well known, that the popular cause of something is often the real one. Both are demonstrated well by the events of 1857 in India. Wars have raged over the control of commodities crucial to life, like water, or salt, or precious metals, or, indeed, oil; but no other fighting, let alone any as savage as these 18 months, was sparked by animal fat.

The East India Company had been trading in India for 150 years, and had gained such a foothold that in the 1830s other companies had demanded an end to its monopoly. Expansion had brought Sind under British rule in 1843, the Punjab in 1849, and the colony extended to the foothills of the Himalayas. There was concern about Russian expansion towards the north-west frontier, and the British had just concluded the Crimean War, fighting the Russians for control of the Black Sea. But the 1850s were the start of the golden age of imperialism, and the British government expected a lot from India, the "jewel in the crown" of empire. It was partly a question of prestige — within 20 years Queen Victoria would declare herself "Empress of India," perhaps the high point of the empire. Partly it was financial, especially as the East India Company itself was under pressure to pay more money to the London government. The Americas were lost but were not a threat, embroiled in their own affairs leading up to the Civil War. Western Europe was peaceful — Napoleon had been defeated, Germany did not yet exist as a nation. Queen Victoria's reign of prosperity and utter self-belief was in full swing. Britannia did indeed rule the waves.

Pressure built on the individual kings and maharajahs of India to pass power to the British and pay substantial taxes. More than a dozen independent rajes were annexed between 1848 and 1854. Most of this was little more than a land grab. Karl Marx, writing in 1853 for the *New York Daily Tribune*, excoriated the British for their hypocrisy:

> While they prated in Europe about the inviolable sanctity of the national debt, did they not confiscate in India the dividends of the rajahs, who had invested their private savings in the Company's own funds? Did they not, in India, resort to atrocious extortion when simple corruption could not keep pace with their rapacity?

© David Bailey | Dreamstime.com

QUEEN VICTORIA MEMORIAL
The Queen Victoria Memorial, by sculptor Thomas Brock, is situated in front of Buckingham Palace, London. It was commissioned, shortly after Victoria's death, as the symbolic hub of the empire. Completed in 1911 it incorporates a statue of the Queen, alongside representations of such Victorian virtues as charity, justice, truth, motherhood, and courage, while it is topped by a winged victory.

ON A MISSION

But there were other pressures on traditional India, too. The British Empire had a missionary bent, not just in terms of converting "the natives" to Christianity, but of imposing the values of Victorian England. The famous historian Thomas Babington Macaulay laid the issue out in two speeches to the British Parliament in a debate on India in 1833 and 1835:

> It is scarcely possible to calculate the benefits which we might derive from the diffusion of European civilization among the vast population of the East. It would be, on the selfish view of the case, far better for us that the people of India were well governed and independent of us, than ill governed and subject to us; that they were ruled by their own kings, but wearing our broadcloth, and working with our cutlery, than that they were performing their salams to English collectors and English magistrates, but were too ignorant to value, or too poor to buy, English manufactures. To trade with civilized men is infinitely more profitable than to govern savages. That would make it an useless and costly dependency, which would keep a hundred million men from being our customers in order that they might continue to be our slaves. It is impossible for us, with our limited means, to attempt to educate the body of the people. We must at present do our best to form a class who may be interpreters between us and the millions whom we govern; a class of persons, Indian in blood and color, but English in taste, in opinions, in morals, and in intellect.

By the 1850s this educational mission had shown itself mostly in attacks on the Hindu rituals most alien to the British sensibility, especially the custom of *suttee*, the burning of widows after the death of their husbands. Stamping this out had caused widespread unrest among local populations.

However, all of this failed to spark more than hostility. It was an act of plain insensitivity that set off what the British call the Indian Mutiny, the Indians call the First War of Indian Independence, and is often now referred to as the Sepoy Rebellion. These days we might call it an insurgency. By 1857 there were 40,000 British troops in India, but these were not nearly enough to control an area and a population of that size; so they had trained and established a local army of some 200,000 soldiers, known as *sepoys*.

LEE-ENFIELD

The Lee-Enfield rifle is one of the most famous weapons in the history of warfare. It was named for Enfield, just north of London, where the factory was located, and for James Paris Lee (1831–1904), a Scottish-born American arms inventor who designed, amongst other things, the box magazine that allowed for the development of bolt-action repeating rifles. The rifle was still in its infancy in the 1850s when it was deployed for British Army use around the world. It fired .303 calibre ammunition that had to be loaded manually. This involved biting the greased end of the cartridge, for which the manufacturers used pork and beef fat. The pig, of course, is forbidden to Muslims; the cow is sacred to Hindus. Perhaps if less attention had been paid to Macaulay's arrogant dismissal of Indian culture, and if even a little thought had gone into the situation, what followed would have been averted. It's hardly as if these religious beliefs were secret.

In January 1857, Captain Wright of the Rifle Instruction Depot overheard a *khalasi*—a lower-caste laborer—berating a Brahmin who would not share water with him: "You will soon lose your caste, as ere long you will have to bite cartridges covered with the fat of cows." Out of pride, the British Army overlooked a crucial fact of the lives and beliefs of the soldiers whom they expected to protect not only their empire but their families as well.

Throughout the early months of 1857, small rebellions took place across British India. By May soldiers were imprisoned if they refused to bite the cartridges. The Commander-in-Chief, General George Anson reacted to this crisis by saying, "I'll never give in to their beastly prejudices," and refused to compromise.

On May 10 members of the Third Light Cavalry regiment in Meerut were jailed, but the 11th and 20th regiments, called to guard them, turned on their commanding officers and freed their compatriots. All hell broke loose. Indian regiments and then rajahs joined the revolt. Indian forces massacred British families at Cawnpore in June and laid siege to Lucknow for two terrible months. That month Anson died of cholera, during the march on Indian mutineers at Delhi, but British vengeance was still terrible—prisoners were at best hanged, at worst tied in front of the muzzles of cannons, which were then fired. By year's end the insurgents were losing, though given the might of the British Empire

THE COMMANDER-IN-CHIEF, GENERAL GEORGE ANSON REACTED TO THIS CRISIS BY SAYING, "I'LL NEVER GIVE IN TO THEIR BEASTLY PREJUDICES," AND REFUSED TO COMPROMISE.

THOUSANDS DIED IN BLOODY BATTLES AND THE ACTS OF REVENGE THAT FOLLOWED UNTIL A PEACE DEAL WAS SIGNED ON JULY 8, 1858. BRITISH CASUALTIES AMOUNTED TO SOME 11,000—INDIANS, AND SEPOYS, MANY THOUSANDS MORE.

they did well to last as long as they had. Thousands died in bloody battles and the acts of revenge that followed until a peace deal was signed on July 8, 1858. British casualties amounted to some 11,000— Indians, and sepoys, many thousands more. Much of the country was ruined and plunged into enormous debt. In 1859 the British Crown established direct rule over the whole of India, no longer trusting the East India Company to rule on its behalf.

Resonance of the importance of this issue was seen 150 years later. In 2001 three American-based Hindu businessmen sued McDonald's, claiming it used beef fat in the initial stages of preparing its French fries, sold widely throughout India. Right-wing Hindu extremists attacked a McDonald's in Bombay and called on the Indian prime minister to shut down the franchises. Finally the company admitted its mistake and agreed that it had failed to give "complete" information when it switched to vegetable oil in 1990, as it still used a "minuscule" amount of beef fat for flavoring in the supply stage.

An apology and subsequent backdown was something that the British Army should have considered. The McDonald's India website now proudly insists on the purity of its vegetable oil alongside the McAloo Tikka and Broccoli 'n' Mushroom Vegetable McCurry Pan. The recent opening of McDonald's Lucknow offers more ground for philosophical consideration of the world's ironies than this volume will allow.

THOMAS AUSTIN'S RABBITS

Christmas 1859 – present day

MOTIVATION
anger
charity
envy
faith
gluttony
greed
hope
lust
pride
sloth

Main Culprit: Thomas Austin (d.1871)

Damage Done: Millions of acres of land and up to 70 percent of domestic species destroyed

Why: Rabbits brought in for recreational hunting purposes did what rabbits do best

'E sort o' takes it personal, yeh see.
'E used to 'awk 'em fer a crust, did Mick.
Now, makin' 'im play rabbits seems to be
A narsty trick.
To shove 'im like a bunny down a 'ole
It looks like chuckin' orf, an' sours 'is soul.
"Fair doos," 'e sez, "I joined the bloomin' ranks
To git away frum rabbits: thinks I'm done
Wiv them Australian pests, an' 'ere's their thanks:
They makes me one!
An' 'ere I'm squattin', scared to shift about;
Jist waitin' fer me little tail to sprout."

"Ar, strike me up a wattle! but it's tough!
But 'ere's the dizzy limit, fer a cert—
To live this bunny's life is bad enough,
But 'ere's reel dirt:
Some tart at 'ome 'as sent, wiv lovin' care,
A coat uv rabbit-skins fer me to wear!"

from "Rabbits,"
The Moods of Ginger Mick
by C. J. Dennis

In 1859 Thomas Austin, a member of the Victorian Acclimatization Society, decided to have a Christmas hunt on his land at Winchelsea, near Geelong, Victoria, west of Melbourne, Australia. Envy of the life in the mother country and gluttony for hunting precipitated one of the great ecological disasters in history, coupled with the forlorn hope of migrants and settlers the world over, that the alien and hostile landscape they found themselves trapped in could be made more like their homeland with the addition of familiar flora and fauna. He had asked his brother to send 24 rabbits from England, and released them onto his property. They came out on the *Lightning*, sailing from Liverpool to the newly established port of Geelong, where, oddly, given the consequences, the contents are celebrated in one of a series of bronze and glass "cargo boxes"—public art sculptures adorning the waterfront. The rabbits bred. In 1866 more than 14,000 were shot on Austin's estate alone. He had also been shooting all the possible predators—hawks, eagles and cats—on his land. So the rabbits spread. In another two years, 3,120 square miles (8,080 sq. km) of farmland surrounding his estate had to be abandoned, stripped bare by the rabbits. By 1886, the devastation spread as far north as Queensland. By 1900 it was 3,000 miles (4,800 km) across the desert to Western Australia and the Northern Territory. The migration of rabbits in Australia was the fastest of any colonizing mammal anywhere in the world. By contrast, rabbits were introduced into southern England by the Normans in 1066 and, as late as 1950, had scarcely made it 500 miles (310 km) north to Scotland.

RABBITS RULE Rabbits turned out to be perfectly attuned to the dry Australian landscape. They are one of the most fertile animals on earth, and the lack of natural predators, coupled with the protection from the heat offered by their warrens, led to their enormous success. The affected area is now estimated at over 1.5 million square miles (3.9 million sq. km).

Early efforts at control included shooting, poisoning, and the rabbit-proof fence. By 1883 the Rabbit Nuisance Act in New South Wales could put a child in prison for six months for letting loose a tame rabbit. In 1907 the West Australian government finished the longest anti-rabbit fence—715 miles (1150 km) long. It ran between Cape Keraudren in the north and Starvation Boat Harbour in the south, and was followed by two more. Though hardly a perfect solution, thousands of rabbits could be found piled up against one side of a fence, with none on the other side, and apparently the resulting differences in vegetation growth can now be seen from space. An entire trade of rabbit killers and skinners came into being; to this day one of the founding clubs of the Australian Rugby League is known as the "Rabbitohs," from the cry of the rabbit skinners as they went through the town. Rabbits were often the main source of protein for Australians during the Depression, and indeed, their commercial potential for skins and furs (in particular the Australian Akubra hat) frequently mitigated the more stringent calls for their extermination.

By the 1940s the population was estimated be as high as 800 million, and each rabbit was figured to cost the country one Australian dollar in damage. Rabbits have particularly devastating effects on local fauna and flora; on one island off the southern coast of Australia, their presence from 1906 to 1936 destroyed all three species of parrot and 23 of the 26 types of tree found on the island. In other areas it is estimated that 66 to 75 percent of native mammal species have vanished as a direct result of rabbit infestation.

POPULATION EXPLOSION

Famously, the introduction of myxomatosis in the 1950s killed about 95 percent of Australia's rabbit population. But that turned out not to be enough—the remaining 5 percent developed immunity and started all over again. Since 1996 the introduction of the controversial Chinese calcivirus, called perhaps unfortunately on an Australian government website a "final solution," together with the European rabbit flea, is starting again to reduce numbers, but the government's Environmental Management Authority still reports plague conditions in the northwest suburbs of Sydney, with considerable property damage and serious injuries, as citizens fall down rabbit warrens.

Such is the continued hatred for the rabbit in Australia that there is a strong move to expel it from its traditional Easter role. The Easter Bilby is being promoted, particularly by a pressure group (the Foundation for a Rabbit-Free Australia), to the point of having its chocolate image now vigorously sold in stores. The bilby is a highly endangered species of bandicoot, an Australian marsupial, ironically also known as a rabbit-eared bandicoot. The rabbit is largely responsible for the fact that there are a lot more chocolate bilbies than real ones.

The same year that Thomas Austin called for his rabbits, Charles Darwin published *The Origin of Species* and transformed the way we think about animals and adaptation. Marsupials had puzzled him somewhat on his trip in 1836. On seeing the marsupials in Australia for the first time and comparing them to placental mammals he noted that "A Disbeliever in everything beyond his own reason, might exclaim, 'Surely two distinct Creators must have been at work: their object however has been the same and certainly in each case the end is complete.'" In *The Descent of Man*, he clearly places the marsupials on a lower order than other mammals. It is perhaps not all that surprising that Australia had an ambivalent attitude to the local animals, and set about doing something about it. There was a purpose to the Victorian Acclimatization Society—to "civilize the Australian bush." This included introducing European fish—salmon, trout, tench—as well as plant life. Its counterpart in New South Wales had the aim of "spreading over the length and breadth of the land inestimable acquisitions to the wealth and comfort of the people"—trying to assist in the manufacture of red dye, which comes from the cochineal insect, by introducing its host plant, the prickly pear, which also spread disastrously. The Victorian Society didn't just import trouble; it exported four possums to New Zealand in 1863. They wreaked havoc and grew to a population of millions. The Society also dumped carp into the Murray-Darling River system, causing ecological devastation. Some scholars have termed this "ecological imperialism," but it still counts as idiocy in this book.

Thomas Austin's uncle James had been transported to Australia in 1803 for stealing beehives and honey. Thomas himself moved to the new city created around Port Philip—what would become Melbourne—in 1845, and married the sister of a landowner, building an estate, Barwon Park. He had visited his brother in England and enjoyed shooting rabbits, among other things—so much so that he asked his brother to ship the rabbits over to him, along with hares, partridges, sparrows, starlings, thrushes, and the hawthorn bush, all of which were introduced into an alien landscape for the first time. But his interest seems to have been less that of an ecological imperialist than a man who simply enjoyed shooting animals. And it wasn't as if the risk was unknown; it was hardly a scientific revelation that rabbits bred. Some had come over with the First Fleet and ravaged the island of Tasmania—so ignorance cannot exculpate Mr. Austin. Indeed, even after the damage became self-evident, Austin would gladly ship a box or two of rabbits to anyone who asked for them, and even promoted his game to royalty. Alfred, Duke of Edinburgh, came not once but twice to "The Shooting at the Rabbit Warren."

Austin built an impressive mansion, bred winning racehorses, and dispensed largesse around the neighborhood—including a hospital in Melbourne, still named for its benefactor—little suspecting the devastation his desire for blood sport would wreak in the century and a half that lay ahead. He died with his grand house unfinished—ironically, like Nero before him, having created a wonderful building on top of the devastation he himself had caused.

THE SPREAD OF RABBITS THROUGHOUT AUSTRALIA

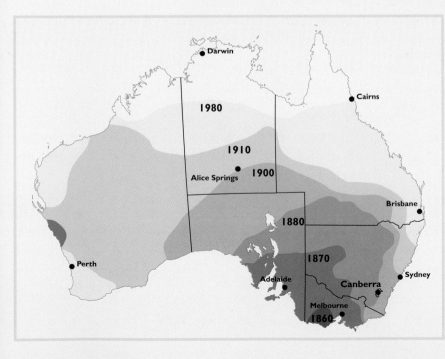

Originally released in Christmas 1859 the spread of rabbits from Austin's estate in what is now Melbourne was prolific. Reaching Adelaide within 10 years, Sydney and Alice Springs within 40 years, and Cairns and Perth in just over 100 years.

MOTIVATION
anger
charity
envy
faith
gluttony
greed
hope
lust
pride
sloth

GENERAL CUSTER AND LITTLE BIGHORN

June 26, 1876

Main Culprit: General George Custer (1839–1876)

Damage Done: Destroyed his own division to the last man, and the repercussions destroyed the Lakota

Why: Overenthusiasm and contempt for his opponents led to one of the great self-destructions in American history

The only good Indian is a dead Indian.

General Philip Sheridan

Colonists often like to portray the expansion of their early settlements as very different from the evil imperialism of their former masters in Europe. Certainly it was different in that the goal was takeover of the land for settlement—impossible in the case of most of Australia—rather than economic exploitation of the local inhabitants as labor or a potential marketplace. As a result, the outcome for the native peoples of America and Australia was, if anything, worse than those who were colonized by the Europeans. They were not there to be exploited; they were just in the way. Attempts at wholesale genocide—the distribution of smallpox-covered blankets—or simply all-out crushing warfare largely succeeded in forcing the natives onto small reservations on land so poor that it was of no use to settlers. Today, the role of these unfortunate populations is often reduced to a parody of their former selves, the stuff of trashy television, cartoon films, and mass merchandising. Commercial opportunities are exploited, often at the expense of the original population, while many of the more recent arrivals derive pleasure from their supposed closeness with nature and their indigenous predecessors by buying "natural" and "authentic" products.

Only 130 years ago the Lakota people were engaged in a visceral struggle. Manifest Destiny, the *Lebensraum* of its day, saw the American settlers, once they had dispensed with their own local dispute of the Civil War, moving rapidly across the continent. They took over the land and pushed the tribes collectively known as the Plains Indians onto reservations with little or no compensation, backed by whatever military or legislative power they cared to invent. Much of the groundwork was laid during the Civil War itself. The coast-to-coast telegraph line was finished in 1861; the Pacific Railroad Act in 1862; the same year as the Homestead Act allowed citizens to settle on up to 160 acres of unclaimed "public" land and receive title to it after five years. In 1862 President Lincoln, the great liberator of slaves, had no problem ordering the mass hanging of 38 Santee Sioux after the New Ulm uprising. In 1864 Kit Carson force-marched 8,000 Navajo across New Mexico to their new "home." While in the same year the Sand Creek massacre saw 200 Cheyenne

© The Art Archive | National Archives Washington DC

GENERAL CUSTER
General George Armstrong Custer, photographed c.1863 by Mathew Brady.

and Arapaho men, women, and children ambushed and slaughtered by troops of the Colorado militia and New Mexico volunteers under the command of Colonel Chivington.

General Sheridan, whose words open this piece, was appointed commander of United States forces in the West in 1866. His peace plan was to exterminate the buffalo, which in his view also meant exterminating the native population. The 1867 Medicine Lodge treaty and 1868 Fort Laramie treaty essentially created reservations, whereby Native American tribes surrendered their land rights in exchange for designated properties where they could theoretically live in peace. Those tribes, or groups of tribes, who would not abide by these enforced treaties were left in little doubt as to the likely outcome. The Fort Laramie treaty, in particular, settled with the Lakota tribe their rights over the Black Hills.

Colonel George Custer, before the outbreak of misguidedness that led him into these pages, had the rare distinction of being court-martialed twice. At West Point, from which he graduated at the bottom of his class, he failed to stop a fight between two cadets he was responsible for. He was saved because of the desperate need for Civil War officers, and indeed, distinguished himself in the first Battle of Bull Run. He came to the attention of General Sheridan, who appointed him a lieutenant colonel of the 7th Cavalry in the western arena. He was again court-martialed after a muddled campaign against the Southern Cheyenne in 1866. Reprieved by Sheridan, he was sent to the Northern Plains in 1873, and in 1874 commanded an expedition to the Black Hills against the Lakota, whose only crime appeared to be occupying the land they had been granted six years earlier.

"Indian Inspector" E. C. Watkins had issued a report in late 1875 that the Lakota and Northern Cheyenne had joined forces and were hostile. Perhaps more to the point, as ever, gold had been discovered in the Black Hills, and the Lakota had turned down an offer of US $6 million from the United States senate to move on out—indeed, they had the temerity to proclaim that they would defend their lands if attacked. On January 31, 1876, all Lakota chiefs were required by federal authorities to report to their designated reservations, and refused. Three army columns, under Brigadier General Crook, Colonel Gibbon, and Brigadier General Terry (whose column included Custer's 7th Cavalry), were supposed to act in

GENERAL SHERIDAN, WAS APPOINTED COMMANDER OF UNITED STATES FORCES IN THE WEST IN 1866. HIS PEACE PLAN WAS TO EXTERMINATE THE BUFFALO, WHICH IN HIS VIEW ALSO MEANT EXTERMINATING THE NATIVE POPULATION.

concert, surrounding the Lakota and then crushing them. Crook's column, though, was held up by Crazy Horse at Rosebud Creek. Custer, having split from the main column, had moved faster than he was supposed to. His brand of fearlessness or foolhardiness had cost every one of his units in the Civil War higher than average casualty rates. His cavalry had far out-paced Gibbons's infantry, and when scouts reported the presence of Lakota and Cheyenne forces at an encampment on the Little Big Horn River, in Montana country, on June 24, Custer was unwilling to await the larger force. Spurred on to commit one of the more famous acts of tactical ineptitude in history, a mixture of pride coupled with ambition and arrogance prompted Custer to ignore his orders, the advice of his scouts, and believe the rhetoric of his leaders that the Lakota were incapable of putting up much of a fight. Details are hard to come by, and much debated, but Custer essentially divided his force in an attempt to make simultaneous assaults from either side of the encampment. However, in the face of a force at least three times stronger than his, and under the able command of Sitting Bull, the coordination of the attacks failed. Every last man of Custer's detachment was killed, and Custer's Last Stand became part of history.

The skirmish alone, though, does not get Custer into this book; this would be a very lengthy tome if every impetuous general who rode with his men to their deaths on a futile and misguided mission was included—though to his credit, at least Custer did ride and die with his men. Their casualties numbered 268, the Lakota's around 50—not especially high given the total killed during what are now known as the Indian Wars. But the totality of defeat, the larger-than-life reputation of Custer, and his apparent embodiment of the values of the new American West, together with the propaganda that followed, meant that this act of impetuosity had tragic consequences that far outweighed the bloodshed of one day's brief fighting.

Custer was already famous throughout the country before his last stand. He had published a book, *My Life on the Plains*, with a New York publisher in 1874. Immensely tall and strong, in great physical condition, he was renowned as an athlete might be today, his idiosyncrasies ignored because of his exploits—11 horses had been shot from under him, and so forth. His wife of 12 years, Elizabeth Bacon Custer, had accompanied him to the West. News of the defeat, soon dubbed a massacre, reached

CUSTER'S LEGEND

the East Coast on July 4, 1876, the centennial of the Declaration of Independence. Fueled by a grieving widow, it didn't require modern media coverage to whip the American public into a frenzied need for revenge and an end to the scourge of the vicious Indians. "Libbie" was only 34, but devoted to her husband, beloved throughout the army, and well known in Washington. Spurred into action by Grant's decision to hold Custer culpable for the shambles at Little Bighorn, Elizabeth Custer devoted the rest of her life to rewriting the events not only of that day, but his entire career—and by extension, arguing the righteousness of the Indian Wars. Poets, painters, novelists, and songwriters weighed in to commemorate the disaster and extol the bravery of the few, who, it was now recalled, were so outnumbered (ignoring the fact that it was no one's fault but Custer's that he had failed to wait for reinforcements). One epitaph simply read: "This was a man."

ONE EPITAPH SIMPLY READ, "THIS WAS A MAN."

The Bismarck Tribune led the media frenzy:

> MASSACRED.
>
> GEN. CUSTER AND 261 MEN THE VICTIMS.
>
> NO OFFICER OR MAN OF 5 COMPANIES LEFT TO TELL THE TALE.
>
> 3 DAYS OF DESPERATE FIGHTING BY MAJ. RENO AND THE REMAINDER OF THE SEVENTH.
>
> SQUAWS MUTILATE AND ROB THE DEAD.
>
> VICTIMS CAPTURED ALIVE AND TORTURED IN MOST FIENDISH MANNER.
>
> WHAT WILL CONGRESS DO ABOUT IT?
>
> SHALL THIS BE THE BEGINNING OF THE END?

Elizabeth Custer's *Following the Guidon*, published by Harper in 1890, is still in print, as are her diaries. She remained alive until 1933, and so powerful was her reputation that it was only after her death that Custer and his actions were reassessed. She was buried next to her husband at West Point. Even within recent years, the decision to rename the Custer Battlefield National Monument as the Little Bighorn Battlefield

National Park, and incorporate sculptures commemorating the Lakota warriors alongside those remember the dead cavalrymen, aroused a great deal of controversy.

The repercussions for the Lakota were immediate and deadly. As much as 40 percent of the entire United States Army was assigned to the Black Hills. Within a year, the Lakota were forced into total and bloody surrender, and Congress repealed the Fort Laramie treaty, annexing 40 million more acres (160,000 sq. km) of Lakota land for good measure. The Battle of Wounded Knee in 1890 was the final chapter in the wholesale destruction of the tribe.

Sitting Bull had managed to escape to Canada, whence he re-emerged on occasion, once to star in Buffalo Bill's Wild West Show, before finally being killed during a skirmish following his arrest for failing to suppress the Ghost Dance ritual that had swept through the Native American tribes. This, as well as several other factors, led to the Wounded Knee Massacre on December 15, 1890, the last major conflict between the Lakota and the United States government. That same year a cartographer declared that for the first time, no frontier line need be drawn on the map of North America. Whether the end result would have been any different had Custer not lost his head is highly doubtful. But the end was bloodier and came faster as a result, catapulting what was seen in on the East Coast as a distant and rather unnecessary conflict into a matter of national significance.

LAKOTA'S DEMISE

KING LEOPOLD AND THE SCRAMBLE FOR AFRICA

1879–1900

Main Culprit: King Leopold II of the Belgians (1835–1909)

Damage Done: Pillage of a continent

Why: The ultimate in copycat crime: "I want an empire too"

There are no small nations ... only small minds.

King Leopold II of the Belgians

Listen to the yell of Leopold's ghost
Burning in Hell for his hand-maimed host
Hear how the demons chuckle and yell
Cutting his hands off, down in Hell.

Vachel Lindsay

The infamous and fatuous "Scramble for Africa," was an undignified, costly, and bloody land grab at the end of the nineteenth century that resembled something from *Alice in Wonderland*'s tea party—a board game played by the insane, but with real people. The whole sordid affair was born of envy—that European powers had what the latecomers did not—and, of course, the colonial staple of greed. Ironically enough, it was the weakest and cruelest empires that in the end took the longest to fall apart, clinging late into the twentieth century to African countries they still claimed as their own. The legacy for these countries has not been burgeoning economies or stable governmental systems, but decades of war, poverty and death. A later entry in this volume relates one of the disasters of post-colonial Africa—Robert Mugabe in Zimbabwe.

The "Scramble" came against the backdrop of surging nationalism in Europe. Three of the worst-behaved powers in Africa—Belgium, Germany, and Italy—had been born as independent nations only within the previous 50 years and were keen to demonstrate their prowess as world powers against the likes of Britain, Spain, France, and the Netherlands. And some, like Portugal, which had long since lost their empires, came in late just to prove that the tide of history had not left them behind, with the most horrific consequences for the unfortunate lands they occupied: Angola and Mozambique. At the same time, simmering tensions in the Balkans, the failing Ottoman Empire, and problems in Central Europe caused by the unification of Germany under Prussian control, meant that the countries involved were in many cases taking out animosities and frustrations that, for the moment, they felt unable or unwilling to fight out in Europe itself. For some of the fatuous rulers of the new Europe not satisfied with their lot, Africa provided an appealing blank space on the map to carve up between them.

© The Art Archive | Culver Pictures

KING LEOPOLD II
Leopold Louis Philippe Marie Victor (born April 9, 1835) was the eldest surviving son of Leopold I, and ruled as King Leopold II of the Belgians from December 10, 1865, until his death on December 17, 1909.

Up until around 1850, colonial activity in Africa had been limited by a number of factors: lack of knowledge of the interior, coupled with a lack of resources worth pilfering. The importance of coastal settlements in West Africa had diminished with the abolition of the slave trade, belatedly in the United States. The British controlled—or tried to control—much of southern Africa for its importance as a trade route on the way to India, until the Suez Canal was built; thereafter, the discovery of gold and diamonds took over. Northern Africa had clear geopolitical significance even before the discovery of oil, especially as the Ottoman Empire declined in power. For centuries, but more significantly during the nineteenth century, Islam was spreading southwards through the continent, to the horror of the growing Christian missionary movement, especially in the United Kingdom. Added to growing missionary zeal was the upshot of Darwin's scientific discoveries and explanations of the appearance of civilization. Africa appeared to many in Europe to be not only a vast "dark continent," which might offer resources and riches—the essential motivation behind earlier exploration and exploitation—but a target for the combined Victorian passions of science and Christian zeal. The development of the machine gun gave added muscle to the dissemination of these ideals.

Africa needed to be explored, claimed for God and country, and rescued from both the Muslim expansion and its own heathen ways. So, during mid-century, Africa was examined and taken over. The expeditions of Mungo Park in the early years, the search for the source of the Nile, then the missionary expeditions of Dr. Livingstone, opened up much of the heartland. The Great Trek saw the Dutch Boers move north and east from the English-dominated Cape Colony in South Africa to carve out new lands for themselves.

NEW LAND OLD POWERS

Much of this newly discovered land was indeed claimed by the old colonial powers—the British and French in West Africa, the British in Kenya, the French in Morocco and Algeria. A great deal lay unclaimed by 1879, mostly too impenetrable, hostile or resource-poor to be of use to the established powers. Within 20 years only Ethiopia, which had famously defeated the hapless Italians at the Battle of Adwa in 1896, and Liberia, with some protection from its origins and links with the United States, remained independent.

The chief culprit in sparking the partition and the land grab was King Leopold II of the Belgians. Belgium had become independent in 1830, after years of association with the Netherlands and being under the rule of half the countries of Europe. Seizing the opportunity of the new Europe following the defeat of Napoleon, the largely Catholic region of Belgium rebelled against the Dutch Protestants in 1830. Napoleon had seized the region from the Austrians, who had previously controlled what was then called the Austrian Netherlands. The Dutch had been in control of Belgium only since the Congress of Vienna in 1815, and then only to help create a stronger buffer state against the French, and to compensate them for the British walking away with the valuable colonies of Ceylon and Cape Colony. Rather unfairly, the Dutch had been deemed to be on Napoleon's side during the long war. The Belgians, though, were less than thrilled at being under Protestant rule. Not known for their bellicose nature, they were finally impelled to riot by an opera, known as *The Dumb Girl of Portici*, in 1830. They fought for independence for nine years, and in the end the countries of Europe deemed the region not to be worth any more bloodshed, and forced the Dutch to grant the Belgians their independence.

Their first king, Leopold I, was a popular and reforming king, one of the first to introduce child labor laws, for example. He was succeeded in 1865 by his second son, who became Leopold II. The second Leopold was obsessed with two things (aside from the fact that in later life he illegally married a prostitute)—building great, imposing, ugly edifices in Brussels, and an empire abroad—supposedly to help defend his country. His subjects were reasonably excited about the first obsession, but not in the least by the second. However, Leopold was not one to give up easily. After the American explorer Henry Morton Stanley returned from presuming correctly and saving Dr. Livingstone, he remarkably entered the personal employ of King Leopold in 1879, with the job of carving out a colony from the region around the Congo River where he had tracked down Livingstone. Stanley, originally an illegitimate Welsh child named John Rowlands, had gone to the United States, and worked for both sides in the American Civil War before becoming a journalist. He was a bounty hunter, for want of a better description. He had found Livingstone for the sake of the ample reward offered by his newspaper and had already gained a reputation for being unusually cruel to his entourage when on expeditions. Stanley did as he was asked and delivered to the eager Leopold a territory that was 80 times the size of Belgium itself. This land was deemed to be Leopold's private property, a personal domain of the kind that is arguably without precedent in history.

LEOPOLD I WAS A POPULAR AND REFORMING KING.

It sparked a huge land grab throughout the region. The first chancellor of Germany, Otto von Bismarck took the first four areas he could get and then tried to negotiate land from other colonizing states to create a wide swathe of German Empire across the middle of Africa. The Portuguese, French and British anxiously annexed anything and everything they could find. The notorious Conference of Berlin of 1884–1885 confirmed the European powers' seizure of this land in its entirety, including the granting of the "Congo Free State" to King Leopold. It also laid down ground rules for what was left — planting flags was not enough; genuine exploitation of the land and country was required to prove ownership. This didn't turn out to be a problem for Leopold; he was in any case now personally in debt, having financed the entire expedition himself. He embarked on a regime probably unparalleled in its pointlessness and cruelty. Tax collectors were sent to extract whatever they could from the unfortunate Congolese, who probably weren't aware whose property the far-away conference had made them. Rubber and ivory were collected, slavery established to ensure greater productivity, and intense cruelty marked the whole enterprise. One estimate sees the population of the Congo reduced from 20 million to 10 million over a 20-year period as a result of Leopold's rule. Gradually, word got out to a horrified world. Vachel Lindsay, Arthur Conan Doyle, and Booker T. Washington all spoke up. Oddly, so did Roger Casement, later hanged by the British in Ireland for treason, but at that time British consul in Kinchasa, who wrote a horrifying indictment of the cruelty he witnessed:

> A careful investigation of the conditions of native life around (Lake Mantumba) confirmed the truth of the statements made to me — that the great decrease in population, the dirty and ill-kept towns, and the complete absence of goats, sheep, or fowls — once very plentiful in this country — were to be attributed, above all else, to the continued effort made during many years to compel the natives to work india-rubber.

Finally the Belgian parliament demanded that Leopold cede his land to the government, which he did in 1908, after spending two weeks burning records of his extortions, and remaining unrepentant. Stanley, meanwhile, had gone back to Wales, married a poet, and become a member of parliament, while the victims of his work died in millions.

RUBBER AND IVORY WERE COLLECTED, SLAVERY ESTABLISHED TO ENSURE GREATER PRODUCTIVITY, AND INTENSE CRUELTY MARKED THE WHOLE ENTERPRISE.

By then the African land grab was falling apart. Organized ethnic groups began to revolt. Soon the Europeans would be killing each other, forgetting for the most part their African spoils. But the Congolese did not forget—as late as 2005, a newly erected statue of Leopold disappeared after just hours after being unveiled.

COLONIAL POWERS IN AFRICA c.1914

SPANISH MOROCCO
TUNISIA
MOROCCO
SPANISH SAHARA
ALGERIA
LIBYA
EGYPT
RIO DE ORO
Nile R.
FRENCH WEST AFRICA
SENEGAL
GAMBIA
PORT. GUINEA
GUINEA
UPPER VOLTA
Niger R.
ANGLO-EGYPTIAN SUDAN
ERITREA
FRENCH SOMALILAND
BRITISH SOMALILAND
SIERRA LEONE
IVORY COAST
GOLD COAST
TOGO
NIGERIA
FRENCH EQUATORIAL AFRICA
LIBERIA
CAMEROON
RIO MUNI
Congo R.
ABYSSINIA
ITALIAN SOMALILAND
UGANDA
BRITISH EAST AFRICA
BELGIAN CONGO
GERMAN EAST AFRICA
NYASALAND
ANGOLA
NORTHERN RHODESIA
MOZAMBIQUE
Zambezi R.
GERMAN SOUTH-WEST AFRICA
SOUTHERN RHODESIA
MADAGASCAR
BECHUANALAND
SWAZILAND
UNION OF SOUTH AFRICA
BASUTOLAND

BRITISH
FRENCH
SPANISH
PORTUGUESE
BELGIAN
GERMAN
ITALIAN
INDEPENDENT

Colonialism in Africa was at its height in 1914, following the "Scramble for Africa." Vast swathes of the north-west were held by the French, while Britain possessed territories ranging from Sierra Leone in the west to British Somaliland in the East, and Egypt in the north to South Africa. The rest of Africa was divided among the other colonial powers, including the Belgians. The only states to retain their independence were Abyssinia, now Ethiopia, and Liberia.

MOTIVATION
anger
charity
envy
faith
gluttony
greed
hope
lust
pride
sloth

NICHOLAS, ALEXANDRA, AND THE MAD MONK

1902 – December 16, 1916, around midnight

Main Culprits: Nicholas II (Nikolai Alexandrovich Romanov), Emperor and Autocrat of All the Russias (1868 – July 17, 1918); Czarina Alexandra of Russia (née Her Grand Ducal Highness Princess Alix von Hessen und beim Rhein)

Damage Done: The end of the Romanov dynasty

Why: Nicholas and Alexandra relied on a lunatic sexual predator not only to cure their ills but also for political advice

His death came too late to change the course of events. His dreadful name had become too thoroughly a symbol of disaster. The daring of those who killed him to save their country was miscalculated . . . in raising their hands to preserve the old regime they struck it, in reality, its final blow.

Grand Duchess Maria Pavlova

There lived a certain man in Russia long ago
He was big and strong, in his eyes a flaming glow
Most people looked at him with terror and with fear
But to Moscow chicks he was such a lovely dear
He could preach the Bible like a preacher
Full of ecstasy and fire
But he also was the kind of teacher
Women would desire

RA RA RASPUTIN
Lover of the Russian queen
There was a cat that really was gone
RA RA RASPUTIN
Russia's greatest love machine
It was a shame how he carried on

Boney M, "Rasputin"

It is unusual in the annals of history for a pop song to celebrate one of the main protagonists, let alone one that so accurately reflects reality. More unusual still is that the protagonist's pickled penis has recently been put on display in a new museum in Moscow. But Rasputin was no ordinary man. Many argue about how potent his influence over the Russian court really was, but in hindsight that is less important than what people believed it to be at the time, and what the consequences of that belief were. The now-legendary death of Rasputin and the decline of the tsars are, in any event, dramatic enough to strain belief.

Gregory Efimovich Rasputin (1869–1916) was born on January 10, 1869, in a Siberian village, Prokovskoe, to a typical peasant family. As an apparently exceptionally dissolute youth, he became fascinated with a peculiar offbeat sect of the Russian Orthodox Church, the Skopsty, which held that the best way to reach God was by committing sins and then confessing and repenting. This suited young Gregory well, and he did his holy best to become a highly accomplished sinner within their ranks, adopting the monk's habit and soon getting a local and then national reputation as a *starets* or holy man. After a pilgrimage to the Holy Land, he came to St. Petersburg in 1902 accompanied by glowing recommendations to the higher clergy of the Russian Empire. He was no less dissolute than before, but was much more accomplished as a speaker and blessed with apparent healing powers. However, his reputation soon dissuaded the Orthodox establishment from having anything to do with him, and although he made some friends (female, naturally) in high places, he soon left, seemingly never to return.

NICHOLAS II
A Russian engraving of the coronation of Nicholas II —Nikolai Alexandrovich Romanov—on May 14, 1896.

© The Art Archive | Bibliothèque des Arts Décoratifs Paris | Gianni Dagli Orti

Europe was approaching the turmoil that was to culminate in World War I, and most countries were busily rearming and preparing for some sort of conflict. Many, such as the Austro-Hungarian and Ottoman Empires, were internally rent with conflict and in no shape to enter such a battle. The great tsarist empire in Russia was not in much better condition. The proud inheritors of the legacy of Ivan the Terrible, Peter the Great, and Catherine the Great had become dissolute and, more crucially, interbreeding with too many European princesses had introduced a terrible disease—hemophilia—into the royal line. The emancipation of the serfs in 1861 had initiated a series of democratic reforms that had done little but excite the middle classes as well as the peasants, and weaken royal power. To a great extent, tsarist power depended on the character of the tsar and tsarina themselves. To put it mildly, Nicholas and Alexandra were the wrong couple for the job. Utterly devoted to each other, disorganized, antisocial, preferring the company of dogs to humans, they would have made, as was said at the time, excellent country squires.

AN HEIR OF UNCERTAINTY

Tsar Alexander III, apparently a healthy and robust man, died suddenly of nephritis in 1894, in his early 50s. Neither he nor anyone in the royal court, especially his son and heir, had expected this, and Nicholas, now 26, had been given no direction in running the affairs of state, having been coddled by an overprotective mother. The only thing he had done on his own was to find a princess to marry, against his parents' wishes. In the end they consented, only because the need to produce an heir to the Romanov dynasty was of such importance and they doubted their son's ability to find anyone else. Nicholas even made a mess of handing out the traditional gifts at his coronation celebrations—massive crowds gathered in anticipation, but rumors spread that there would not be enough beer to go around and the crowds rioted, causing over a thousand deaths.

The new tsarina was Princess Alexandra (Alix) of Hesse, one of Queen Victoria's favorite granddaughters, and also Nicholas's third cousin. Although the dynastic link with Britain was a good thing, her melancholy nature and her German nationality worked against her throughout her life—much as Marie Antoinette's Austrian ancestry had been used against her during the French Revolution a century earlier. The couple was by all accounts very happy, but also isolated and remote both from their subjects and their court. They rapidly produced four daughters, confirming Nicholas's mother's worst fears about her son and his wife, but also causing real concern in the court as to the need to produce a son and heir. After the fourth daughter's birth in 1901, a desperate Alexandra started to look beyond the medical profession for help. Her brother, Alexander Mikhailovich, said "She turned toward religion . . . but her prayers were tainted with a certain hysteria."

Alexandra's beliefs were enhanced by the subsequent birth of a son and heir, Alexis, on July 30, 1904. But the happiness of the royal couple soon turned to dismay as the boy showed signs of hemophilia, which ran in the bloodline of Queen Victoria. Doctors warned there was no hope of a cure, and a great likelihood of death. One of the tsarina's closest friends, Anna Vryubova, was a major supporter of Rasputin, whom she credited with her recovery after a bad train accident, and she suggested that he visit Alexis in secret. The idea of using holy healers was not that strange at the time; Nicholas's father had sent to Kronstadt for a famous healer when his diagnosis was made. Rasputin was eccentric, but he was also effective, and brought the small boy almost instant relief. However, his boasting of his relationship with the family soon reached the tsar's ears and he was banished, only to return, for good, in 1905 after Alexis fell dangerously ill once more.

Totally distracted by his son's illness, the state of Nicholas's mind and his inability to rule began to have serious consequences. A nonsensical war against Japan only showed how weak Russia was compared to the level of militarization of other countries. Nicholas had nearly been killed on a royal trip to Japan and hated the place. Although nominally allied with England and France, Nicholas was heavily influenced by his wife's connections with the Kaiser and the German royals. In January 1905 more than 1,000 demonstrators had been killed in a tragic overreaction by police. A year later a constitution had been declared, and the tsar had to contend with a genuine reform movement emanating from the *Duma*—part of the Russian parliament. Rasputin acquired more and more influence at the Russian court; Nicholas referred to him as "our friend." Rumors circulated of affairs that Rasputin was supposedly having with the tsarina, with her young daughters, with almost every woman in the court, insinuations often circulated by him in endless drunken orgies. He seems not to have had a particular political agenda, other than retaining his own privileged position, but it was not surprising that others, especially aristocrats who now found their expected access to the tsar blocked, were suspicious. Nicholas and Alexandra seemed as oblivious to the worsening situation in Europe as they were to the domestic political chaos that would overwhelm them. When war broke out, the Russian army was hopelessly ill prepared. With the blessing of Rasputin, Nicholas appointed his cousin, Grand Duke Nicholas, to head the army. Hearing that things were going badly, Rasputin

TOTALLY DISTRACTED BY HIS SON'S ILLNESS, THE STATE OF NICHOLAS'S MIND AND HIS INABILITY TO RULE BEGAN TO HAVE SERIOUS CONSEQUENCES.

telegraphed an offer to help by coming to bless the troops. He received the curt reply: "Do come. I'll hang you." Shortly thereafter, Rasputin had a vision that only the tsar himself could save his country by leading them in war. Nicholas shuffled off to the front, leaving government in the hands of Alexandra and, effectively, Rasputin. Leading public officials were fired and replaced with cronies.

Finally, the court had had enough. Prince Felix Yusupov, *duma* member Vladimir Purishkevich, and the tsar's cousin, Grand Duke Dmitri Pavlovich Romanov, decided the country must be rid of the "evil genius." In December 1916, Yusupov invited Rasputin to his home, ostensibly to meet his beautiful wife, then poisoned him. The plotters shot Rasputin, tied him up, wrapped him in a blanket, and then threw him into the Neva River. He was seen trying to swim through the icy waters, but finally, his body was found three days later. The conspirators were banished by the furious tsar—which turned out to be a lucky break for them, in fact, as they avoided the fate that awaited the rest of the royal family a few months later.

Rasputin had predicted that in the event of his death, the tsar and his family would fall. He saw himself, it seems, as something of a revolutionary, proof that a peasant could hold his own against the aristocracy. It is not uncommon, of course, for seers and mystics to predict doom should anything unfortunate befall them, but it is certainly true that the loss of their confidant destroyed any remaining resolve the royals had to avoid the impending end of Romanov rule in Russia. The speed of his abdication, barely three months after Rasputin's death, seems ample evidence of his dependence on the charismatic Rasputin.

ISMAY'S LIFEBOATS

11:40 P.M., April 14, 1912 – 2:20 A.M., April 15, 1912

MOTIVATION

anger

charity

envy

faith

gluttony

greed

hope

lust

pride

sloth

Main Culprit: J. Bruce Ismay (1862–1937)

Damage Done: 1,503 deaths

Why: The "unsinkable" ship failed to carry enough lifeboats for its passengers

I remember Titanic. Everything was so stately and beautiful. The linens were of a fine white and as soft as the clouds. I remember my mother having such a sense of dread and my father exclaiming that this ship was unsinkable. My mother told him that we should all perish because that was flying in the face of God himself.

> **Edith, survivor**

This is exactly what might take place and what will take place, if the liners are sent to sea short of boats.

> **William T. Stead** (*Pall Mall Gazette* 1886, "How the Mad Steamer Went Down in the Mid-Atlantic, by a Survivor." Stead was a British spiritualist and writer who in 1912 was on his way to a conference at Carnegie Hall . . . on the *Titanic*.) He did not survive.

Just because an event is famous enough to become a cliché—"Ship Sunk by Huge Metaphor" as the spoof headline from *The Onion* later described it—does not mean its place in this book is not deserved. The extraordinary pride and arrogance that led to the destruction of *Titanic* on its maiden voyage makes it a natural for these pages. It was not so much the design fault that led to the flooding of the lower levels; mistakes in themselves are not idiotic. Nor was it even the route taken—the ship, after all, hit a particularly wayward southern-located iceberg that had no business being there. But the failure of the designers and owners of the ship to believe in the possibility of an accident and to put enough lifeboats on *Titanic* was an act of gigantic foolishness that cost the lives of all 1,503 who died on that fateful night.

THE TITANIC SINKING
A watercolor by British artist C. J. Ashford of lifeboats leaving the *Titanic*, after it hit the iceberg.

There have been many engineering catastrophes over the years. Victorian technology at its height yielded amazing results: the spanning of waterways, the coming of the railways, tunnels and bridges around the world. Disasters were inevitable, many commemorated in poetry and literature, from the dreadful William McGonagall tribute to those who died on the Tay Bridge to the works of more talented writers. Boat travel also had its fair share of tragedies over the years, though mostly in bad weather or through enemy action in wartime. Certainly the death toll of *Titanic* was substantially less than that of German refugees fleeing the Russian advance on Danzig on the *Wilhelm Gustloff* in 1945, with an estimated loss of life of between 7,000 and 10,000.

HUBRIS DEFINED

Titanic, though, was different. It was perhaps understandable that the "unsinkable" phrase was coined as an early example of PR hype. There was a considerable battle going on between the Cunard Line, whose flagship *Lusitania* would meet its own terrible fate sometime later, and the White Star Line, which, determined to win the corporate battle at any cost, and funded by J. P. Morgan, decided to build the ultimate ship. Actually, *Titanic* was to be one of three sister ships aimed at dominating the transatlantic route. The construction was a joint project between J. Bruce Ismay, president of White Star, and Lord Pirrie, chairman of Harland and Wolff shipbuilders in Belfast, Ireland (as it was then). Bruce Andrews, managing director of Harland and Wolff, was the ship's designer and went down with the ship, not before realizing exactly what had gone wrong and giving the captain and crew the precise time at which the ship would sink. A crew of 14,000 men worked on the construction, which took three years. At the time, *Titanic* was the world's largest movable object.

At 880 feet (268 m) long, 92 feet (28 m) wide, 60 feet (18 m) from waterline to boat deck, Titanic was about the same length and height as London's Tower Bridge. Its 29 boilers were fired by 159 coal-burning furnaces, and a top speed of 23 knots ensured a quick crossing of the Atlantic. Of the famous four funnels, only three were actually usable; one was just for ostentation. In addition to the usual luxuries, a Turkish bath, squash court, and four lifts were installed. The design and function of the watertight compartments, tragically flawed as they turned out to be, led the trade magazine *Shipbuilder* to hail *Titanic* as "practically unsinkable." The phrase soon stuck in everyone's mind, especially as it set off for its maiden voyage from Southampton, via Cherbourg, on April 10, 1912.

Capacity was supposed to be in excess of 3,500 people, but it was carrying only 2,210—in fact, more than expected, because of a coal strike that led to poorer passengers being transferred. The cost of the trip in first class lived up to the marketing hype. Despite being at only two-thirds capacity, the provision of lifeboats was woefully inadequate. *Titanic* carried a total of 20 lifeboats: 14 of them wooden, each with a capacity of 65; two were woodcutters with a capacity of 40 people each; and four were collapsibles (wood bottoms and canvas sides), capable of carrying 47 people. The total capacity of all 20 lifeboats was 1,178 people. If every lifeboat left *Titanic* filled to capacity, 1,023 people would have been left behind.

The cause of the disaster is well known—hitting an iceberg on the side and at full speed ruptured too many of the watertight compartments. *Titanic* could withstand four of the compartments being filled with water, but the hole in the hull was so big that six compartments were filled and the ship was doomed. Unfortunately, for the first two hours of the tragedy, that fact was not apparent to the passengers, who in first class were less than enthused at the prospect of leaving their staterooms

THE DESIGN AND FUNCTIONING OF THE WATERTIGHT COMPARTMENTS, TRAGICALLY FLAWED AS THEY TURNED OUT TO BE, LED THE TRADE MAGAZINE *SHIPBUILDER* **TO HAIL** *TITANIC* **AS "PRACTICALLY UNSINKABLE."**

for wooden lifeboats on an icy Atlantic night; in third class, most people didn't have the opportunity anyway.

Very few lifeboats were completely filled when they were lowered from *Titanic* into the icy water. This caused the death toll to rise dramatically. When the order came from Captain Smith to commence loading the lifeboats, *Titanic*'s officers were probably unaware of the magnitude of the situation. There were never any lifeboat drills and the crew had not been informed that each lifeboat could be safely lowered when filled to capacity.

COMFORT BEFORE SAFETY

But why were there so few lifeboats? As ships increased in size over the years, the lifeboat requirements stayed the same. *Titanic* was designed to carry a total of 48, but the White Star Line decided that passenger comfort was more important. They believed that an increase in the number of lifeboats would have cluttered the decks and taken up valuable space. Harland and Wolff tried to persuade the White Star Line to install more lifeboats, but eventually gave up the fight. Moreover, it was widely believed that White Star chairman Ismay, the one who overruled Harland and Wolff on the number of lifeboats, also insisted that Captain Smith keep sailing full steam ahead on the same course, despite reports of icebergs. Ismay famously found himself, almost by accident by his own account, one of the few men actually in a lifeboat, and survived the tragedy, staying on as an executive of the White Star holding company. He lived another 25 years but may have wished he had indeed gone down with the ship. He was held responsible by all for the disaster; a town in Texas called Ismay even changed its name. One of his critics said, "He is one of those human hogs whose animal desires swallow up all finer feelings . . . whose heart is atrophied by selfishness."

Many maritime laws were introduced as a result of the disaster, such as more lifeboats, better distress signals, and 24-hour ship-to-ship radio communications. And a legend of corporate greed was born.

GAVRILO PRINCIP'S DELI SANDWICH: THE ASSASSINATION OF FRANZ FERDINAND

June 28, 1914

MOTIVATION

anger
charity
envy
faith
gluttony
greed
hope
lust
pride
sloth

Main Culprit: Gavrilo Princip (1894–1918)

Damage Done: The beginning of World War I

Why: The infamous spark that ignited the conflagration—assassination that went beyond its aims

What is the good of your speeches? I come to Sarajevo on a visit, and I get bombs thrown at me. It is outrageous!

Franz Ferdinand, Sarajevo, 1914

Our ghosts will walk though Vienna
And roam through the palace
Frightening the lords.

Gavrilo Princip, 1918

It is doubtful that any period in world history offers so prolonged, useless, pointless, and terrible an example of waste as Europe from 1914 to 1918. World War I wins almost every conceivable award for idiocy that one can imagine. The causes, 90 years later, are still obscure. The casualties are mind-boggling.

Not only that, but a muddled conclusion meant that within a mere two decades the grand masters of Europe were ready to go at it all over again, this time involving almost every country of the world. A whole panoply of books, movies, TV shows, and mythology has sprung from World War II, which had its share of atrocities, dreadful enough, and also its share of terrible decisions. However, "man's inhumanity to man" was rarely more evident than during World War I. At a rough estimate, the dead numbered more than 8 million in combat alone. It is doubtful that more than a handful could have explained what they were truly fighting for, other than their country.

A DOUBLE-EDGED SWORD

Political assassination has always been a double-edged sword. Frequently, within the plan lies the hope of redemption, but all too often the mistaken notion that removing one person somehow makes a difference proves itself horribly wrong. All too often it is a suicide mission; in more recent decades, the prelude to the 15 minutes of fame. Usually, history remembers the dead leader, no matter how evil, as the victim of a dastardly plot, and the assassin, no matter how heroic, or well intentioned, as the wicked or crazed perpetrator. And unintended consequences have a tendency to backfire on the assassin and his or her cause, especially if their aim is not true. Countless leaders are remembered for their survival, rather than the grievances that led people to want them dead. And, like rock stars, the legacy of certain victims may even shine brighter for their untimely and bloody end.

At the beginning of the twentieth century, assassination was in vogue. President McKinley had been shot; Teddy Roosevelt was saved by his diary; in Ireland and throughout much of Europe, improved gun technology had rendered the assassination of rivals a lot easier than it had been previously.

In hindsight, the nineteenth century had been a period of peace and prosperity throughout Europe. The diplomatic peace of the Congress of Vienna of 1815, masterminded by Metternich and Talleyrand, had created the concept of the balance of power to prevent the emergence of another Napoleon, and the peace had held pretty well. Europe had held together through the crises of 1848. The emergence in the later years of two unified countries, Italy and Germany, had changed the players somewhat, but a complex, ever-changing series of alliances held the balance intact. Leaders were more keen to industrialize their countries and find and exploit their new worldwide colonies than to fight one another again. But by 1914 the giant Austro-Hungarian and Ottoman Empires were creaking and failing, and the power vacuum was apparent to emergent nationalists. The still young and expansionist German regime stood ready to take any advantage that might accrue from this power failure in the center and east of Europe. Modern technology had provided much that was new and deadly in the period since the Napoleonic wars, including the machine gun, the railway, the submarine, and by the end of the war, the airplane. War became much bloodier and more protracted than ever before. Indeed, it was the exact workings of the balance of power that made the whole thing so terrible—neither side, or group of alliances, was ever really strong enough to wipe out the other. In the end, it took the entrance of the United States into the war and the true globalization of the conflict to provide enough of a shift in power to produce what was in essence a temporary result.

War was by no means inevitable in 1914, but it was very close. Diplomacy was wearing thin as a means of resolving issues. The Germans had kept a war plan in place since at least 1905, which they assumed assured them of victory in a few months. This was a serious miscalculation though, resulting in what then became a bloody stalemate. But the assumption at the time was that the sabre-rattling of early 1914 would, if it came to blows, produce a conflict that would be over quickly.

During the late nineteenth century the hotbed of nationalism had been, not for the first or last time, the Balkans. The Ottoman Empire began to fall apart; Serbia and the Balkan region were the most insistent on autonomy, emboldened by the successful independence movement in Greece, so beloved of Lord Byron and his pals, which succeeded in 1830. To the north, the Hungarians were granted equal footing

THE GERMANS HAD KEPT A WAR PLAN IN PLACE SINCE AT LEAST 1905, WHICH THEY ASSUMED ASSURED THEM OF VICTORY IN A FEW MONTHS.

with the Austrians in 1867; the Russians were supporting uprisings in Turkish regions throughout the Balkans. Part of the compromise following the Crimean War, which the British and French had fought to hold back Russian expansionism in the Near East, was to force the Turks to grant more autonomy to the Balkans. At the Congress of Berlin in 1878, Serbia, Montenegro, and Romania were granted independence. The Serbians immediately laid claim to more land than they had been given, as did the Bulgarians, who had been somewhat short-changed. They annexed land to their south immediately and in the Second Balkan War of 1913, in conjunction with the Greeks, they took the area around Skopje, their part of Macedonia. By then, the Ottomans had been thrown off the mainland of Europe and their part in the upcoming war was at best peripheral, though as we shall shortly see, many soldiers laid down their lives for their cause.

EYES ON BOSNIA

More significantly and fatally—and again, not for the last time—the Serbs laid claim to Bosnia and its capital, Sarajevo, which had been handed to the Austro-Hungarian Empire at Berlin. The Slavs of Bosnia and Herzegovina had been perfectly content to accept the imperial trade, but Serbian nationalists continued to stir up agitation. However, their opponent was no longer the failing Ottoman Empire, whose Sultans perhaps had a vague appreciation that their days were numbered, it was the still powerful Austro-Hungarian Empire. Bosnia was of little significance to anyone but the ruling Hapsburgs.

Although the Great War was to prove to be the Hapsburgs' undoing, that was far from obvious to anyone in 1900. Vienna, if anywhere, was the world's pre-eminent cultural and intellectual city at that time. The Western powers were mightily sick of the unstable Balkans in any case by now. The Austrians sought to take advantage of this by annexing Bosnia completely in 1908, and indeed were fighting Serbia off and on through to 1911. The Russians were as alarmed by this as the Austrians were by the Serbian and Greek land grab of Macedonia in 1913. Meanwhile, fear of German expansionism had led Britain, France, and Russia to form an alliance. The Russians formally abandoned their close relations with Austria and Germany. Though this was not widely realized at the time, the Berlin government had made it clear to the Viennese leadership that no more diplomatic compromises would be reached. The world would remain at peace only so long as no one tried anything foolish. On June 28, 1914, someone did.

Franz Ferdinand was heir apparent to the Hapsburg Empire. He had been third in line to the throne, but Crown Prince Rudolf had infamously died in the hunting lodge of the palace at Mayerling with his mistress, Marie Vetsera. Conspiracy theorists inevitably claim they were murdered, to the point that the body of the unfortunate 19-year-old Baroness Vetsera was stolen in 1992 and subsequently examined by experts to determine cause of death, which, oddly enough, favored murder rather than the double-suicide theory. Rudolf had decidedly liberal tendencies compared with his arch-conservative father. The emperor's brother Karl Ludwig, already in his 60s, suddenly became heir, and decided—perhaps in preparation for this unexpected role—to make a pilgrimage to Jerusalem, where he drank from the River Jordan, promptly contracted typhus and died. His son, Franz Ferdinand, then became heir. Two years later his aunt, the emperor's wife Elisabeth, was stabbed by an Italian anarchist as she boarded a steamer on Lake Geneva. And two years after that, in 1900, his marriage to a mere countess so infuriated the emperor that Franz Ferdinand was forced to revoke his children's rights of succession, perhaps not the wisest of moves for a dynasty already under nationalist pressure and with an increasingly short life expectancy.

Although Franz Ferdinand was initially favorable to liberal causes, the pressure of his uncle began to bear down upon him, and he was seen as increasingly conservative and opposed to aspirations of self-rule. By 1914, still not emperor,

GAVRILO PRINCIP
The arrest of Gavrilo Princip for the assassination of Archduke Franz Ferdinand in Sarajevo on June 28, 1914.

Franz Ferdinand was a solid and morose 50-year-old, in no mood for a trip to Sarajevo; he was still outraged at being booed and rioted against on a previous visit in 1906. The only thing that continued to make him happy was his devotion to the wife he had defied the emperor to marry. He had very little influence at court in Vienna, though, and it was far from clear that he ever would.

Austro-Hungary's 1908 annexation of Bosnia seemed proof of all this to young men in Sarajevo, who were attracted to a rather disunited rebel movement, Young Bosnia. Most of the new adherents to this old movement were sons of men who had moved from peasant life into the cities, scraped together the rudiments of an education, but found themselves blocked from any real advancement in life by political and economic rule from an apathetic Vienna. They traveled, also. Danilo Ilie ventured to Switzerland to meet with Russian Mensheviks. Their activities were mostly talk, of course, but a group of three Young Bosnians—Ilie, Gavrilo Princip, and Vladimir Gaciovie—fell under the spell of a more shadowy and sinister Serbian, Colonel Apis, founder of the Black Hand movement. Black Hand was more genuinely anarchist and revolutionary than any group in Bosnia; indeed, Apis had played a major role in the assassination of King Alexander of Serbia in 1903. He was easily able to pull together the Bosnians and persuade them that assassinating Franz Ferdinand would be the prelude to a great Bosnian nationalist uprising that would strike a fatal blow at the heart of the Hapsburg Empire. It all blew up with an act of enormous rashness based on foolish hope for a better future; the assassins were not so much evil as acting on misplaced belief. A contributing factor may have been that Princip, was terminally ill at only 19 with tuberculosis.

THE ASSASSINATION

The actual attempt was a fiasco. The initial troika had recruited four more conspirators, armed with guns and bombs supplied by Colonel Apis. As Franz Ferdinand and his wife Sophie's car rolled through the city, the first conspirator found a policeman next to him; the second lost his nerve, not realizing a woman would be in the car; the third threw his bomb but it bounced off the car and exploded in the crowd, injuring many. In the chaos, Princip, armed with a pistol, failed to recognise the car and another conspirator was overwhelmed by the panicked crowd. The archduke reached the town hall, gave his speech, and then decided to go to the hospital to visit the wounded, who included Austrian officers. Ninety minutes had passed and the conspirators had basically given up by now. Princip had gone to buy a sandwich, and, walking out of Moritz Schiller's delicatessen, was astonished to see the archduke's car he had failed to recognize earlier. It had taken the wrong route to the hospital, without its escort, and slowed to a crawl directly in front of him. He pulled out his Browning and fired. The first shot missed the archduke but bounced off the side of the car and hit Sophie in the abdomen. The second shattered Franz Ferdinand's jugular vein and, with his last words to Sophie, he died. Princip was too young to be executed, but, sick as he was with tuberculosis, survived only a few years in the Austrian fortress of Theresienstadt in what is now the Czech Republic. (It was later used by the Nazis as their infamous "model" concentration camp.)

The consequences of this rather pathetic incident were horrific, and not at all what the conspirators had in mind. The warmongers in Berlin and Vienna, who couldn't care less about Franz Ferdinand, jumped at the opportunity. Serbia, which had done nothing more than be the home of Colonel Apis, was blamed, given impossible conditions to fulfil, and then invaded anyway. Half a million Serbs, a huge proportion of the population, died in the impending invasion; well over a million Austrians would die, and the Hapsburg Empire would indeed be doomed, though not in the way Princip might have expected. His goal of Bosnian independence remained many years and bloody wars away.

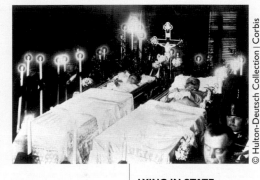

© Hulton–Deutsch Collection | Corbis

LYING IN STATE
Austro-Hungarian Archduke Franz Ferdinand lying in an open coffin beside his wife Sophie, the Duchess of Hohenburg, after their assassination.

MOTIVATION

anger
charity
envy
faith
gluttony
greed
hope
lust
pride
sloth

WINSTON CHURCHILL AND THE DISASTER AT GALLIPOLI

February 1915 – November 1915

Main Culprit: Winston Churchill (1874–1965)

Damage Done: At least 400,000 dead on both sides; over a third of the ANZAC forces in their first-ever battles

Why: Vainglorious and pointless attack on an impregnable peninsula

And the band played "Waltzing Matilda,"
As the ship pulled away from the quay,
And amidst all the tears, the flag-waving and cheers, we sailed off for Gallipoli.

How well I remember that terrible day
How our blood stained the sand and the water,
And how in that hell that they called Suvla Bay
We were butchered like lambs at the slaughter.
Johnny Turk, he was ready, he'd primed himself well,
He showered us with bullets and he rained us with shell,
And in five minutes flat, he'd blown us all to hell;
Nearly blew us right back to Australia.

And the band played "Waltzing Matilda," when we stopped to bury our slain,
We buried ours, and the Turks buried theirs, then we started all over again.

Eric Boyle, *The Band Played Waltzing Matilda*

We have seen the peripheral status of the Ottoman Empire in the prelude to the war; nonetheless, the region became one of the arenas of battle in the conflict. The Dardanelles was a 31-mile (50 km) strip of land that controlled the passageway from the Aegean Sea into the Sea of Marmara, which itself passed into the Black Sea at Constantinople. Gallipoli was a mountainous area under Turkish control, and extremely defensible, with high mountains and small beaches.

The young Winston Churchill, whose name will reappear later, was First Lord of the Admiralty. He was itching to get into the fray somehow, but the war was a land affair. There was only one major naval battle — Jutland. Later, the pioneering use of submarines by the Germans would cast a different light on everything, but in the early years there wasn't much for a bellicose First Lord of the Admiralty to sink his teeth into. Before the Ottoman Empire even formally entered the war, in October 1914, Churchill ordered the bombardment of the Dardanelles, an action that reminded the Turks of the importance of mining the waterways and building up their defensive positions. The war council had rejected Churchill's immediate request for an attack as being too risky, but after the Russians requested help by the terms of their alliance against an invading Turkish force, they decided to let Churchill have his way, albeit with limited support. The Russians soon beat the weak Turkish army. The strategic possessions that were of importance within the Turkish Empire — Suez, Jerusalem, the Iranian oil wells — were fought for successfully by Allenby and his men on land. There were vague hopes of inducing the Balkan states and Italy to attack Austria, but it is not clear to this day that there was the least strategic value in getting through the Dardanelles. It was little more than pride and vainglory that propelled Churchill onward, even Carden, vice-admiral in charge of the eastern Mediterranean region, condemned the idea's recklessness.

© The Art Archive | Imperial War Museum

DAWN OF ANZAC DAY
A watercolor by Herbert Hillier showing the battleship H.M.S. *Queen Elizabeth* (on the left) in the Aegean Sea off the Gallipoli Peninsula, on the dawn of the ANZAC landings.

Resources were limited. Most of the fleet had to stay in the North Sea. Army supplies were extremely limited because of the bloodbath on the western front. Only one division of British forces, the 29th, was not needed in France. The Royal Naval division sent by Churchill was a hodgepodge of irregulars and marines, barely a fighting force. Australian and New

Zealanders, just arrived in Greece and barely trained were co-opted. No one expected them necessarily to fight. They were to be garrison forces, sent in once the naval bombardment had done its work. But it did not. Between February 19 and March 18, 1915 six of the sixteen ships assigned to the bombardment had been destroyed by Turkish mines, and apart from breaching the limited coastal defences, no real progress was made. Carden was replaced and it was determined that the assault would be made by the army, on the beaches of Gallipoli.

What happened next lives on in history — not so much for the British, who were used to their men being sacrificed by their generals, but for the New Zealanders and Australians. For them, April 25, 1915 is known as ANZAC Day, the first day those newly independent nations saw battle. And for the Turks, the genesis of the new secular country of Turkey under Kamal Ataturk would start with the fierce defence of Gallipoli, a source of pride for a homeland defended in stark contrast to the decadent and weak rule of the Ottoman Empire. Churchill, too, would go on to greatness in World War II. Three countries would create legends from the thousands about to give their lives in a hopeless assault on impregnable terrain.

ERRORS OF JUDGEMENT

The dreadful details, the errors of judgment — half the Australians landed at the wrong beach — and the awful death toll tell their own story. One fifth of the New Zealand force died that first day. None of the assaults, brave as they were, made significant headway. Many troops had not even made it ashore. A recommendation for evacuation was rejected. The scenario — soon to be repeated at the Somme — of sending thousands of men across No Man's Land in an attempt to take heavily fortified defences, saw many deaths and no progress. By November, casualties were high enough for London to take notice; more troops had been requested, but Lord Kitchener himself visited Gallipoli in November 1915 and ordered evacuation instead.

Casualties were high: 120,000 British, 27,000 French, fewer in total for the ANZACs, but 25 percent of the New Zealanders, more of the Australians. Turkish casualties numbered perhaps 250,000.

Churchill was initially held responsible for the debacle, lost his position in the War Cabinet and he was excluded from government. Indeed, he went to the trenches in France as a lieutenant colonel, before returning

ACTION ON THE GALLIPOLI PENINSULA

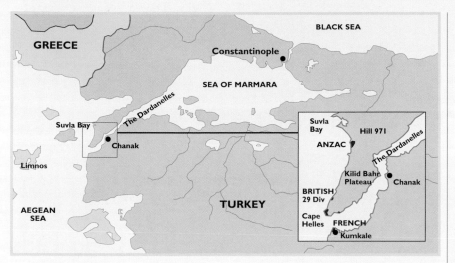

The 1915 assault on Gallipoli commenced with an attempt to force the Dardanelles by a flotilla containing 16 battleships in February and March. Heavy losses were sustained and no real progress was made, leaving the job of opening a supply route to the Russian army via the Black Sea to land forces.

Assaults on April 25, 1915 at Cape Helles, Anzac Cove, and Kumkale were met by Turkish resistance and made little ground. A stalemate ensued and casualties numbered around 200,000 on both sides—the Allied evacuation was made that winter.

to office as Minister for Munitions in 1917. He was reappointed to the Admiralty position on the first day of World War II—a signal went out to all ships: "Winston's back"—and of course went on from there to glory. He never appeared to have any remorse about Gallipoli; indeed, his eastern Mediterranean strategy was markedly similar. On the eve of the 1944 Anzio landing, the commander in charge, Major General John Lucas, wrote in his diary: "This whole affair has a strong odor of Gallipoli and apparently the amateur is still on the coach's bench."

Defenders of Churchill point to lack of support from the War Office in London and poor leadership on the scene. Since he was both part of the War Cabinet and in charge of the appointment of officers, these arguments seem weak at best. In the lustrous career that was to follow—eventually—Gallipoli is seen as a blip. But similar characteristics of Churchill's—fight to the last man, attack the impregnable, Britain at all costs—will be seen again within these pages. His view of troops from the empire as cannon fodder did much during World War II to turn Australia and New Zealand away from Britain towards the protection of MacArthur and the American sphere of influence. Gallipoli never has been forgotten in Australia and New Zealand.

ON THE EVE OF THE 1944 ANZIO LANDING, THE COMMANDER IN CHARGE, MAJOR GENERAL JOHN LUCAS, WROTE IN HIS DIARY: "THIS WHOLE AFFAIR HAS A STRONG ODOR OF GALLIPOLI AND APPARENTLY THE AMATEUR IS STILL ON THE COACH'S BENCH."

MOTIVATION
anger
charity
envy
faith
gluttony
greed
hope
lust
pride
sloth

TRENCH WARFARE, GENERAL HAIG, AND THE BATTLE OF THE SOMME

July 1, 1916 – November 9, 1916

Main Culprit: Field Marshal Douglas Haig (1861–1928)

Damage Done: Over one million dead, including 420,000 of his own army

Why: Suicidal attacks over No Man's Land for month after month

If you want to find the old battalion
I know where they are, I know where they are
If you want to find the old battalion
I know where they are,
They're hanging on the old barbed wire.
I've seen 'em, I've seen 'em
Hanging on the old barbed wire

"Over The Top," anonymous soldiers' song

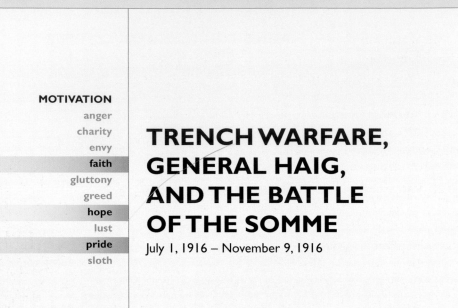

Of all the perpetrators of stupidity within these pages, it is hard to beat General Sir Douglas Haig, commander of the British Expeditionary Force. Much of World War I was turning out to be a virtual stalemate. The Germans had quickly advanced and taken Belgium and northern France, and the Allies sought to remove them. Repeated French and British offensives in 1915 had gained little and lost little. The Germans, though, struck a blow against the French in a successful attack on Verdun in February 1916. French commander Marshal Joffre had planned an attack on the Somme but was forced to hand over control of the operation to Haig, whose early strategy was simply a mistake, but to continue in the mass slaughter thereafter was the height of idiocy. Assuming that he wasn't a murderous psychopath, he was presumably drawn to his continued strategy through pride and, to put it charitably, hope that the day would somehow be won despite all evidence to the contrary. And presumably he had faith, too, that the men he consigned to near-certain death day after day after day somehow were going to a better place than the trenches of northern France.

GENERAL HAIG
A portrait of General Douglas Haig in 1916 by the French war artist Lucien Jonas.

Haig had at his command 750,000 men in 27 divisions. The plan was to use the modern British guns to bombard the German forward defences for eight straight days and then mount a full-frontal assault. The Germans were in a better position, on higher ground, and had strongly fortified positions. The bombardment had no effect at all on the barbed wire and concrete defensive positions.

On the first day of the charge, at 7:30 A.M. on July 1, Haig ordered General Rawlinson's men forward. By the day's end 58,000 British casualties were counted, the worst single day of losses in the entire history of the British Army. Incredibly, he ordered a repeat performance for the next day—and the next. The British Army HQ in Paris issued this statement on July 3:

> The first day of the offensive is very satisfactory. The success is not a thunderbolt, as has happened earlier in similar operations, but it is important above all because it is rich in promises. It is no longer a question here of attempts to pierce as with a knife. It is rather a slow, continuous, and methodical push, sparing in lives, until the

day when the enemy's resistance, incessantly hammered at, will crumple up at some point. From today the first results of the new tactics permit one to await developments with confidence.

On July 13 they made a small gain but German reinforcements repelled them; on July 27, Pozières was captured. By September, French forces using tanks were able to join in, but still made little progress. As winter drew on, Haig ordered attacks every day the weather would allow, until he finally gave up in December. He had killed 420,000 of his own troops, maybe 620,000 Germans, and around 200,000 French. At the very height of the success of the Somme campaign, 7 miles (12 km) of territory were gained; by the end, practically none. Over one million casualties in six months for absolutely no gain whatsoever.

Was there method to the madness, as some claim? Here is Haig himself explaining his battle orders before it all started in May:

THE COURSE OF THE BATTLE OF THE SOMME

Commencing on July 1, 1916, the Battle of the Somme was an Allied attempt to break through German lines. However, gains were minimal and resulted in a slight bulging in of the German positions, rather than the envisaged break through. By the time the front stabilized on November 19, 1916, well over a million lives had been lost in total, in an advance that measured approximately 7 miles (12 km) at its greatest extent.

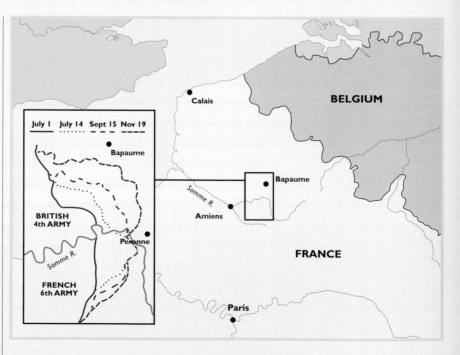

The First, Second, and Third Armies will take steps to deceive the enemy as to the real front of attack, to wear him out, and reduce his fighting efficiency both during the three days prior to the assault and during the subsequent operations. Preparations for deceiving the enemy should be made without delay. This will be effected by means of—

(a) Preliminary preparations such as advancing our trenches and saps, construction of dummy assembling trenches, gun emplacements, etc.

(b) Wire cutting at intervals along the entire front with a view to inducing the enemy to man his defences and causing fatigue.

(c) Gas discharges, where possible, at selected places along the whole British front, accompanied by a discharge of smoke, with a view to causing the enemy to wear his gas helmets and inducing fatigue and causing casualties.

(d) Artillery barrages on important communications with a view to rendering reinforcements, relief, and supply difficult.

(e) Bombardment of rest billets by night.

(f) Intermittent smoke discharges by day, accompanied by shrapnel fire on the enemy's front defences with a view to inflicting loss.

(g) Raids by night, of the strength of a company and upwards, on an extensive scale, into the enemy's front system of defences. These to be prepared by intense artillery and trench-mortar bombardments.

THE PLAN

Philip Gibbs, a journalist, who was nominated as one of the army's five official war correspondents, watched the preparation for the major offensive at the Somme in July, 1916.

> Before dawn there was a great silence. We spoke to each other in whispers, if we spoke. Then suddenly our guns opened out in a barrage of fire of colossal intensity. Never before, and I think never since, even in the Second World War, had so many guns been massed behind any battle front. It was a rolling thunder of shell fire, and the earth vomited flame, and the sky was alight with bursting shells. It seemed as though nothing could live, not an ant, under that stupendous artillery storm. But Germans in their deep dugouts lived, and when our waves of men went over they were met by deadly machine-gun and mortar fire.

Our men got nowhere on the first day. They had been mown down like grass by German machine-gunners who, after our barrage had lifted, rushed out to meet our men in the open. Many of the best battalions were almost annihilated, and our casualties were terrible.

George Coppard, a machine-gunner at the Battle of the Somme, described what he saw on the July 2, 1916 in his book *With A Machine Gun to Cambrai*:

Concentrated machine gun fire from sufficient guns to command every inch of the wire, had done its terrible work. The Germans must have been reinforcing the wire for months. It was so dense that daylight could barely be seen through it. Through the glasses it looked a black mass. The German faith in massed wire had paid off.

How did our planners imagine that Tommies, having survived all other hazards—and there were plenty in crossing No Man's Land—would get through the German wire? Had they studied the black density of it through their powerful binoculars? Who told them that artillery fire would pound such wire to pieces, making it possible to get through? Any Tommy could have told them that shell fire lifts wire up and drops it down, often in a worse tangle than before.

Perhaps one of the most telling assessments of the futility of the Somme is in the official German account by General von Steinacker:

The great Battle of the Somme was ended without bringing about a decision. The result was limited to a "bulging in" of the German position, so to speak, a result achieved at a cost of approximately three quarters of a million lives. The losses of the defender were well below half a million, which is the more remarkable in view of the fact that, according to official reports, about 76 percent of all the wounded were able within a relatively short time to return to the front in fighting condition.

A utilization of the successful defence made was impossible for the German command owing to the relative strength of the two armies. There was no decision reached on this theater of war.

Sixteen months later the Germans launched a furious artillery attack firing over 3,000 shells per minute. This was followed by storm troopers—lightly equipped, but with devastating weaponry including

THROUGH THE GLASSES IT LOOKED A BLACK MASS. THE GERMAN FAITH IN MASSED WIRE HAD PAID OFF.

flame-throwers and machine guns — who routed the Allies. Over 21,000 British soldiers were taken prisoner on the first day of the offensive, and their commanders lost control of a situation that so many had died for.

After the war, Haig was posted as commander-in-chief of home forces until his retirement in 1921. He devoted the rest of his life to the welfare of ex-servicemen via the Royal British Legion. He was made Earl Haig in 1919 and then Baron Haig of Bemersyde in 1921. Douglas Haig died in 1928. To this day he remains a highly controversial figure — excoriated by many for the catastrophic loss of life of those men under his command, still defended by some for his leadership.

HONORED FOR HIS ROLE

MOTIVATION
anger
charity
envy
faith
gluttony
greed
hope
lust
pride
sloth

MAGINOT'S LINE
1929–1940

Main Culprit: André Maginot (1877–1932)

Damage Done: Millions of francs spent building the wrong type of fortifications in the wrong places

Why: Fighting the last war instead of preparing for the new technologies of the next one

Fixed fortifications are a monument to the stupidity of man.

General George S. Patton

The philosopher George Santayana wisely wrote: "Those who are ignorant of the past are condemned to repeat it." Rarely was this more true than in the case of the Maginot Line, a string of fortifications built by the French after World War I to protect themselves from another invasion by German forces. The fierce fighting, which had seen Alsace-Lorraine change hands after the Franco–Prussian War and then go back to the French after World War I had been won, left the French determined never to allow such an invasion to happen so easily again. The Germans had, at the beginning of World War I, made a lightning sweep into France by way of Belgium, essentially going around the north of France and coming in from the side. The French, in their wisdom, decided not to fortify the Belgian border but to focus their defences on the direct route. Unsurprisingly, in 1940 the Germans followed the same route—through Belgium—and rather than tackle the Maginot Line head on, they simply went around the side, but this time with tanks. Rarely can such an expensive and complex system of defense have been rendered so totally useless so quickly. The German *Blitzkrieg* had them in Paris in days. The thinking behind the Maginot Line is not that easy to deduce. It mixed pride and arrogance with faith that history would not repeat itself.

ANDRÉ MAGINOT
A portrait of André Maginot at his desk from the Parisian Roger-Viollet collection.

André Maginot had been an under-secretary of war at the outbreak of World War I, a position he resigned to fight with honor in the trenches. After the conclusion of that war the French government was in the hands of the generals who proclaimed that they had won it. Marshal Joffre first proposed a new defense plan, though there was resistance both from pacifists and from those such as General de Gaulle, who wanted investment in aircraft and heavy tanks, both of which had come into play towards the end of the war. Marshal Pétain persuaded Maginot to rejoin the War Department in 1928 to become minister of war, finding a ready ally in his insistence that the "War to End All Wars" was no such thing and that the Germans still posed a threat. Appeasers had agreed that the French would withdraw early from the occupied Rhineland, which gave added impetus to the program. Indeed, Maginot was spectacularly successful in his fund-raising. He convinced the right wing that it would be good for the military, and the left wing that it would create jobs—this was the time of the development of the New Deal. The forts were specifically for defensive purposes, so even the pacifists were willing to agree. Three billion francs were allotted to build a series of fortifications along a line from the Swiss border in the south to the Ardennes Forest in the north—108 massive forts at 9-mile (15 km) intervals, connected by a series of tunnels, totalling over 62 miles (100 km) in length, and hundreds of artillery emplacements, all to be manned by thousands of soldiers. French pride in this achievement, built quickly and effectively in only a few years, was enormous; the phrase "Maginot Line" meant something impregnable, at least before the war; afterwards, Maginot's name became linked with the shortsightedness of depending upon only one course of events.

The certainty in French minds that they were protected had a major impact on their foreign policy, when a clearer, more aggressive stance against Hitler's remilitarization might have been more effective. Indeed, when Hitler invaded France, the Germans did not dare attempt a direct assault on the Maginot Line; in fact, only one of the 50 forts was ever taken by force. But by then the Germans were on the other side of the fortifications. Despite giving the French a false sense of security, the Line did not extend far enough in the north, and was based on the World War I concept of a war fought by soldiers in trenches attacking fortified lines; while World War II was to be fought using more mobile forces, which the Germans used to simply bypass the Line through the Low Countries to the north. The Ardennes Forest, the end of the Line, was judged to be impenetrable and probably was by traditional infantry, but the Panzer divisions rolled straight through it and into France. The name Maginot became synonymous with a recurrent military shortsightedness in planning for the last war, rather than the next one.

WHEN HITLER INVADED FRANCE, THE GERMANS DID NOT DARE ATTEMPT A DIRECT ASSAULT ON THE MAGINOT LINE.

Another problem had been placing trust in the alliance with Belgium, which seemed firm until 1936 when Belgium abrogated the treaty and declared neutrality. Having been decimated in the previous war, the Belgians responded to German rearmament largely by hiding and hoping no one remembered them. It didn't work, of course. But the Line was hastily and not very well extended a little to cover the border, although the Ardennes section was left unguarded. The Germans were well aware of the strengths and weaknesses of the Line. The forces lined up against the border were nothing but a decoy when the *Blitzkrieg* opened up on May 10, 1940.

The Manstein Plan, as it was known, was approved by Hitler in February 1940. Oddly enough, the whole idea of using tanks in this way had been developed in the early 1920s by a Briton, Colonel John Fuller, in two books on warfare published after the British army had shown no interest in the strategy. The Germans, however, most certainly did take notice, and the Manstein Plan was designed around the capabilities of the Panzer tank divisions, with the aim of avoiding the Maginot Line and reaching the English Channel instead. Erwin Johannes Rommel, then a young lieutenant colonel but a student of infantry warfare with a book of his own on the subject, published in 1937, led the assault through the forest, which, to be fair for a moment to the hapless French, was a raid of unprecedented speed and brilliance. Even Rommel, soon to be promoted to general, writing in his own journal, was perhaps a little surprised by the results:

THE MANSTEIN PLAN

> The people in the houses were rudely awoken by the din of our tanks, the clatter and roar of tracks and engines. Troops lay bivouacked beside the road, military vehicles stood parked in farmyards and in some places on the road itself. Civilians and French troops, their faces distorted with terror, lay huddled in the ditches, alongside hedges and in every hollow beside the road. We passed refugee columns, the carts abandoned by their owners, who had fled in panic into the fields. On we went, at a steady speed, towards our objective. Every so often a quick glance at the map by a shaded light and a short wireless message to Divisional HQ to report the position and thus the success of 25th Panzer Regiment and to assure myself that there was still no resistance and that contact was being maintained to the rear. The flat countryside lay spread out around us under the cold light of the moon. We were through the Maginot Line! It was hardly conceivable. Twenty-two years before we had stood for four and a half long years before this self-same enemy and had won victory after victory and yet finally lost the war. And now we had broken through the renowned Maginot Line and were driving deep into enemy territory. It was not just a beautiful dream. It was reality.

French defences were totally compromised within five days, and while the Alpine section of the Line held the Italians back, the Germans took control of the whole of northern France, and the surrender on June 25 came with barely a shot fired from the Maginot Line. Maginot himself died in 1932, blissfully unaware that his masterpiece would be turned into a laughing stock. Shockingly, the French remanned the Line after the end of the war and only when they had built up their independent nuclear deterrent was it abandoned in 1969.

THE GERMAN INVASION OF FRANCE IN MAY 1940

The German invasion of the Low Countries began on May 10, 1940. Essentially two maneuvers, the first drove a wedge between Allied forces in France and those fighting further north—forcing the more northerly troops' evacuation from Dunkirk in late May and early June. The second thrust swept southwards from June 5, successfully bypassing the Maginot Line, and the fast-moving *Blitzkrieg* meant Paris fell on June 14, followed by the total surrender of France on June 25.

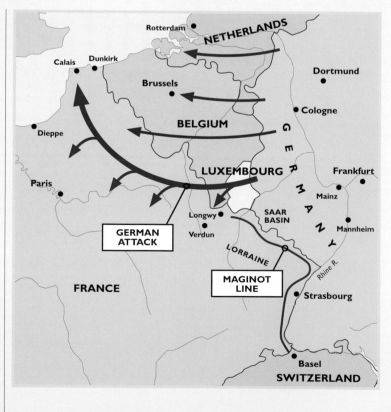

MOTIVATION

anger
charity
envy
faith
gluttony
greed
hope
lust
pride
sloth

WINSTON CHURCHILL STRIKES AGAIN: THE MAP OF IRAQ

March 12, 1921 – present

Main Culprit: Winston Churchill (1874–1965)

Damage Done: An artificial country was created from totally disparate communities with disastrous consequences to this day

Why: Ignorance and failure to care about the fate of the decolonizing nations

I do not understand this squeamishness about the use of gas. I am strongly in favor of using poisoned gas against uncivilized tribes.

Winston Churchill

One result of World War I was that the Ottomans' foolish last-minute alliance with the Kaiser and the Austrians led to the almost complete dismemberment of their empire. Turkey itself, empowered to some extent by the victory in the Dardanelles, became a secular state. The rest of the empire was left without rule, but not entirely in chaos. The empire's complex structure meant that provinces were to some extent self-governing and could soldier along on their own. The British had effectively won the war in the Middle East, though with large forces from India, alongside groups of, for want of a better word, adventurers such as T. E. Lawrence. But, with Britain shattered by the loss of manpower and money from the European campaign, there was a lack of will or ability to simply move in and claim the Middle East for the Empire—not all of it, anyway. Implicit support of Jewish claims for a sovereign state in Palestine in 1917, in the Balfour Declaration, had embittered many Arabs and infuriated many in the Colonial Office in Britain who were pro-Arab. Threats from other countries that might expand north from their African colonies had effectively evaporated; the British had literally the last empire standing. The new nationalisms that had exploded in the Balkans and had begun the decline of the Ottoman Empire spread swiftly into the newly liberated Ottoman provinces, and bitter riots against any attempt at British rule began. The home audience had no stomach for this: "How much longer are valuable lives to be sacrificed in the vain endeavor to impose upon the Arab population an elaborate and expensive administration which they never asked for and do not want?" asked *The Times* of London.

Had the British realized that the rumored oil reserves in the region held the key to world power for the next century they might have been a little more concerned. Perhaps the only one who really did care was Sir Mark Sykes appointed by General Kitchener in 1915 as his personal representative to a prime ministerial committee to determine the future of the Middle East. He had worked tirelessly to establish British control in the region, backed by Prime Minister David Lloyd George, plotting to ensure that local leaders would be on the side of the British, matching the aspirations of sheikhs and other aspirants to power, working essentially to take over the Ottoman Empire. But in 1919 Sykes died unexpectedly. Lloyd George could not find anyone to

THE BRITISH HAD
EFFECTIVELY WON THE
WAR IN THE MIDDLE
EAST, THOUGH WITH
LARGE FORCES FROM
INDIA, ALONGSIDE
GROUPS OF, FOR WANT
OF A BETTER WORD,
ADVENTURERS SUCH AS
T. E. LAWRENCE.

take on the role, and under political pressure, turned in the end to the man who became Colonial Secretary in 1921 — Winston Churchill.

Churchill had no time for any of this. He wanted the army demobilized; he wanted Arab rebellions put down, and the map redrawn. Egypt was to remain British; control over the Suez Canal and the route to India was of massive importance. The Syria-Lebanon area was complicated by French refusal to give up any remaining colonial influence. But the rest of Arabia had to be dealt with, and as it was deemed to have no particular value, to be dealt with as quickly as possible.

British forces had rather halfheartedly taken Baghdad in 1917, having suffered a particularly bad defeat at Kut, to the south, in 1916; where in a half-flooded cemetery the graves of some 40,000 British soldiers can still be seen. A British protectorate was finally set up in 1917, but the hold on Iraq was tenuous. There was strong opposition throughout the region to British rule, partly because the British proved a great deal more adept at tax collection than the Turks had been. The Ottomans had divided the region into three provinces, ethnically centered around Mosul, Baghdad, and Basra, in an attempt to keep the warring Sunni and Shiite populations apart. Baghdad also had a sizeable Jewish population and a significant Assyrian Christian one; this is not counting the Kurds, whose province was the closest to Turkey but who opposed British dominion even more fiercely than Turkish. By 1920 all of this had boiled over into full-scale revolt across the region. Horrifically, Churchill was not the least bit interested in working out what to do with whom. His view was pithily expressed in this chapter's epigraph, and indeed, despite official denials, there seems little doubt that Saddam Hussein was far from being the first to use chemical weapons against the Kurds. Led by some young generals, poison gas was regularly used across the region to put down the revolt.

WINSTON CHURCHILL
A portrait of Winston Churchill taken around 1941 when he would have be aged about 67.

Public Domain

"If the Kurds hadn't learnt by our example to behave themselves in a civilized way then we had to spank their bottoms," said Wing Commander Gale. Wing Commander Harris, notable in later life for the firebombing of Dresden, also noted: "The Arab and Kurd now know what real bombing means in casualties and damage. Within forty-five minutes a full-size village can be practically wiped out and a third of the inhabitants killed or injured." Airpower, particularly the dropping of bombs containing gas, was used extensively for almost the first time in history to save ground forces and expense; indeed, the whole revolt was put down with the loss of 2,000 British soldiers, a tiny fraction of the casualties of World War I. Gas was also used around the same time to keep down revolts in Afghanistan. Indeed, recent documents reveal that Churchill, even in 1940, was buying huge stocks of chemical weapons for potential use in Germany. ("It is absurd to consider morality on this topic when everybody used it in the last war without a word of complaint from the moralists or the Church.")

The problem remained of what to do once the revolt had been put down. Essentially, the decision was made to hand over all of Arabia to local strongmen in return for their support of Britain. It didn't really matter which populations, whether they wanted to be under that leader, or who their new countrymen might be. The careful planning of Sykes was all for naught. Churchill held a 10-day conference in Cairo in March 1921, to work out the new frontiers.

THE HOUSE OF SAUD

Ibn Saud was one such man and was effectively given the heart of Arabia to reinstate the rule of the House of Saud (Saudi Arabia). Two Hashemite brothers from Mecca, Faisal and Abdullah, were recruited to be kings of Iraq and Transjordan respectively. The separate Ottoman provinces of Mosul, Baghdad, and Basra were thrown into the new state of Iraq, a word that ironically meant "well-rooted country." Local observers were horrified. An American missionary noted, "You are flying in the face of four millennia of history." The British civil commissioner in Baghdad, Captain Arnold Wilson, warned that it was a recipe for disaster because the enduring Shia–Sunni conflict would result in "the antithesis of democratic government." But since Churchill was not the least bit interested in democratic government anyway, it was of little importance. The Kurds were lured into the new kingdom by promises of self-rule, not the first or last time such a promise was quickly broken.

Abdullah had already assumed power in Transjordan, but French hostility kept Faisal out of Syria, so he was handed Iraq instead. In order to create borders that could be more easily protected for the two new kingdoms, the conference blithely gave a large portion of what should have been Saudi Arabia—west of the Euphrates—to Iraq. In return, Ibn Saud was given control of most of the historic Kuwaiti kingdom, all but cutting off Iraq from wide access to the Persian Gulf.

The consequences are all too apparent today. Rivalry between Saudi Arabia and Iraq remains. Three times Iraq has laid claim to Kuwait, the most recent precipitating the First Gulf War. The total lack of interest in laying down sensible borders resulted in the predicted rivalry between Shiites and Sunnis. This was complicated by the uncomfortable presence of the Kurds; the imposition as king of someone who was considered an outsider; and the lack of interest on behalf of the British in imposing any proper governmental system. This catastrophe eventually led, via a succession of coups, to the rule of Saddam Hussein.

The chances for democracy arising from this series of decisions was, and maybe is, remote while the borders of Iraq remain so artificial and internally challenged. But the legacy in Iran turned out differently. Within 30 years the Iranians had instituted a democratically elected government, a beacon for progress in the region, and a harbinger of promise for the future, although it was short lived, as we shall see.

A CURRENT MAP OF THE MIDDLE EAST

A current map of the Middle East, showing Basra, Baghdad, and Mosul—the centers of three provinces under the Ottoman Empire—subsumed within Iraq.

MOTIVATION

anger
charity
envy
faith
gluttony
greed
hope
lust
pride
sloth

STALIN
AND THE GREAT PURGE
(1936–1938)

Main Culprit: Joseph Stalin (1879–1953)

Damage Done: Destruction of the elite of the army, as well as millions of Russians

Why: The paranoia of the all-powerful at full throttle

These scenes of terror and slaughter were not what they had looked forward to that night when old Major first stirred them to rebellion. If she herself had had any picture of the future, it had been of a society of animals set free from hunger and the whip, all equal, each according to his own capacity . . . instead—she did not know why—they had come to a time when no one dared speak his mind, when fierce, growling dogs roamed everywhere, and then you had to watch your comrades torn to pieces after confessing to shocking crimes.

George Orwell, *Animal Farm*

With the eyes of Yezhov—the eyes of the people.
Yezhov is on the watch for all poisonous snakes
And he smoked out vermin from den and lair.
He annihilated all types of scorpions.
With hands of Yezhov—the hands of the people.
And the Order of Lenin, burning flame,
Was given to you, faithful Stalinist People's Commissar,
You—a sword, unsheathed, calm and stern . . .
You—a bullet for all scorpions and snakes,

You—eyes of the country, clearer than a diamond.

Grey chronicler, witness of an era . . .
The million-voiced resounding word
Will fly from the people to the fighter Yezhov;
Thank you, Yezhov, that, raising the alarm,
You stood on guard for the country and the leader!

Dzhambul, Bard of Kazakhstan

History is full of purges, "ethnic cleansing," forced deportations, and great evils committed against their own subjects by rulers of all ages, castes, beliefs, and races. Improvements in technology and communication over the centuries have only seemed to make the process of slaughter more intense and, in the end, more public; but no matter how fierce the barbarity of those who have gone before, each genocide is rapidly pursued by one just as bad right behind it. The reasoning behind these "cleansings" is frequently warped and always evil, but not normally idiotic as such. There is usually, in the eyes of the perpetrators, some genuine sense of injustice or fear that mutates itself into the need to utterly destroy their own subjects or neighbors. Even the horrors of the Holocaust have done nothing to stop others from pursuing similar paths—Rwanda, Cambodia, even the descent of supposedly civilized Europe back into the medieval Dark Ages in the Balkans in the 1990s, stand as testimony to this.

© Swim Ink | Corbis

JOSEPH STALIN
Iosif Vissarionovich Dzhugashvili, better known by his adopted name Joseph Stalin, meaning "man of steel," ruled as First Secretary of the Central Committee of the Communist Party of the Soviet Union from April 3, 1922 until his death on March 5, 1953.

Not surprisingly, Hitler and Stalin, arguably the two worst tyrants of the twentieth century, stand head and shoulders above the others. Interestingly, both of their worst excesses were at best disbelieved, at worst deliberately ignored, by those in other countries whose vested political interests deemed it better to be looking in another direction. Hitler's crimes are now well known, the numbers and extent documented by dint of German efficiency, even in the matter of mass extermination. The untold millions who died as a direct result of Stalin's tyranny are even to this day highly debated. Hitler had a point to prove, no matter how evil, and some sort of plan in place. Stalin's terror in retrospect was scattered, insane, and in one specific aspect, utterly reckless, with severe consequences not only for those unfortunate victims but for world affairs in general. Leaving aside sheer insanity, it was essentially paranoia and fear that led Stalin not only to dispose of many millions of his own people—many of those who had helped him win the Revolution—but also on an unprecedented level to wipe out the upper echelons of his own armed forces. The purge of the Red Army left the Russians apparently unprepared to defend their own territory and prompted Hitler to think he could outdo Napoleon and successfully invade Russia. The failure of Hitler's Operation Barbarossa was no thanks to Stalin's idiocy in destroying his own generals.

The Red Army emerged as an organized form of the Red Guards, armed groups of workers who were the troops at the forefront of the Russian Revolution and the ensuing civil war. Originally, the army was thought to symbolise too much governmental power, but of course, as in all revolutions, the moment an oppressed group seizes power from an evil government, it rapidly acquires the means, techniques and terminology of the old regime. The Red Guards were not organized enough to take on the resistance of the White Army, but under Leon Trotsky—the People's Commissar for War—they were rapidly organized into what became known as the Red Army, formally coming into being on February 23, 1918, known and celebrated thenceforth as Red Army Day (later, Defenders of the Motherland Day). From the beginning there was fear about setting up a professional military cadre that might challenge or question the Revolution. Each army unit therefore had a political commissar working alongside the unit commander. Many of the units were essentially formed and run by pre-revolutionary tsarist officers in the early years, so to some degree caution may have been justified. A professional officer corps was seen as part of the "heritage of tsarism." By 1935, though, with the active cooperation of German experts, this decision was reversed and a general staff came into being. The situation in Europe and its increasing volatility made the haphazard nature of the Red Army a little too weak for comfort.

THERE WAS FEAR ABOUT SETTING UP A PROFESSIONAL MILITARY CADRE THAT MIGHT CHALLENGE OR QUESTION THE REVOLUTION.

This professionalization of the army coincided uneasily with the height of the power of the NKVD, the Soviet secret police, responsible among other things for internal security and the *gulag* forced labor camps. For years, hundreds of thousands of Soviet citizens had been deported to far reaches of the Soviet Union, ostensibly for political disobedience or what was known as "wrecking," a loose term for failing to meet economic targets, among other things, which could be applied to almost anybody at will. Article 58 of 1927 deemed punishable any action that could be seen as making one an "enemy of the workers"—not just Soviet workers but the international solidarity of workers. There was also massive relocation on ethnic lines of populations, resulting in millions of deaths on forced marches and inhumane conditions. But by the mid-

1930s, the power of the NKVD reached new heights under Nikolai Yezhov, and a reign of terror began, reaching deep into Soviet society but more crucially into the higher echelons of the party itself. Yezhov typified the new Soviet regime in many ways. A tailor's assistant in St. Petersburg, he joined the Bolsheviks at Vitebsk in May 1917. He worked his way through the bureaucratic ranks, holding positions such as Deputy People's Commissar for Agriculture and acting head of the accounting and distribution department for the Communist party. He rose to Secretary for the Central Committee in 1934, and in 1935 wrote a paper for Stalin arguing that political opposition must inevitably lead to violence and terrorism and must ruthlessly be purged. This approach appealed to Stalin's increasing concern about his own authority—the continuing thorn in his side of the other founders of the Revolution—as much as it appealed to Yezhov. In 1936 he became People's Commissar for Internal Affairs (head of the NKVD); to the surprise of few, his predecessor was found guilty of treason at one of the famous show trials in 1938 and shot. A glorious revolutionary history was invented for Yezhov, the savior of Kazakhstan during the Civil War, but it is far from clear that he ever actually went there.

NO OPPOSITION

It did not take long for the new professional Red Army to fall foul of what became known as *Yezhovshchina*. They were far from alone; it is thought that at least half the entire leadership of the country, the political and military establishment at all levels, were killed during the next two years. The infamous Order NO. 00486 of August 15, 1937 extended automatic guilty verdicts against anyone—and their wives and children over 15—who were deemed "socially dangerous." There was, in particular, deep suspicion of anyone negotiating with or influenced by outside powers. Since the new corps of the Red Army were German-trained, that essentially included all of them. It was this kind of idiocy— creating a corps with German assistance to train the army against the growing German threat, then killing them for consorting with Germans—that passed beyond even the normal barbarism of internal security forces. The purge was supported by fabricated evidence that German counterintelligence had introduced through an intermediary, President Bene of Czechoslovakia. These forgeries purported to be correspondence between Marshal Tukhachevsky and members of the

German High Command. Tukhachesky had in fact just returned to Russia from leading a delegation to London for the funeral of King George V, and visiting also France and Germany, when he was recalled to Moscow, arrested, and executed two days later. He was widely credited with the modernization of the army, and had been one of the chief architects of the victories against the White Army and the Russian army in 1920–1; having at the same time had a furious disagreement with Stalin over Poland. The purge of the army removed three out of five marshals, 13 out of 15 army generals, eight out of nine admirals (the navy was suspected of exploiting its opportunity for foreign contacts), 50 out of 57 army corps generals, 154 out of 186 division generals, all 16 army commissars, and 25 of the 28 army corps commissars.

HITLER'S FOLLY

It seems likely that Hitler was, in the end, persuaded that this self-destruction of the Soviet army presented an opportunity too good to miss. Indeed, so demoralized and leaderless was the Red Army that Hitler's early gains were enormous; the Soviet air force barely left the ground and hundreds of thousands of the initial 1.5 million soldiers were rapidly surrounded and killed. Only by declaring a Great Patriotic War, abandoning for the moment the tenets of class struggle and extolling defense of the Motherland, was Stalin able to mobilize an army of 15 to 20 million to defeat the Germans, and perhaps lose 7 to 10 million of those in the process. Yezhov, the architect of the stupidity, a bureaucrat with power gone to his head, willing to lap up Stalin's distortions, lies, and self-destruction, was long dead, a victim of false accusations, betrayed by his own successor, Beria. Famously, well before the advent of computer technology, he was "disappeared" from a photo which showed him walking with Stalin. That the damage he inflicted on his own cause was not fatal to the Revolution was no credit to Stalin; it was due only to the sheer number of the Russian population and their willingness to die for their country.

SHENTON THOMAS'S LITTLE MEN AND THE FALL OF SINGAPORE

December 8, 1941 – February 15, 1942

MOTIVATION

anger
charity
envy
faith
gluttony
greed
hope
lust
pride
sloth

Main Culprit: Sir Shenton Thomas (1879–1962)

Damage Done: What Churchill called the "worst disaster" of British history

Why: Main fortifications facing the wrong way

Well I suppose you'll shove the little men off.

Sir Shenton Thomas, December 8, 1941

Everyone remembers December 7, 1941, the day the Japanese attacked Pearl Harbor and precipitated the American entry into World War II. The very next day, Japanese forces landed on the east coast of South Thailand and North Malaya, embarking on an invasion that no one, especially those about to be invaded, had imagined possible. Fifty-five days later, the cornerstone of the British Empire in South-east Asia would fall to a small Japanese force, undermanned, underfed, and travelling mostly by bicycle. A combination of pride and sloth, contempt for a misunderstood enemy, and total lack of foresight takes the fall of Singapore above and beyond the realm of normal military blunders.

Some blame lies with Churchill, his generals and various colonial leaders, some with Lieutenant-General Arthur Percival, in charge of Allied forces in Malaya. But Percival didn't arrive until 1941, and while he made tactical errors, probably nothing, by that point, could have stopped the advance. However, partly as the Crown's representative in Singapore since 1934, and partly on behalf of the many men at the end of the colonial era who had no business in running other people's countries, the chief responsibility belongs to Governor and Commander-in-Chief of the Straits Settlements and High Commissioner of the Malay States from 1934 to 1942, Sir Shenton Thomas.

FROM THE CLASSROOM TO THE WAR ROOM

He had no military experience; his position as commander-in-chief was just a title. Shenton Thomas was educated at St. John's at Leatherhead in England, which specialized in educating the clergy. His father was a vicar. He graduated from Queens' College, Cambridge, and was a teacher for seven years at Aysgarth Preparatory School in Yorkshire. He joined the Colonial Service in 1909, serving in Kenya, Uganda, Nigeria, and the Gold Coast before becoming governor of Nyasaland in 1929. He returned to the Gold Coast in 1932 as governor until 1934, when he was appointed governor and commander-in-chief of Malaya. A. H. Dickinson, inspector-general of police in Singapore and close friend of Shenton Thomas, said of him that he would have made a first-class headmaster. After the fall, a report was assembled by General Wavell and issued on May 30, 1942. Of Shenton Thomas, it said:

> The name of Sir Shenton Thomas will go down to history as the most abused Englishman and the Malayan Civil Service will be named as one of the most incompetent institutions which has

ever existed. Most civilians resent what they regard as gross and calculated deception on the part of Sir Shenton Thomas in that he repeated, both in public announcements and privately, assurances that there was no need to think of evacuation as Singapore would not fall.

At the beginning of 1941 no one in London was paying much heed to the Asian situation. The Japanese had entered the war but were preoccupied in Manchuria and Indochina, and everyone expected any ongoing hostilities to be with the Russians. The Americans were concerned, but expected to be able to repel the Japanese by economic blockade. The situation in Europe was much more serious; the Germans had overrun almost all of the continent. The British had evacuated from Dunkirk and, despite winning the Battle of Britain, had little hope of taking back any of the losses. Australian troops, far from protecting Southeast Asia, had been summoned to defend North Africa. But the collapse of Europe had left the French and Dutch colonies wide open to invasion. In October 1941 General Hideki Tojo, an aggressive expansionist, became prime minister of Japan and embarked on a rapid war plan to take the whole region and destroy American naval power. Everyone in Europe was too preoccupied with Hitler's decision to invade the Soviet Union to notice much of this. Anyway, Singapore was impregnable to the only possible route of attack, from the sea. As unprepared as the Americans were for Pearl Harbor, the residents and generals sipping gin in the Raffles Hotel were equally unaware and unprepared for the Japanese.

The island of Singapore lies at the southern tip of the Malay Peninsula. When Sir Stamford Raffles landed in 1819, it was almost uninhabited and mostly jungle. Singapura — Lion City — had supposedly been named by a Sumatran prince who landed there in the thirteenth century and saw what was probably a tiger. It had been a minor trading post for various empires over the following centuries. The British, however, had seen the Straits of Malacca as a major sea route early in the eighteenth century — on the trade route from China through to India — and Raffles, on behalf of the British East India Company, had been given a free hand to establish bases for British imperial expansion. Singapore was set up

© Bettmann | Corbis

SHENTON THOMAS
Shenton Thomas inspecting British cadets in Singapore on December 12, 1941, four days after the Japanese invasion of Malaya.

as a tariff-free port and rapidly became both an important British colony and trading center. Indeed, as an independent country, it has made its mark in the world in much the same way centuries later. Singapore was ruled as part of the Straits Settlements, along with Malaya, rich in tin and rubber. British colonial rule was as secure as any in the world. The population was, as it remains, an eclectic mix of Malays, Chinese and Indians, ruled over by a reasonably benign series of second sons of wealthy vicars and third-rate generals.

In 1921 the Committee of Imperial Defence recommended that a major British naval base be built in Singapore. It was finished in 1938. Even though Japan left the League of Nations in 1933 and was clearly a military threat, it had been determined that the only threat to the island came from the sea. Vast, dense Malayan jungle lay to the north, over a causeway, supposedly securing the landward approaches. Large guns were placed around the naval base to fire on enemy ships. These were static and could not be turned.

LARGE GUNS WERE PLACED AROUND THE NAVAL BASE TO FIRE ON ENEMY SHIPS. THEY WERE STATIC AND COULD NOT BE TURNED.

The essential idea was that Fortress Singapore could hold out for a "period before relief" when land forces could be sent down from India, in the unlikely event of attack. Malaya was left unprotected—a country which in 1939 was producing 40 percent of the world's rubber and 60 percent of the world's tin. Belatedly, in August 1937, according to a memorandum from Lieutenant-General Sir Henry Pownall, who had been sent to Singapore in 1941, the British government decided to build proper airbases and send warships to defend Malaya. But there was no coordination between the army, navy and air force. Pownall warned: "It was obviously not only wasteful but dangerous to make new airfields unless there was a reasonable certainty of a strong and efficient air force to use them and to cooperate in the defense as a whole." In August 1940 Pownall found 84 aircraft in Malaya; by December 7, 1941, despite an assurance of 582 aircraft, there were only 158, a fourth of them obsolete. The fleet that was supposed to provide the "relief" had mostly been recalled to the Mediterranean. Still, even Pownall did not foresee an attack from the north, through the jungle. And Churchill wasn't interested. He wrote: "The political situation in the Far East does not seem to require, and the strength of the air force by no means permits, the maintenance of such large forces in the Far East at this time." On

November 6 all Japanese civilians were evacuated from Singapore. British Intelligence reports of Japanese troop movements throughout November were largely ignored. Finally, on December 2, two British warships, the new battleship *Prince of Wales* and the *Repulse*, arrived.

Recent and still unconfirmed findings suggest that something more sinister than ignorance was at work. Top-secret War Cabinet memoranda from 1940, apparently incorporating some of Shenton Thomas's more gloomy predictions from a prewar visit, were apparently en route—via the real slow boat to China—when they were intercepted by Japanese agents. It is possible, therefore, that the London government was well aware of the shortfalls in Singapore's defences, and that the Japanese knew them too. Either way, Shenton Thomas's fatuous remarks to the citizens of Singapore that it was impregnable, coupled with his failure to erect even the most rudimentary fortifications, look even more foolhardy.

IGNORANCE AND MORE

On December 5, interestingly for Americans two full days before Pearl Harbor, Thomas met with Air Chief Brooke-Popham to discuss clear indications that an invasion was about to be mounted. There was a defence plan for Malaya of a sort, but they decided it would be wrong to proceed, as it might worry the citizens too much.

Japanese Zero fighters attacked British air bases in Singapore on the same day as the attack on Pearl Harbor, destroying 90 percent of the aircraft. No air-raid sirens went off in the city, and the lights remained helpfully on all night long. When the Japanese army landed, Sir Shenton Thomas said to the army commanders, "Well I suppose you'll shove the little men off." The British army had a fleet of World War I Rolls-Royce armored cars against lightweight Japanese tanks. *The Prince of Wales* and the *Repulse* sailed on December 8 to take on the invading force, but without air support. Both ships were sunk two days later. Churchill reported, "I put the telephone down. I was thankful to be alone. In all the war I never received a more direct shock."

Within two days the one and only major land battle of the campaign had been lost decisively by the British, but still there was certainty that the Japanese could never make it through the jungle into Singapore, and still nothing was done to shore up the defenses. Churchill commanded, "There must be no thought of sparing the troops or population;

commanders and senior offices should die with their troops. The honor of the British Empire and the British Army is at stake." As it turned out, the Japanese army had no intention of sparing anyone. Japanese soldiers were instructed: "When you encounter the enemy after landing, think of yourself as an avenger coming face to face at last with your father's murderer. Here is a man whose death will lighten your heart." Part of the speed of the invasion force was due to a directive that prisoners and the wounded should be killed rather than slow the advance. On December 30, Governor Thomas had the belated idea of asking the Chinese population to help build defenses around the perimeter. He still insisted that all was well. The extent to which he was ignorant of events right up to the surrender was shown when G. Weisberg, the pre-war colonial treasurer, dropped in and asked how the war was going. Shenton Thomas replied, "Honestly, Weisie, I don't know. They tell me nothing, although I am a member of the War Council."

By the end of the following month, January 1942, the Japanese were at the causeway linking Singapore with Malaya. The British soldiers retreated over the causeway, which was then blown up. General Percival had three times as many troops as the Japanese, part of whose quest

THE EXTENT OF THE JAPANESE ADVANCE OF 1941–2

Japanese advances in 1941–2 —including the capture of Singapore—threatened Australia, which had large numbers of troops and equipment committed in Europe and North Africa. However, over-extension on the part of the Japanese, and the increasing power of the United States Navy turned the tide in mid-1942, first by rebuffing a Japanese invasion force bound for New Guinea at the Battle of the Coral Sea, and later inflicting a decisive defeat on June 4, 1942 at the Battle of Midway. The later Battle of Milne Bay saw the first land defeat of the Japanese, inflicted upon them by Australian troops.

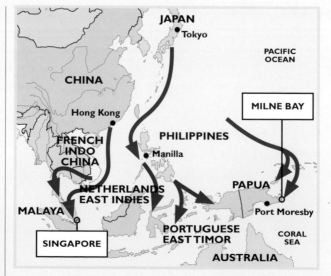

for speed lay in the knowledge that they had only days of food supplies left. But without air power, sea power or, crucially, any artillery, there was nothing Percival could do to stop the Japanese from crossing into Singapore. The Japanese forces were battle-hardened, experienced from years of fighting in Manchuria, and well used to jungle warfare, invasions, and rapid movement. Percival had little of help to say to the population: "Our task is to hold this fortress until help can come, as assuredly it will come; this we are determined to do." At the same time, the brand new and unused naval base was abandoned without a fight. The forces that were in Singapore had never been in combat before and were in shock. Everyone knew no help was coming. The last boatload of evacuated civilians never made it out of the harbor.

The island was lost within six days. Everyone in the Alexandra Hospital—patients, nurses, and doctors—was massacred. On February 15 Percival surrendered unconditionally. Over 100,000 men were taken prisoner, along with the entire British civilian population. Many of the military prisoners, perhaps 9,000, died during the forced construction of the Burma–Thailand railroad. The Chinese civilian population of Singapore, though, were even less fortunate. And up to 50,000 of them were slaughtered.

It was the Americans who eventually turned the tide of the war at the Battle of the Coral Sea and the Battle of Midway. Both symbolically and strategically, the whole hemisphere slipped from British control the day the guns failed to turn.

On September 5, 1945, when the Japanese surrendered to Lord Louis Mountbatten, the prisoners in Sime Road Camp (who included this author's father, grandmother, and aunt) held their own ceremony. In the place of honor, by the flagstaff, was Lady Daisy Thomas who had been interned there. When the Union Jack was hoisted, the freed prisoners cheered three times for King George V and three times for Lady Thomas.

> MANY OF THE MILITARY PRISONERS, PERHAPS 9,000, DIED DURING THE FORCED CONSTRUCTION OF THE BURMA–THAILAND RAILROAD. THE CHINESE CIVILIAN POPULATION OF SINGAPORE, THOUGH, WERE EVEN LESS FORTUNATE. UP TO 50,000 OF THEM WERE SLAUGHTERED.

MOTIVATION
anger
charity
envy
faith
gluttony
greed
hope
lust
pride
sloth

SUHRAWARDY, PARTITION, AND THE BENGAL RICE FAMINE

October 1942 – October 1943

Main Culprit: Huseyn Shaheed Suhrawardy (1892–1963)

Damage Done: 4–5 million dead of famine during good growing weather

Why: Deliberate hoarding of crops to avoid them getting into the hands of an enemy that never came

Bengal famine was one of the greatest disasters that has befallen any people under British rule and damage to our reputation here both among Indians and foreigners in India is incalculable.

Field-Marshal Lord Wavell

There have been many famines throughout history, not least in India. A disastrous famine in the eighteenth century killed as many as ten million. A catastrophe not far short of that befell India during World War II, killing maybe four to five million. Initially it was just considered to be, well, one of those famines. But later research has established that it was far different, one of the most bitterly debated yet at the same time least-known disasters in modern history, with casualties totalling almost 60 percent of those who died in the Holocaust at the same time, yet in a country almost entirely untouched by the ravages of the war in terms of battle. Its aftermath led to some extraordinary scholarly, political and economic developments. As with any disaster of this magnitude, there are complex reasons for its coming about, but amongst them we can certainly identify greed. It defies belief that those who created the problem appeared oblivious to its unfolding before them and then were incapable of stopping it. Many have been blamed for this famine, but we can isolate at least one man as the cause, a man who rose later to substantial political power and remains much revered—by some—as a founder of his nation, though his idiotic actions in 1943 would seem to have killed many of his would-be countrymen before his nation was even born.

Bengal under the British Empire included what is now North India and Bangladesh, or what was to become East Pakistan at Partition in 1947. Its history dates back many thousands of years and it had its own empire before the arrival of the Mughals and then the British, and a substantial culture. It stretches from the foothills of the Himalayas through to the populous Ganges delta. Calcutta (now Kolkata), its main city, was to all intents and purposes the capital of British India,

HUSEYN SHAHEED SUHRAWARDY
The Indian wing of the Statutory Commission c.1928. Suhrawardy stands at the left.

being the center of commercial trade for the British East India Company. In all, it is one of the most densely populated parts of the world. Dating back to the battle of Nabadwip in the thirteenth century, it has had both sizeable Hindu and Muslim populations and competing rulers. Bengal, and Calcutta, had for years been the intellectual and literary heart of India, and the birthplace of the nationalist movement in the twentieth century. In 1906 the Muslim League was born in Dhaka and, briefly and disastrously, East and West Bengal were partitioned. The capital of British India moved to Delhi after the subsequent riots. Gandhi's peaceful campaigns of civil disobedience were born in Calcutta, and the fight for independence was given strength by the advent of the war; one Indian leader even joined with the Japanese and set up a provisional government in exile to encourage Indians to fight against the Allies. Calcutta in 1946 was the scene of terrible riots as the full force of independence and partition split Bengal in two. By then, though, the province had suffered tremendously from the Bengal Famine.

A FAILING POWER

The roots of this disaster can no doubt be traced to the worsening turn in the war situation. Singapore had fallen early in 1942, ending British dominance in Southeast Asia and seriously diminishing the aura of power that the British Empire possessed, including its ability to protect its dominions, of which India was the jewel in the crown.

As it was, there had been rising demands for independence and tensions between nationalists and the imperial forces, as well as a growing push by the Muslim minority for self-rule in certain provinces, and unrest among the Hindu population. The capture of Burma by the Japanese in early 1942 had led to the sudden cessation of imports of much-needed rice into the Bengal region. At the same time, in a far more sinister development, the British decided to institute a policy of "denial" within the area of India — Bengal again — deemed to be most vulnerable to Japanese invasion. This included destroying or removing products deemed essential to an invading force, including foodstuffs. Rice, in particular, was targeted, and supplies were diverted to the major city of Calcutta, which was deemed more important and more defensible, leaving many of the rural provinces short.

For some years afterwards, it was claimed that a drought led to the famine. This was fundamentally disproved by the Indian economist Amartya Sen, who showed that the rainfall figures were at the least normal, if not above normal, during 1942–3. He developed a complex economic theory of scarce resources and their distribution according to social standing in the community. There was no shortage of rice. This theory, in part, earned him a Nobel Prize for Economics. However, later research has pointed out that there was a dip in rice production, partly because of the higher rainfall noted by Sen and a serious outbreak of the fungus *Helminthosporium oryzae*, which causes brown spots in rice and could conceivably have ruined 90 percent of the crop. Other theories abound, and hostility between Hindus and Muslims still pervades heated discussions about the famine to this day.

There is no doubt that unusual natural problems and the British denial policy played their part in the famine. But while hindsight is a useful tool, it is often the case that the contemporary view of events is closer to the truth than subsequent political or religious explanations with an axe to grind. And locals seemed in no doubt about who to blame for allowing four million people to die while food was available. The Calcutta newspaper *The Statesman* and other local despatches blamed the local provincial government and its leader, H. S. Suhrawardy, a controversial figure at the time and even more so when he later became the fifth prime minister of the new country of Pakistan.

Once the 1937 elections were over, Suhrawardy became the minister for labor and by 1943 was the minister for civil supplies. He formed the only Muslim League government on the subcontinent. In 1949 he founded the East Pakistan Awami Muslim League, and in 1953, the United Front in Dhaka, which won the 1954 general elections. The same year he joined Muhammad Ali Bogra's ministry as law minister. However, with the change of government in 1955, Suhrawardy became leader of the opposition. H. S. Suhrawardy rose to become the fifth prime minister of Pakistan on September 12, 1956. During his tenure, he tried to remove economic disparity between the two separate parts of the country. In October 1957, Suhrawardy resigned from his premiership due to the president's refusal to convene a meeting of parliament to seek a vote of confidence. Suffering from a chronic heart conditions, he died on December 5, 1963.

Most accounts agree that his policies led to the hoarding of rice supplies, and heavy profiteering by some of his political allies. Much less than Sen's market forces, it was deliberate manipulation of the war situation and the food supplies for personal—and perhaps political—gain that led to the situation getting out of hand. Rice prices doubled every week or so and soon rose way beyond the ability of the average citizen to buy. The famine, which affected the rural areas, swept out of control

WHILE HINDSIGHT IS A USEFUL TOOL, IT IS OFTEN THE CASE THAT THE CONTEMPORARY VIEW OF EVENTS IS CLOSER TO THE REAL TRUTH THAN SUBSEQUENT POLITICAL OR RELIGIOUS EXPLANATIONS.

as hundreds of thousands descended on Calcutta, hearing that food was available there. M. H. Ispahani, a friend of Suhrawardy and a leading Calcutta-based Muslim business magnate, was appointed the sole procuring agent. The Famine Enquiry Commission later noted: "Government control over purchase made by this (Ispahani) firm was inadequate and undue profits were made by this firm." In the debate in the Bengal Assembly, Dr. Shyama Prasad Mukherjee identified Ispahani and company as the main culprit. Dr. Mukherjee also spoke against the preferential treatment of Calcutta and its urban hinterland. In his opinion, "the activities of the government seem to suggest that whatever food grains may be available will be kept in the greater Calcutta area and the rest of the province will be left to its own tragic fate." It later turned out that Ispahani was a major financial backer of Jinnah's Muslim League, leading to at least the suggestion that there was a political edge to all this. The fact that the majority of the dead were Muslims rather than Hindus is a tragic irony.

CATASTROPHE CONDEMNED

The Statesman declared: "This sickening catastrophe is man-made. So far as we are aware, all of India's previous famines originated primarily from calamities of Nature. But this one is accounted for by no climatic failure; rainfall has been generally plentiful. What the province's state would now be had drought been added to governmental bungling is an appalling thought." British Field Marshal Wavell, appointed Viceroy of India in 1943, was appalled when he realized what had happened and protested to Churchill; but even after his intervention, Suhrawardy was reluctant to open up supplies or use anything other than distribution networks controlled by the government. Finally, a combination of British pressure and local demands got the situation under control, only after between two and four million Indians had died needlessly.

WAKEFIELD'S NUTS

1949–1950

MOTIVATION

anger

charity

envy

faith

gluttony

greed

hope

lust

pride

sloth

Main Culprit: John Wakefield

Damage Done: US $100 million worth of a cash-strapped post-war Britain's money and a discouragement of later aid efforts

Why: Massive aid effort to grow peanuts where peanuts can't grow

On the Groundnut Scheme, I think they could have gone ahead with many other schemes of that nature—both from the point of view of trying to assist the countries in Africa as well as to help the food policy here. Because that scheme failed they rather got cold feet, but I think that was a pity.

Michael Foot,
Former Leader of the British Labour Party, 2002

© Razvanjp | Dreamstime.com

At the end of World War II perhaps the only true socialist government in British history was elected, under Clement Attlee as prime minister. The British Empire by now was lost for good and the process of decolonization had begun in earnest. At the same time, food rationing prevailed in Britain and many basic goods were in short supply. Unlike some other colonial powers, many in the British government were determined to try to help their former colonies to establish themselves as independent nations with some chance of survival. They did not often succeed, as the history of Africa attests, but with a genuine desire for charity, they often invested money in schemes. Unfortunately, the utter ignorance of the officials who put together the plan to grow groundnuts—better known as peanuts—in Tanganyika, now Tanzania, not only cost a great deal of money but to some degree put an end to the whole concept of promoting self-sufficiency in decolonized countries. The basic problem—the word "basic" is used advisedly—was that they initially spent half a million pounds—many millions in today's currency—trying to grow a crop on land where it couldn't actually grow.

The original proposal came from the managing director of the United Africa Company, Frank Samuel. He was charged with finding vegetable oil for Unilever's soap and margarine. The oil was in short supply and there was significant rationing of these products in Britain, which was politically uncomfortable for the government. Samuel realized that a project of the scale he was thinking of could be handled only by a government, so he presented a five-year plan to the new Labour government to clear 20,000 acres (80 sq. km) for a test project. A government study was commissioned and former Director of Agriculture John Wakefield was put in charge of the study.

Wakefield immediately saw the huge potential in Samuel's plan, less to bring profit to Unilever, or even soap to the by-then long unwashed British public, but more as a way to solve major economic problems in African nations, including famine and problems of cultivation of the land. He was concerned that solutions had to be found to prevent major crises in the future as the countries became independent. African farmers could not just be told about modern agricultural techniques; they had to see them in a practical demonstration of their superiority, and be shown how marginal land could be brought into use by promoting new crops. He was, in short, proposing the peanut plan as the base for a massive agricultural revolution. And given what happened in Africa over the subsequent 50 years, and the number of lives lost to famines in those years, the disaster that overwhelmed the plan may indeed have caused a loss higher than its purely financial one.

The importance of the plan for Wakefield was the main theme of his report. The land he chose, the Kongwa region in the Central Highlands of Tanganyika, had major problems, not the least being that the adequacy of the rainfall was marginal. Massive clearing of the native brush was needed; it was assumed in the report that the government could both find and pay for the major machinery to clear the land. The explorer Henry Morton Stanley—the one who found Dr. Livingstone—called this scrub "an interminable jungle of thornbushes." It was almost impenetrable, even for animals, except snakes. The southern region was in fact much more suitable, but had no port or rail connection, whereas Kongwa could be reached relatively easily from Dar es Salaam, the capital. Wakefield, in his enthusiasm to do good, ignored the obstacles and put through a positive report, which the government, equally enthusiastic, put rapidly into effect. By the time Wakefield had finished, Samuel's planned 20,000 acres (80 sq. km) had become 3.25 million acres (13,150 sq. km).

They hit trouble almost immediately. The scrubland turned out to hide hordes of very unpleasant bees. Ship anchor chains were needed to link bulldozers together to clear the trees; then the roots proved almost impossible to remove. Within the first hours, the roots destroyed the machinery that had been sent over. Finally, a fraction of the land planned for, just 10,000 acres (40 sq. km), was successfully cleared and the crop planted. Unfortunately, the soil, though fertile, was rock-hard underneath, and although the peanut plants grew above the ground just fine, the actual nut grows underground and turned out to be virtually impossible to harvest. The entire project had failed completely because no one had considered the fact that the land could not actually sustain the crop. No matter how hard they worked, how much money they put into it, how badly the operation might have been run—and much blame was showered on all of those culprits—nothing could overcome

THE EXPLORER HENRY MORTON STANLEY CALLED THIS SCRUB "AN INTERMINABLE JUNGLE OF THORNBUSHES."

the essential problem of trying to force the land to grow a crop that was entirely unsuited for it. Worse still, peanuts are grown successfully in other regions of Africa—just not there. Wakefield was so overcome with the importance of what he was trying to do, and had such faith in the burgeoning technologies of the post-war world, that he assumed all obstacles could be overcome for the greater good. The scheme was touching in its faith but utterly disastrous in its execution.

Not one nut in any form ever reached the British marketplace. Around four thousand tons of peanuts had been purchased in 1947 to produce seed. By 1949 only half that amount had been harvested. A staggering total of £49 million—then worth well in excess of US $100 million, and in today's terms massively more—was spent to produce half of what had been purchased as seed. By 1950, in an attempt to salvage something from the land, sunflowers were planted. The next year saw a total failure of the crop through a lack of rain. The plan was officially abandoned.

To this day, economists argue about what went wrong with the peanut plan. It is offered as proof that private companies, not governments, should tackle big ventures of this sort. Bureaucrats were blamed, and blamed each other. But it did have a greater impact in seriously undermining future plans that might really have made a difference in the region. Certainly, other plans followed, especially during the Cold War as the Americans and Soviets competed in the region, but their interest was always in political influence and not in helping subsistence agriculture. The unfortunate Tanzanians were also subjected to the Canadian wheat plan of the 1970s—the Barbeig cattle herders were moved off land they had tended for centuries for a large-scale effort to plant prairie wheat that proved slightly more successful than the peanuts, but less fruitful than the cattle herds that were there before. And Lake Victoria is still under threat after perch, put into adjacent ponds to encourage fish-farming, escaped into the main lake, and subsequently ate 180 of the 300 species that once lived there.

More significantly, the failure of the groundnut scheme has been used to argue against intervening in the affairs of developing nations and as proof of the foolishness of foreign aid plans. In early 2005 peanuts were again in the news as the Senegalese government came under pressure from the International Monetary Fund and the World Bank to privatize its peanut industry, the second biggest export of the country, in exchange for relief from debt. Its initial attempt to do so only a few years previously left millions of peanut farmers and their dependents on the brink of starvation, and the government was reluctant to take the route once more, but had little choice. The grand charitable plans of the John Wakefields have been replaced by a far different way of extracting money from nuts.

As Michael Foot, leader of the Labour party and a major figure in British and world politics for more than 40 years, notes in the epigraph to this chapter, the tragic legacy of the failure of the groundnut scheme was profound indeed. The litany of debt, disaster, war and famine in Africa could perhaps have been avoided, at least in part, if the grand plan envisaged by John Wakefield had actually come to fruition. But he allowed his enthusiasm to overcome his own good judgement and disaster resulted instead.

MOTIVATION
anger
charity
envy
faith
gluttony
greed
hope
lust
pride
sloth

MOHAMMED MOSSADEGH, *TIME*'S MAN OF THE YEAR, AND DEMOCRACY IN IRAN

April 28, 1951 – August 19, 1953

Main Culprit: Allen Welsh Dulles (1893–1969) and Kermit Roosevelt (1916–2000)

Damage Done: A laughing stock made of the concept of democracy in the Middle East

Why: British and CIA meddling

So this is how we will get rid of the madman Mossadegh in Iran.

United States Secretary of State John Foster Dulles, 1953

The United States played a significant role in orchestrating the overthrow of Iran's popular prime minister, Mohammed Mossadegh. The Eisenhower administration believed its actions were justified for strategic reasons. But the coup was clearly a setback for Iran's political development and it is easy to see why so many Iranians continue to resent this intervention by America in their internal affairs.

United States Secretary of State Madeline Albright, March 16, 2000

Although oil played only a peripheral part in the events surrounding the creation of Iraq, it had become by World War II highly significant. World War I had shown the world the importance of oil reserves in keeping a fighting machine going long enough to win the type of war that was being fought. Indeed, Germany's inability to control the flow of raw materials was highly significant in its eventual defeat. As oil reserves began to appear in the Middle East, American commercial and political interests began to bring the Americans into conflict with their British allies. The United States had been happy to allow British control over the region for a while, but as America's domestic oil reserves, which had been 70 percent of global oil production in 1914, began to dwindle, and oil started to gush from the Arabian desert, the situation changed; today 67 percent of global oil reserves are in the Gulf region. American oil companies made a huge deal with Ibn Saud, cementing his dynasty's power and also involving the United States inextricably in the affairs of the region—and equally inextricably, with one of the most despotic regimes in the world. Arrangements were made, cleverly, with the Emir of Bahrain before oil was actually discovered. Soon the British found themselves outflanked in many parts of a region which they has previously considered their domain, but hadn't taken the trouble to secure.

The aftermath of World War II brought even more significant changes. The Cold War saw both geopolitical threats to the stability of the region, and the disappearance of many rich oil fields firmly behind the Iron Curtain. The British remained confident, though, of their influence, both in Iraq under the regime they had set up, and in Iran where a constitutional monarchy, with the Pahlavi family established as shahs, kept reasonably firm control over affairs. The Anglo-Iranian Oil Company, set up by treaty in 1919, was of huge importance both to the Iranian economy and the British, though very much weighted toward British interests. In 1941 the British and Russians, now allies against Germany, moved into Iran to secure the oilfields in a joint operation. In 1943, indeed, the Iranian capital of Tehran was the seat of the first major conference between Stalin, Roosevelt, and Churchill to discuss strategy for the remainder of the war, and to offer Iran particular protection and guarantee its independence.

AMERICAN OIL COMPANIES MADE A HUGE DEAL WITH IBN SAUD, CEMENTING HIS DYNASTY'S POWER AND ALSO INVOLVING THE UNITED STATES INEXTRICABLY IN THE AFFAIRS OF THE REGION—AND EQUALLY INEXTRICABLY, WITH ONE OF THE MOST DESPOTIC REGIMES IN THE WORLD.

The postwar situation did not work out as planned, however. Soviet troops refused to leave northern Iran without oil concessions. Iran suddenly became an important pawn in the Cold War, a buffer state between the Soviet Union and western influence elsewhere in the Middle East. And having got the Russians out of the country, there was increasing nationalist anger in Iran that they could get no better deal on their oil from the British government, which they felt was exploiting their oil resources.

COMETH THE HOUR

Onto this scene came Mohammed Mossadegh, a French-educated Iranian politician who had been in and out of minor political offices and intermittently in exile since 1914. He had been a strong opponent of the imposed oil deal in 1919, and consistently opposed the shah's acquiescence to the agreement. After the abdication of the first Pahlavi shah in 1941, and the succession of his son, Mossadegh was allowed again to run for Parliament and was elected easily. His opposition to foreign intervention in Iranian oil matters became very popular, and with an unlikely coalition of socialists who sympathized with the Soviets and the radical Muslim ayatollahs, he was elected prime minister in March 1951. He immediately tried, and failed, to renegotiate the oil royalty deals. Within months his National Front alliance had moved to nationalize Iranian oil and throw out foreign control from the oilfields and the Abadan refinery, the largest in the world. Although this was a unilateral and radical action, it was not necessarily illegal. Indeed, Mossadegh won the approval of the International Court in The Hague in June 1952, which ruled in favor of Iran. By this time his charm and idiosyncratic ways, which included turning up at parliament in his bathrobe, had won him worldwide notice. He was *Time* magazine's Man of the Year in 1951.

© Bettmann | Corbis

ALLEN WELSH DULLES
The director of the CIA photographed at his desk on January 14, 1953, just seven months before the overthrow of Mohammed Mossadegh

The British, though, were not impressed. They immediately put into place a massive economic blockade on Iranian oil, backed by the British navy in force, effectively shutting down the economy. A substantial propaganda campaign was launched against Mossadegh, focusing on his supposed ties with the Soviet Union. By the time of The Hague court decision, the British—under Prime Minister Winston Churchill, had persuaded Allen Welsh Dulles, director of the CIA, to support them in a plot to overthrow Mossadegh who, just to be clear, was a democratically elected prime minister whose policies were uniformly popular within his own country.

Operation Ajax was essentially a CIA operation once the Americans had signed on to the plan. It was run by Kermit Roosevelt, grandson of President Theodore Roosevelt. An Iranian general, Zahedi, was chosen to succeed to power in Iran after the coup. After several abortive attempts to displace Mossadegh, the prime minister demanded control over the military. The coup was moved forward, but still without success. On August 16, 1953 the shah unilaterally removed Mossadegh from office. Massive rioting broke out on the streets of Tehran when word got out, and within hours the shah was forced to flee to Italy. Statues of the shah and his father were torn down around Iran. Three days later General Zahedi mobilized tanks and charged through the streets to the prime minister's residence, plundered and burned it to the ground, arrested the prime minister, and the shah flew back to Iran and power—until the Americans their withdrew support for him too, some 26 years later.

Mossadegh refused to engineer a rival coup, and be partly responsible for the inevitable bloodshed, and gave himself up, remaining under house arrest until his death in 1967.

In itself, the coup was not especially illogical; it may be emblematic of a number of similar covert CIA operations across the globe during the Cold War. But there were clearly strategic considerations, both political and economic, which strongly indicated that Mossadegh was a danger to Western interests. And the immediate aftermath was not especially bloody, mostly through Mossadegh's refusal to allow it to be, when he accepted his fate in order to avoid bloodshed. And in that Iranian oil continued to flow steadily into the West from that point on, including during the oil crisis of the early 1970s, no doubt many in the United States government considered the coup a success—though the truth about the CIA's involvement in the matter was kept secret successfully for many decades.

MOSSADEGH REFUSED TO ENGINEER A RIVAL COUP OR CAUSE BLOODSHED AND GAVE HIMSELF UP, REMAINING UNDER HOUSE ARREST UNTIL HIS DEATH.

TODAY, HUNDREDS OF
WEB SITES HAIL THE
LEGACY OF MOSSADEGH
AS A MARTYR, A
HERO OF NATIONAL
SOVEREIGNTY AND
DEMOCRACY WHOSE
NAME STANDS
ALONGSIDE GANDHI,
MANDELA, AND KING AS
A SYMBOL OF PEACEFUL
RESISTANCE

But from the vantage point of half a century later, the consequences seem more dire and the coup more foolhardy than ever. Certainly, greed was involved, and the refusal to allow countries to exploit their own resources was a throwback to the old colonial days. Certainly, pride dictated that an upstart politician could not be allowed to thumb his nose at government or corporate control. But overwhelming those, the rampant hypocrisy of deliberately overthrowing the only democratic regime in the region showed everyone living in the Middle East precisely what democracy and freedom as offered by the West actually meant in practice, if that democracy did not agree with what the West wanted. The lesson did not go unlearned. Today, hundreds of websites hail the legacy of Mossadegh as a martyr, a hero of national sovereignty and democracy whose name stands alongside Gandhi, Mandela, and King as a symbol of resistance and demand for respect from the world for their cause and country. It is hardly surprising, as Madelaine Albright herself admitted in the epigraph to this chapter, that the Iranians show no great enthusiasm for democracy or the overthrow of the radical government they embraced once the Americans dumped the shah, the same shah who, as puppet, oversaw the end of democracy in the Middle East.

THE BRITISH NUCLEAR LEGACY: THE BLACK MIST OF MARALINGA

1952–1963

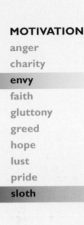

MOTIVATION
anger
charity
envy
faith
gluttony
greed
hope
lust
pride
sloth

Main Culprit: Sir Robert Menzies (1894–1978), Prime Minister of Australia

Damage Done: Unknown numbers of British and Australian servicemen and aborigines died as a result

Why: Last chance for the Brits to keep up their pretensions of world power—at any cost

The Americans bagged around 50 grams [1 ¾ oz] of plutonium-contaminated soil and put it into a military repository under lock, key and guard. Australia, by comparison, has put 100 times that amount of plutonium into several large unlined, unguarded holes in the ground.

Gregg Borschmann, ABC Radio

Between 1952 and 1963 the British government, with the agreement and support of Australia, carried out nuclear tests at three sites in Australia: the Monte Bello islands off the coast of Western Australia, and two sites in South Australia. By 1956 Maralinga was the permanent site for all nuclear testing. Two major trials, Operation Buffalo in 1956 and Operation Antler in 1957, and a number of smaller operations were carried out at the facility until 1963. Maralinga was officially closed following a clean-up operation in 1967, and remains closed to this day. It will probably take the better part of the next 250,000 years for the land to cease to be radioactive, despite continued reassurances that it will be handed back safely.

GOING NUCLEAR

The successful explosions at Hiroshima and Nagasaki, and later H-bomb tests at Bikini Atoll, had alarmed the British government, still clinging to the grandeur of Empire and desperate to develop its own independent nuclear deterrent—presumably partly out of envy at American success, and partly the fear of the Soviet ability to match them. They were determined to speed the process no matter the cost, and that process involved testing. Australian premier Sir Robert Menzies tended towards Anglophilia and would do whatever he was told, perhaps in the hope that Australia might pick up a weapon or two. Although his nation later ended up with a number of American missile bases on Australian soil instead.

In 1984, after a great deal of pressure from veterans who served at Maralinga—essentially as human guinea pigs in an operation that ten years after Hiroshima and Nagasaki, was obviously fraught with serious danger—a royal commission was established. In general, it takes 25 to 30 years after exposure to radiation for the victim to die. The closeness of the commission to that 30-year date and the likelihood that most victims would be dead by the time the deliberations were over was not felt to be a coincidence by many. The servicemen, though, were not the only casualties.

© Hulton-Deutsch Collection | Corbis

SIR ROBERT MENZIES
The Australian Liberal Prime Minister Sir Robert Menzies (1894–1978) during a July 1, 1964 press conference in London. Menzies retained power until January 26, 1966. Operations at Maralinga ceased in 1963.

Maralinga is in the center of the arid wastelands of South Australia. A geopolitical map from the 1980s marks it as "no significant use c.1960," unless you count the explosion of nine major nuclear bombs, and six other tests. And the fact that not only were servicemen stationed there, but thousands of the Tjarutja, Pitjanjatjara, and Kokatha peoples were living there at the time of the tests. They were forcibly removed from their land, but through miscalculation, ignorance, and simple indifference, an untold number died in the immediate aftermath or from airborne radiation over the following decades. Blindness and cancer are common amongst the peoples whose oral memories refer to the "black mist" that came from nowhere. Of the 8,000 known to have been moved, fewer than 2,000 remain alive today. Some were given one-way rail tickets to Kalgoorlie in Western Australia; others were herded into camps or reservations. Others were clearly left to their fate.

Government admissions as to what happened and why have been remarkably slow in coming, and are contradicted by eyewitness accounts. There remains a refusal to admit that experiments were carried out to examine the effect of radiation on humans and that servicemen were simply used as guinea pigs. In 2001 the British government finally admitted to what it described as "clothing trials." It admitted that 76 Australian and New Zealand servicemen were required to crawl, walk, or drive through zones contaminated by a bomb the size of Hiroshima in a variety of protective and non-protective clothing. As late as 1997 a government spokesman in court had denied even this and said it would have been "an act of indefensible callousness" to have done so. Too right. Additionally, some thousands of servicemen were required to observe the blast from a supposedly safe distance, some watching through dark glasses. One soldier described a "vivid flash and even with your eyes shut and you're looking through your hands, you can see an X-ray of your hands." Trucks were assigned to drive through the dust and shower the men with contaminated soil. British and Australian air force personnel were ordered to fly planes into the mushroom clouds, taking air samples and photos. One hour after the blast, servicemen were walking freely into the zone, eating food and drinking water entirely covered in red dust.

It has become clear that experiments including swallowing radioactive substances were carried out at the Aldermaston base in England and other locations around the British Empire in the 1950s. This was revealed after a government agency announced it had had to erase its database of 40,000 veterans who served in these areas. Other documents proving that plans existed to run an even bigger experiment in 1959 were found in a garden shed in Western Australia. None of these were provided by the British or Australian governments to the 1984 royal commission.

76 AUSTRALIAN AND NEW ZEALAND SERVICEMEN WERE REQUIRED TO CRAWL, WALK OR DRIVE THROUGH ZONES CONTAMINATED BY A BOMB THE SIZE OF HIROSHIMA IN A VARIETY OF PROTECTIVE AND NON-PROTECTIVE CLOTHING.

IN 1967 OPERATION
BRUMBY, CONDUCTED
BY THE BRITISH
GOVERNMENT,
DETERMINED THAT
THE LAND WAS CLEAN,
AND THE AUSTRALIAN
GOVERNMENT MEEKLY
ABSOLVED THE BRITISH
GOVERNMENT OF ANY
FURTHER RESPONSIBILITY.

In 1967 Operation Brumby, conducted by the British government, determined that the land was clean, and the Australian government meekly absolved the British of any further responsibility. Twenty years later a fact-seeking publicity-hungry group of politicians and journalists flew by helicopter over the stricken land. They saw the skeletons of a whole group of aborigines, who were later determined to have been killed after one test, when the wind shifted direction, and whose deaths had previously gone unacknowledged and unknown. They landed at one of the hot-spot sites, eager to prove how clean the land now was, only to sprint back and take off some 30 seconds after the Geiger counters went off the scale. Subsequent more serious investigation points to sloth and total ignorance of the effects of radiation, or even the remotest idea of how to clean it up, as the reason for this massive environmental degradation, the deaths of servicemen, and what many groups call the genocide of many thousands of aboriginal people.

A JOB UNFINISHED

To compound the problem, the later clean-up was grossly inadequate. Most of the contaminated materials were buried in shallow pits, no more than 10 ft (3m) deep; some of the plutonium-contaminated materials were found covered by a scraping of soil. The soil itself in many cases was contaminated, and much of it blew away in subsequent dust storms. The pits were supposed to be concrete-capped but only 19 of the 21 were, and the caps of two were damaged so badly as to be useless. The follow-up to the Royal Commission's report was to hire contractors to deal with these issues, but as late as 1998 these projects were failing to clean up the mess. A former government advisor-turned-whistleblower described what a government official had described as the "world's best practice" as not even suitable for the disposal of household garbage, let alone plutonium. In 2001 it was deemed that all but 329 square miles (530 sq. km) could be handed back safely to the aboriginal peoples, the remainder marked by flags with a life expectancy of 50 years for land that by best estimate will be habitable in 240,000 years. The same government officials and contractors are proposing a massive nuclear waste dump repository in the same state, South Australia.

SIR ANTHONY EDEN, SUEZ, AND SPEED

1956

MOTIVATION
anger
charity
envy
faith
gluttony
greed
hope
lust
pride
sloth

Main Culprit: Sir Anthony Eden (1897–1977)

Damage Done: End of British imperial power

Why: One last imperial foray went wrong

Egypt has resolved to show the world that when small nations decide to preserve their sovereignty, they will do that . . .

President Nasser of Egypt, September 15, 1956

In many ways the Suez Crisis marks a watershed in the recent history of the world. It marks the last time the British tried to do anything on the world stage without the approval of the Americans; even the Falklands War had prior go-ahead from the White House. The crisis started as a very imperial affair, and ended as an example of Cold War détente. From this point on, the pages of this book will be filled more by the malfeasance of global corporations than that of nations.

THE SHORTCUT | The very traffic on the Suez Canal was a mark of the changes the world had experienced. It had been built in 1869 as a French–Egyptian project, but the British government had bought out the Egyptian share when they realized the strategic importance of the canal. It linked the Mediterranean with the Red Sea, cutting out the treacherous and lengthy route around the Cape of Good Hope. It wasn't quite the modern marvel it was claimed to be—the ancient Egyptians had a working canal from the thirteenth to the eighth centuries BCE—but it performed three essential functions for the British Empire: it helped profits by cutting distance and time; it allowed for quicker troop movement to help quell disturbances; and it dramatically lessened the need to protect the overland route and worry so much about Russia. Britain did have to start worrying about the Middle East though, and Africa and protection of Suez became important during the partition of Africa as well as in the World Wars. This accounted for Britain playing such a big role in the redrawing of the map of the Middle East after the fall of the Ottoman Empire. With the loss of India in 1947, many of these considerations became unimportant. The canal, though, had found a new importance. The huge leap in Persian Gulf oil production found its way to Europe straight through the Suez Canal; by 1955 two-thirds of canal traffic was oil and two-thirds of Europe's oil supply came through the canal. Strategic imperial issues were replaced by more straightforward economic ones, as British banks and companies owned 44 percent of the canal, which was pulling in profits of around US $25 million a year.

In the new era of decolonization, and without the huge need for the canal to get to India, Britain was happy to discuss independence with Egypt. It had become a sovereign state after the Ottomans, but with the establishment of a British-supported puppet government under

King Farouk. In 1936 the British were guaranteed a garrison of 10,000 men in the Suez Canal Zone, but in the post-war period the Egyptians became increasingly nationalistic, militant, anti-British and opposed to the monarchy. By 1952 Farouk had been overthrown by generals, and by 1953 Egypt was a republic, bringing to an end the 5,000-year monarchy. The British had to send warships and rattle sabres to hold their own, but were not prepared to intervene further. Under pressure they agreed to withdraw from Suez by 1954. Radical Muslim elements also tried to force their way into power, but by the end of 1954 General Gamal Abdel Nasser had full control of the country. Nasser, taking his cue from Mossadegh in Iran, employed what was to prove a much more aggressive foreign policy.

The other major new post-war components of what was to become the Suez Crisis were the establishment of Israel in the region and the beginnings of the Cold War. The sudden appearance of a new country in the region had seriously destabilized the area, and already a number of skirmishes and wars were breaking out as Arabs tried to deal with an unwanted newcomer in their midst. And the Soviet Union slowly began to realize that the newly independent states offered an opportunity to expand its sphere of influence, perhaps even to establish ports that could free the fleet from the confines of the Black Sea. Oil, as in Iran, had become a complicating factor, bringing the Americans into the picture with substantial economic as well as moral interests and soon economic support for the state of Israel.

Much of this seems to have passed the British government by. Perhaps, given his role in a number of earlier incidents, it will not come as a great surprise that the prime minister in the build-up to all this was Winston Churchill. To a large extent he was no longer the great wartime leader but a figurehead, back in power since 1951 after the Labour government of Attlee. The foreign secretary, and clearly the heir apparent, was Sir Anthony Eden, a dashing and accomplished man who had been instrumental in aggressive foreign policy before the war, becoming the foreign secretary in 1935 at the age of 38. By 1955 he was more than a little frustrated at still being in the same role in the new administration. Churchill showed remarkably little interest in retirement. Additionally, and unknown to anyone at the

IN 1936 THE BRITISH WERE GUARANTEED A GARRISON OF 10,000 MEN IN THE SUEZ CANAL ZONE, BUT IN THE POSTWAR PERIOD THE EGYPTIANS BECAME INCREASINGLY NATIONALISTIC AND MILITANT, ANTI-BRITISH, AND OPPOSED TO THE MONARCHY.

time, Eden had developed an alarming medical problem. In 1953 a routine gallstone operation had gone wrong when doctors ruptured his bile duct. In considerable pain, and prone to infection, he had been prescribed Benzedrine, a new wonder drug. "Bennies" proved popular with writers and the young Bohemians of the late 1950s. Better known as "speed," the drug caused violent mood swings and a tendency towards paranoia, and was highly addictive. Not that much of a problem if you are a poet and artist, rather more so for a prime minister, which is what Eden finally became on April 7, 1955.

© Hulton-Deutsch Collection | Corbis

SIR ANTHONY EDEN
The Conservative politician Sir Anthony Eden photographed in 1951 when he was the secretary of state for foreign affairs, a position that he held until April 7, 1955, when he became the prime minister.

He walked straight into an escalation of the crisis in Egypt. General Nasser started to turn to the Soviet Bloc for trade and to build armed forces against Israel. Arms-for-cotton deals were made with the Soviet Union. Cotton was exported to China. Czechoslovak tanks started to arrive. One month after Britain started its planned withdrawal from Suez, the United States abruptly withdrew its financial support for the huge Aswan Dam project, citing Egyptian connections with the Soviet Union. On July 26, 1956, Nasser nationalized the Suez Canal, claiming the need for the profits to finance the Aswan Dam project. Not only British pride but British financial interests were hurt. Eden imposed a trade embargo, and raised patriotic indignation in Britain, comparing Nasser to Mussolini. Nasser sank ships in the canal to block it, and the British formally reneged on their deal to withdraw.

The British and French started secret talks and came up with a unilateral plan that sounded great in principle—and within its limits worked well. Operation Musketeer called for Israel to attack Egypt, then call for Anglo-French help, which would give them an excuse to invade and take back the canal. The invasions duly took place and by October a substantial force had seized Suez. However, no one had checked first with the new superpower, America.

The United States was highly preoccupied with the Soviet threat, and was busily condemning the Soviets for their brutal suppression of the Hungarian uprising the very same year. Faced with the almost unanimous condemnation of the Anglo-French invasion by the United Nations, the United States found it impossible to endorse one

TROOP MOVEMENTS OF THE SUEZ CRISIS

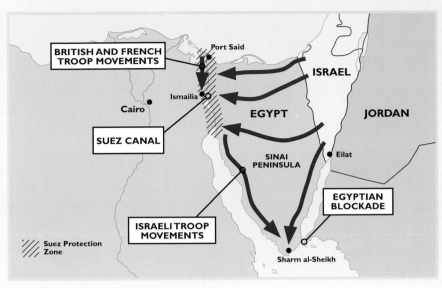

BRITISH AND FRENCH
TROOP MOVEMENTS

Port Said

ISRAEL

Ismailia

Cairo

SUEZ CANAL

EGYPT

JORDAN

SINAI
PENINSULA

Eilat

ISRAELI TROOP
MOVEMENTS

EGYPTIAN
BLOCKADE

Suez Protection
Zone

Sharm al-Sheikh

The Israeli assault started on October 29, 1956. On November 5, British paratroops landed west of Port Said, and French paratroops to the south, on the same day as Israelis captured Sharm al-Sheikh lifting the Egyptian blockade of the Gulf of Aqaba. By November 7, British and French forces had advanced as far as Ismailia on the day when pressure from the United Nations, United States and Soviet Union forced a cease-fire. British and French troops completed their withdrawal at midnight, December 22, while the Israelis remained in the Sinai until March 1957.

invasion while condemning another; moreover, the Soviet Union had substantially raised the stakes by announcing that it would intervene on behalf of Egypt during November. Eden, meanwhile, the architect of the whole operation, had been sent to Jamaica on what appeared to be a vacation but was actually an attempt by doctors to get him off speed.

By December the Americans had forced a cease-fire, and withdrawal by Anglo-French forces came on December 24. Nasser nationalized other British interests in Egypt, and by March 1957 a humiliated Eden was forced to resign. British power and influence in the region—and to some extent in the world—was forever relegated to secondary status. The new world era set up by the events of World War II had really begun, precipitated to no small extent by the pride of Sir Anthony Eden, and his little pills. In 2004 the man who had offered such promise was voted the least effective British prime minister of the twentieth century.

THE UNITED STATES FOUND IT IMPOSSIBLE TO ENDORSE ONE INVASION WHILE CONDEMNING ANOTHER; MOREOVER, THE SOVIET UNION HAD SUBSTANTIALLY RAISED THE SUEZ BAR BY ANNOUNCING THAT THEY WOULD INTERVENE ON BEHALF OF EGYPT DURING NOVEMBER.

MOTIVATION
anger
charity
envy
faith
gluttony
greed
hope
lust
pride
sloth

GRÜNENTHAL'S OUTSTANDINGLY SAFE DRUG: THALIDOMIDE

December 25, 1956 – November 28, 1961

Main Culprit: Grünenthal (drug company)

Damage Done: Horrific birth defects in thousands of children

Why: Bringing untested drugs too soon to market

Distavel [thalidomide] can be given with complete safety to pregnant women and nursing mothers without adverse effect on mother or child ... Outstandingly safe Distavel has been prescribed for nearly three years in this country.

Ad for thalidomide

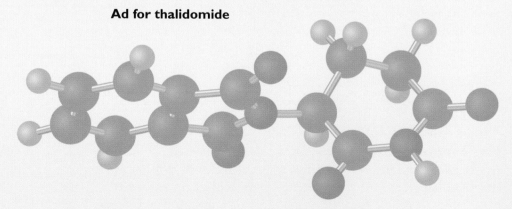

If it weren't for recent examples of pharmaceutical companies marketing drugs that turned out to be deadly, it would perhaps be easier to put the tragedy of thalidomide down to simple error. However, the rapacious greed to get a drug on the market before it had been properly tested is not an isolated incident. Drug companies in many parts of the world jumped on the appearance of an apparent new wonder drug that was to have devastating consequences.

Thalidomide was developed in the 1950s by German drug company, Grünenthal, as a sedative. The end of World War II heralded an era in which factories involved in churning out chemicals for the mass destruction of human beings switched to the development of pharmaceuticals to cure their every ill. In the rubble of war-ravaged Germany in 1946, a factory employing 1,500 workers engaged in producing soap and detergents formed a subsidiary company called Chemie Grünenthal, which began operations in an abandoned copper foundry near Hamburg. For several years it produced antibiotics, some for the American drug company Lederle, with which it had close links. Then, in the early 1950s came a series of failures as a number of its drugs produced severe adverse reactions, including deaths. Though these were well reported and documented by several doctors, Chemie Grünenthal ignored the serious risks and moved into the profitable field of sedatives and hypnotics, which included thalidomide. It proved successful and popular, and was remarkably effective against morning sickness for pregnant women. By 1957 it was being aggressively marketed in 50 countries around the world. In Britain, in particular, the Distillers Company made a special point of its safety and utility for pregnant women.

But thalidomide apparently passed through to the placenta and blocked the development of blood vessels. This led to serious deformities in affected fetuses. It needed to be taken only once during the first trimester to have an impact, especially during the first 25 to 50 days of pregnancy when some women were not even aware they were pregnant. The birth defects normally manifested as missing or badly deformed limbs. It is estimated that a minimum of 15,000 fetuses were affected in 46 countries, of which 12,000 were born with birth defects, and of those, one-third died in their first year. Most of the other victims are still alive today.

THE END OF WORLD WAR II HERALDED AN ERA IN WHICH FACTORIES INVOLVED IN CHURNING OUT CHEMICALS FOR THE MASS DESTRUCTION OF HUMAN BEINGS SWITCHED TO THE DEVELOPMENT OF PHARMACEUTICALS TO CURE THEIR EVERY ILL.

Many have gone on to successful careers in one field or another, but all live with their deformities for life. For example, Thomas Quasthoff, one of Germany's leading baritones, was born in Hanover in 1959, with severe disabilities. His parents, unable to care for him, sent him to a medical institution where he was brought up. Music schools turned him down despite his burgeoning voice because he was unable to meet their entrance requirements—which involved the playing of a musical instrument—due to the fact that he has only vestigial arms. Although Quasthoff went on to create a fine career for himself as a performer, he is the exception rather than the rule.

In retrospect, there was trouble from the very beginning. Although nothing adverse supposedly showed up on tests, there were deformities among children of parents who worked for the pharmaceutical company. The first thalidomide baby is now thought to have been born on Christmas Day, 1956, although the drug did not go onto the market until

© Bettmann | Corbis

THALIDOMIDE
Dr. Samuel Andelman, Chicago Health Commissioner, in 1962 showing thalidomide tablets collected by the Health Department during an investigation into the drug's effects.

October 1, 1957. By 1960 sales of thalidomide were stepped up, despite reports of malformations caused by the drug, which now poured in from all over the world. It was being marketed by 14 firms in many countries under 37 different trade names and sold without prescription. It was combined with other drugs such as aspirin and prescribed widely for headaches, migraine, coughs, colds, flu, asthma, neuralgia, nervous debility, to calm frisky babies, and to give pregnant women a good night's sleep. Globally, thalidomide was the big winner and dominated prescriptions. Distillers produced thalidomide for morning sickness and it was distributed throughout the British Isles, Australia, and New Zealand under the trade name Distavel.

By 1960 thalidomide was so successful around the world that Grünenthal decided to seek an FDA licence to sell in the United States. Part of its success lay in the fact that it was almost impossible to commit suicide with the drug, a big issue for any sedative or sleeping pill. Grünenthal's website still maintains that the drug was useful, and that "the catastrophe was due to a lack of knowledge and perhaps attention." It goes on to tell us that "it exemplifies above all the meaning of 'Post Marketing

Surveillance.'" Subsequent evidence from many hearings casts doubt even on the veracity of the claimed lack of knowledge. In August 1959 a doctor in Basel described thalidomide as "a horrible drug. Never again," because of its impact on the nervous system.

A number of medical heroes swiftly emerged onto the scene. The first was Frances Oldham Kelsey, a young woman who had recently joined the FDA. She was unimpressed by the studies she was shown purporting to demonstrate the safety of the drug, partly because her research area was on toxicity in pregnancy. In theory it had proved safe in animal testing. Many feel that the failure to notice the problem proves the inappropriateness of relying upon animal testing to demonstrate fitness for human use; others suggest that either the tests were not performed properly or their results were misunderstood. The fact remains that Kelsey refused to clear thalidomide for sale in the United States. Despite considerable pressure from a local drug company, it remained off the shelves until the true extent of the disaster was discovered in the rest of the world. Thousands of lives were saved as a result and in 1962 Kelsey was rewarded for her role by President Kennedy with the highest civilian award in the United States. In light of later events one might speculate as to whether the FDA is still as careful today, or whether it was just fortunate that it was a young and enthusiastic woman, who had a specific interest in pregnancy, who was responsible. Whatever the reasoning, the fact remains that later claims by the drug companies in Europe that they had no reason to doubt that thalidomide was safe must be cast in considerable doubt by the refusal of the FDA to grant a license. Interestingly, the French had also refused a license. And as one of the later investigators pointed out, the countries behind the Iron Curtain of the time also did not allow the drug to be marketed, and viruses did not stop at the Berlin Wall. The argument that there was no reason to doubt the safety of the drug seems extremely weak.

In April 1961 a doctor at Crown Street Women's Hospital in Sydney, Australia, Dr. William McBride, was taken aback by limb and bowel deformations in three babies delivered in quick succession. His research soon unveiled thalidomide as the only link he could find between the three mothers. His urgent warnings were generally dismissed. He notified Distillers' representatives in Australia about

HEROES

his suspicions of a link between Distavel (thalidomide) and the deformities. Distillers in England claim they never received the written report. Sales promotion of the drug was stepped up and 250,000 leaflets distributed, saying thalidomide is "harmless even over a long period of use" and "completely harmless even for infants"—this despite later evidence that in December 1959 and January 1960 a Dr. Somers in Distillers' own lab had written internal memos querying the apparent high toxicity of the drug. McBride wrote a letter to *The Lancet* medical journal: "Thalidomide and Congenital Abnormalities," published in December 1961. Coincidentally, in West Germany, a Dr. Widukind Lenz had become concerned by a series of limb and ear malformations and by mid-November had come to the same conclusion as McBride. He called Grünenthal to express his concerns on November 16, but it still took ten days and increasing pressure from the press for anything to happen. The drug in various forms was withdrawn on November 26, 1961, in West Germany and a few days later in Britain and Australia, though in other forms it remained on the shelves until at least March 1962. Inexplicably, it remained for sale in countries including Brazil, Spain, Italy, and Japan, in an over-the-counter form, for many months after the German withdrawal.

What followed was an unimpressive failure by the drug companies to admit fault or properly compensate victims. The Grünenthal website was, at the time of writing, still far from forthcoming and in places positively extraordinary in its indignation. In 1972 the *Sunday Times* of London produced a stunning article, one of the pioneering pieces of activist journalism, openly condemning the failure of Distillers to provide adequate compensation for victims and questioning the motivations that had led them to rush the drug to market. It also unveiled reports from Germany from as far back as 1950 reporting effects of thalidomide on the nervous systems of children. The response was a legal writ, the quashing of follow-up articles, and a court case that ended up in the European Court of Justice in 1979. The result? A victory for journalism and free speech. But even now, pressure groups around the world still protest the inadequate compensation paid by companies that peddled this drug.

There have been books and articles and accusations back and forth over the years as to how this was allowed to happen. Certainly, both

THE DRUG IN VARIOUS FORMS WAS WITHDRAWN ON NOVEMBER 26, 1961, IN WEST GERMANY AND A FEW DAYS LATER IN BRITAIN AND AUSTRALIA, THOUGH IN OTHER FORMS IT REMAINED ON THE SHELVES UNTIL AT LEAST MARCH 1962.

testing and government regulations have been massively tightened as a result. Some of the accusations have been wild indeed, stretching back to suggestions that the scientists who manufactured and tested the drug in the first instance in Germany did not just inherit the Nazi approach to the manufacture and use of drugs, but were actually the same individuals who had escaped prosecution after the war. And it was perhaps ironic that Widukind Lenz himself was the son of one of the first proponents of eugenics; his father writing a book in 1921 that suggested that one-third of the population bearing "unsound hereditary traits" should be sterilized. A more tragic irony is the fact that Widukind Lenz's unseen and unknown fellow discoverer William McBride, still investigating and crusading 40 years later, again wrote to *The Lancet* in 2004, issuing a warning that it appears the toxic nature of thalidomide could be passed on genetically.

There may yet be further consequences because thalidomide has made an astonishing comeback. It turns out that it has very strong and positive effects on AIDS and on leprosy, and may even inhibit cancer growth, oddly through the very same inhibiting characteristics that made it so lethal in pregnant women. It has this time been provisionally approved by the FDA, but only under the name Thalomid to remind everyone of the history and genesis of the drug, rather than the generic name the manufacturers wanted to use.

THE COMEBACK

MOTIVATION
anger
charity
envy
faith
gluttony
greed
hope
lust
pride
sloth

VACCINES, AIDS, AND THE CHIMPS OF THE CONGO

1957–1960

Main Culprits: Scientists unknown

Damage Done: Conceivably, the introduction of AIDS into the human race

Why: Alleged improper care in preparation of vaccines for a massive polio immunization project

Some in our common world consider the questions I and the rest of our government have raised around the HIV/AIDS issue, the subject of the Conference you are attending, as akin to grave criminal and genocidal misconduct. What I hear being said repeatedly, stridently, angrily, is—do not ask any questions!

South African, President Thabo Mbeki, 2000

Much of what we now recognize as stupidity was not recognized as such at the time, either because of lack of information about what really happened, or lack of knowledge of the eventual consequences. Some of the examples may well not be based on what really happened at all, but on the subsequent rewriting of history by later generations. Other events may be seen in very different ways by the perpetrators as opposed to the victims. This chapter does not offer a verdict of any sort as to the truth of the claims made by either side in what has become an increasingly controversial and vitriolic issue. It simply reports the existence of one hypothesis, which, if true, would undoubtedly rank the events in the Congo in the 1950s and 1960s right up there with the worst of them. There is no suggestion of malice, just an attempt to uncover the origins of a disease that has ripped through the human race at a rate almost unprecedented in history—at least 3 million dead and up to 40 million people infected, according to United Nations statistics. These are the casualties of AIDS since its first appearance among humans in the early 1960s. In some countries 40 percent of the adult population is thought to be infected. Not since the "black death" killed two-thirds of the population of China and one-third to one-half of the population of Europe has a pandemic so affected the world. It is noticeable that the fears of population explosion and subsequent global famine that so dominated discussions of 30 years ago are now less frequently heard.

Conspiracy theories abound as to the introduction, spread, and causes of AIDS—and no less as to its cure. A recent study suggested that 12 percent of African-Americans believe AIDS was introduced by the CIA, as many as half that it was deliberately made and targeted at minorities. South African President Thabo Mbeki's statements querying the paramount importance of AIDS in care aid to South Africa has been taken as brutal, uncaring, and detrimental to the population of his country. What he actually said was that AIDS needs to be taken as part of the overall health—and more important, poverty—crisis that is overwhelming the continent of Africa, and that subsidized condoms and expensive medications may not be the most important concentrations for the South African health system.

IN SEARCH OF THE TRUTH

© Gary Woodard | Dreamstime.com

THE RED RIBBON
The Red Ribbon Project was created in 1991 by Visual AIDS, an organization that "strives to increase public awareness of AIDS through the visual arts." The now internationally recognized symbol represents solidarity with AIDS sufferers around the world, and is particularly linked with December 1 —World AIDS Day.

What is beyond most doubt is that the HIV virus originated in Africa and is a variant of the SIV virus, which is prevalent throughout much of the primate population (but does them no harm). The question at issue is how the transmission took place from one species to another with such devastating consequences. Essentially there are two major theories of origin that seek to explain how humans acquired the pandemic AIDS virus (HIV-1) from the common chimpanzee host. These two theories are the natural transfer hypothesis, or bushmeat theory (which has various versions), and the OPV theory. The bushmeat (or "cut hunter") theory proposes that HIV-1 crossed from a chimpanzee to a human in the course of the hunting, butchery, and consumption of chimpanzees. While perfectly plausible, this theory fails to explain why it should suddenly transfer in the 1960s and not hundreds or thousands of years before. There is a variant of this theory, which brings in the appearance of hypodermic needles at around the right time, but it isn't entirely convincing. The alternative theory sounds far-fetched, but it is plausible. Its detractors have been vocal and their attempts to denigrate the theory forcible, but without quite answering all the questions convincingly.

The OPV theory proposes that HIV-1 crossed via an oral polio vaccine (OPV). The United Nations had in the 1950s embarked on a mass polio vaccination programme throughout Africa. It was one of those grand public health projects that signalled to the world that the new United Nations was at work, and that it could do nothing but good. If what is suggested did actually occur, then the entirely laudable aim of saving the lives of a million children, an act of enormous hope and charity that perhaps was less well funded and managed than it might have been, has resulted in a widespread global disaster.

The center of the vaccination operation was in Stanleyville, in the then Belgian Congo. One million Africans received the vaccine in a group of villages in an area now divided between Congo, Rwanda, and Burundi. Around ten years later, the first major incidence of what is now known as AIDS showed up in those same villages; as many as 76 percent of the early cases can be linked back to the area where the vaccine was used. There may have been earlier cases, but these remain in some dispute.

The dispute lies in what happened at the local level. The supervising doctors in the United States were supposed to make all the vaccines;

macaque monkeys were commonly used to provide the tissue culture in which safe quantities of the vaccine were cultivated, and these were shipped over. Not just in Africa, but in other countries, it may have been usual to use the initial shipments as a base from which to increase the amount of vaccine being used. It is suggested that green monkey or chimpanzee kidneys were used at the local level—both are carriers of SIV-1—and that the vaccines therefore became contaminated with the virus that became HIV. There was a chimpanzee research facility a few miles from the laboratory, and there is evidence from other countries that booster cells were used; scientists in French Equatorial Africa, for example, used cells from baboons to top up the vaccines they were receiving from the Pasteur Institute in Paris, without any apparent side effects—baboons are not SIV-1 carriers. Some evidence from local workers at the laboratory confirms that this was happening in a more or less unsupervised operation, with the best of intentions, to allow the vaccine to go further. The supervising doctors deny this, and also deny the possibility that the virus could have been transmitted to humans through an oral intake of a vaccine. (The vaccine was not injected.) However, the vaccine was given to young children for the most part and it is thought, among other things, that AIDS can be transmitted through breast milk, for example, so doubts as to this possibility remain.

Most scientists and AIDS researchers, and certainly the scientific establishment, refute the OPV thesis—and no doubt there are good non-scientific reasons why they should do so, not least the deep, and these days unwarranted, suspicion that vaccinations might be dangerous, which is leading to increasing refusal to accept them and the concurrent return of some contagious diseases. Also the concept that anything so basically well intentioned—we are not talking about profiteering drug companies—could have had such disastrous consequences seems perhaps too dreadful to believe.

LINGERING SUSPICIONS

MAO AND THE GREAT LEAP FORWARD

1958–1960

Main Culprit: Mao Zedong (1893–1976)

Damage Done: 20 to 40 million of own his people died of starvation

Why: Taking all the farmers off the land to initiate an industrial revolution they could not sustain

Struggle hard for three years. Change the face of China. Catch up with Britain and catch up with America.

Official slogan of The Great Leap Forward

It says something for the Chinese people that the most populous nation in the world makes only one appearance in this book. But as might be expected, when something goes wrong, it goes wrong in a big way. The problem for China since time immemorial has been how to feed its huge population. Most regimes have done this by exercising strict central political control in one way or another and restricting the movement of people, and certainly their freedom of expression. At the end of the 1950s, a number of different influences came together to create one of the worst disasters in human history, one caused entirely by man and not by nature—indeed really by one man, Chairman Mao Zedong. The motivation was not that of Stalin in his Great Purge or even of Pol Pot in Cambodia, who sought to re-engineer his people by killing a third of them first. There seems to have been little greed or anger involved. The very phrase—*da yue jin*, the Great Leap Forward—suggests nothing more than an act of faith in the future of his country. Without question it was pride that prevented him from realizing the monumental nature of his error until it was too late.

DA YUE JIN

Since grasping power after the Great March, Mao's Communist regime in China had been closely allied with the Russians. The year 1956, however, saw an end to Stalin's rule and an apparent weakening of Soviet power, with an insurrection in Hungary and uprisings in Poland. Khrushchev was seeking "peaceful coexistence" and that type of policy was not going to get the Chinese anywhere.

Mao decided that the Chinese economy must compete with the West, but on revolutionary terms. The Eighth National Congress of 1956 heard this speech:

> On the basis of actual conditions in our country, the Central Committee has thus defined the Party's general line in the period of transition: to bring about, step by step, socialist industrialization and to accomplish, step by step, the socialist transformation of agriculture.

The aim was to out-produce the British steel industry within 15 years. In essence, he proposed a commune system for the production of steel. Farmers across the country were given quotas for steel production to the exclusion of all else. Rice fields were planted over, lakes filled in, regular agriculture ignored, apart from the revolutionary command to plant three times as many seeds in the same spot for the land to be more productive (in fact, they all died instead). Tens of millions of people were ordered to produce steel, and in their backyards built homemade furnaces that in the end produced almost nothing worthwhile. The villagers had just thrown the whole metal content of their villages—spoons, plates, old machinery, anything—into the furnaces to meet enormous production quotas. As many as 23,500 commune-based plants were set up, but with little or no training and the most basic of equipment, the villagers had no idea how to make the steel. Every available resource was used to support the plan; other factories, even schools and hospitals, turned all their efforts to making the Great Leap Forward.

Indeed, to start with, the statistical gains were impressive: 45 percent growth in 1958, 30 percent over each of the next two years. But once the easily available supply of iron gave out and the side effects of the effort began to take hold, production plummeted again, by 1961 it had fallen below what it had been before the start. By the end of what the Chinese central government named the Three Years of Natural Disasters, coincidentally occurring over exactly the same time period as the Great Leap Forward, horrific famine conditions had overwhelmed China.

Famine was nothing new to the Chinese population—natural disasters, flood, pestilence, earthquake, drought, could easily tip the fragile balance and cause starvation. By 1959 the population was in excess of 680 million people, so it was not surprising that there should be another famine that could be blamed on natural causes. But in fact there was no natural cause. The ploughing up of rice fields and the massive movement of the working population out of agriculture into steel led to a fall in crop production, from an estimated two million tons in 1958 to under one and a half million in 1960. The birth rate dropped, the death rate more than doubled, and by 1961 the population of China had actually dipped to 655 million. Conservative estimates are that 20 to 25 million Chinese starved as a consequence of the Great Leap Forward; some put that figure as high as 40 million.

What was perhaps even more astonishing than the calamity that was unfolding in front of everyone was the complete refusal to admit to it. The Great Leap Forward had followed a strange two-year campaign, the Hundred Flowers, during which Mao, apparently upset that all the local Communist officials and intellectuals were silent about improvements

CONSERVATIVE ESTIMATES ARE THAT 20 TO 25 MILLION CHINESE STARVED AS A CONSEQUENCE OF THE GREAT LEAP FORWARD; SOME PUT THAT FIGURE AS HIGH AS 40 MILLION.

that could be made, and problems within the regime, first encouraged, then demanded, letters from all across the country so that a variety of views could be expressed and changes made. "Our society cannot back down, it could only progress . . . criticism of the bureaucracy is pushing the government towards the better. Let a hundred flowers bloom, let a hundred schools of thought contend." Officials were rightly suspicious of this move from the beginning, and indeed, once the complaints started to flood in, the campaign was swiftly stopped and orthodoxy reigned again. "Counter-revolutionaries" were rounded up, making everyone even less likely to tell the truth when the famine had begun.

MAO ZEDONG
A paramilitary police officer stands guard in front of a huge portrait of late Chinese leader Mao Zedong at the Forbidden City in Beijing.

By 1961 the project was abandoned and everyone returned to what was left of their farms. Mao kept something of a low profile for a while; but as criticism started to mount both within and without the party as the awful truth inexorably came to light, he commenced the terrible crackdown on dissidents and intellectuals known as the Cultural Revolution, which to some extent could be seen as a further consequence of the horrors of the Great Leap Forward. It was only after Mao's death, as after Stalin's, that it was possible to begin to tell the truth about the Great Leap Forward. The Three Years of Natural Disasters became the Three Years of Economic Difficulty—not much of an improvement, to be sure, but a step.

Paradoxically, it is steel that is China's biggest growth industry in the early twenty-first century. China is the world's biggest producer and market. The toll on lives is still considerable, as the staggering death rate in coal mines will testify. The cost to the environment may also be extremely high as China's demand for fossil fuels expands. This time, it is highly unlikely that the people will starve and that the projects will collapse from underfunding. But the essential idea—that China must become an industrial nation to survive and thrive in the globalized world, and cannot continue just to ensure that its people can eat—is the same idea as the one that Mao put forward. Mao managed to kill more of his own subjects than any other leader mentioned in these pages.

MOTIVATION

anger

charity

envy

faith

gluttony

greed

hope

lust

pride

sloth

ROBERT McNAMARA AND AGENT ORANGE

April 12, 1961 – January 1971

Main Culprit: Robert McNamara (b.1916)

Damage Done: Disease and birth defects for thousands of American soldiers, and millions of Vietnamese to this day

Why: Quadrupling the safe dose of a pesticide to clear the Vietnamese rain forest

I don't think that anybody thought much about whether it was contrary to the rules of war. I doubt very much that its toxicity was very much known.

Robert W. McNamara, interviewed in the *Observer*, May 19, 2002

Agent Orange was a herbicide developed in the 1940s and used extensively in agriculture in the United States, in the 1950s especially. It isn't actually orange, but a colorless liquid; the barrels used to transport it sported an orange stripe. No particular problems were associated with its use during crop spraying in the United States.

Some time early in the Vietnam War a bright idea was hatched. The National Liberation Front, the North Vietnamese guerrilla movement, was hiding in the dense jungle, and tracking them from the air was near impossible. If pesticides were so good at clearing land for agribusiness, why not use them to clear the jungle? They turned out to be deadly to humans—not just Vietcong guerrillas, but the civilian population and American and Australian soldiers combing the jungle. Though liability is hotly debated, there is little doubt that the sloth in not bothering to check what was being dropped, and anger in wanting to hasten the war, were responsible for what followed. To this day, contamination remains, especially around Da Nang, and birth defects abound.

Agent Orange was a combination of two chemicals that destroyed plants by interfering with their metabolisms. One chemical also tended to produce high quantities of dioxin, which in high doses is deadly to humans, and also causes birth defects by working itself into the food chain; and the half-life of dioxin within the soil is at least three years, maybe longer.

A full 95 percent of the residents of Bin-hoa near Ho Chi Minh City have 200 times the safe level of dioxin in their bloodstream today. Although attempts have been made to deny links between Agent Orange and the resulting damage, no other cause for this level of poisoning has ever been suggested. The United States government still denies any positive proof of a link, although the Veterans Administration guidelines on disability payments to veterans and their families take a very different line. The likelihood seems to be that only those veterans who came into direct contact with the chemical were affected. The actual spraying was not toxic, but the effect on the food chain continues through generations. It is conservatively estimated that 150,000 Vietnamese children have birth defects stemming from Agent Orange contamination.

© Bettmann | Corbis

ROBERT MCNAMARA
United States Secretary of Defense Robert McNamara onboard an army helicopter in Le My, Vietnam on July 18, 1965 during a five-day inspection trip.

On April 12, 1961, Walt W. Rostow, a foreign affairs adviser, forwarded a memo to President Kennedy recommending nine courses of action, including that a military hardware research and development team go to Vietnam to explore the usefulness of various "techniques and gadgets" then available or under development. Aerial defoliation was one of these unspecified "techniques." By May, White House approval had been given, and test runs started in August 1961. Defense Secretary McNamara approved use in November 1961, and bombing with so-called "Rainbow Herbicides" including Agents Purple and Pink started almost immediately.

Agent Orange appears to have been tested a few times for military use in the late 1950s, but no full-scale testing was done, even on animals, until serious problems began to emerge. It was only after carcinogenic results appeared in rats that its use was curtailed. It was very effective in its military application, known as Operation Ranch Hand—part of the larger Operation Trail Dust, which involved road and riverside clearing of vegetation, and crop destruction. Each plane could destroy 350 acres

"RAINBOW HERBICIDES" USED FROM 1961–71

Agent Orange and other "Rainbow Herbicides" were dropped from late 1961 until early 1971. Alongside Agent Orange other chemicals used included Agents Blue, Green, Pink, Purple, and White, which were collectively intended to defoliate the jungles in which the Vietcong troops operated, and destroy the rice crop upon which they depended.

(1.4 sq. km) of forest in a run, taking less than four minutes to dump 1,000 gallons (3,780 liters) of Agent Orange; often three planes flew side by side. However, in spite of the large-scale deforestation, the Vietcong never had any problem in obtaining the food they needed, and they were much too adept at hiding out in the jungle to be caught out by the clearing of roadside vegetation. The American soldiers, on the other hand, operating on the roads, could be seen easily and became sitting ducks.

In October 1967 the Rand Corporation, which had worked on the original plans in 1961, issued two reports concluding that the program had little effect on Vietcong rice consumption; had not resulted in significant food shortages among Vietcong units; had harmed residents in the vicinity of crop destruction targets; had alienated the rural South Vietnamese population from the government; had aroused much hostility towards the United States and its South Vietnamese allies; was not considered necessary or useful by the rural population; and might well be counterproductive. The Joint Chiefs of Staff rejected this report and kept on spraying. Operation Ranch Hand did not fly its last mission until January 1971, ten years after operations had started and four years after the exercise had been seriously questioned. Indeed, 1968, the height of the war, saw the greatest use of chemical herbicides.

In 2005 Federal Court Judge Jack Weinstein, himself an advocate of class action suits, found he had no option but to refuse a suit on behalf of four million Vietnamese, brought against the companies that manufactured Agent Orange. Many of those companies had reached a settlement with United States veterans for US $180 million in 1984. The judge's ruling stated that the contractors had no control over how the chemical was used and no liability, since they had originally manufactured the herbicide to kill plants and there was no intention to cause pain to humans, and therefore there was no criminal intent on behalf of the companies. The military was using Agent Orange at concentrations many times greater than the safe levels laid down by the companies. The Vietnamese cannot pursue the United States government itself, although at an intergovernmental level there has been significant work done on helping to clean up the damage. The error of Agent Orange lies not in its manufacture or use as a herbicide (though that is now banned too) but in its use as a weapon.

NO LIABILITY

MOTIVATION
anger
charity
envy
faith
gluttony
greed
hope
lust
pride
sloth

MURPHY'S LAW AND THE MISSING HYPHEN

July 22, 1962, 09:21:23 to 09:22:16

Main Culprit: NASA

Damage Done: Destruction of expensive hardware and nearly the end of humankind's exploration of other planets

Why: A missing hyphen caused the *Mariner* rocket to burn too soon

If it can go wrong, it will.

Edward Murphy, Jr.

The most expensive hyphen in history.

Arthur C. Clarke

There have been of course many mishaps in the history of discovery and exploration. Columbus might have graced these pages had he not been fortunate enough to discover a great continent, even though he thought he was on another one. Many died trying to find lakes, passages, and treasures that simply did not exist. Others, such as Burke and Wills, or Captain Scott, or George Mallory, gave their lives attempting to go, literally, where no man had gone before. Space travel was very much the same. Disasters have happened, of varying magnitudes and loss of life, mostly through a combination of human error and technological breakdown, or sometimes almost culpable negligence through cost-cutting in the wrong place. But the fate of several missions in the space program stand out as examples of sloth. One early incident nearly brought an end to planetary exploration. Later ones may have cost a lot more money (see pages 232–4), but this stands out precisely because of its startling similarity to these later mistakes and offers proof, yet again, that those who do not learn from history are condemned to repeat it.

MARINER 1
The launch of the ill-fated Atlas-Agena 5 carrying the Mariner 1 spacecraft on July 22, 1962.

MURPHY'S LAW

Not for nothing, as it turns out, was Murphy's Law promulgated during the rocket-sled "G-force" tests in the 1950s that were early stages of the space program. Edward Murphy, Jr. was an engineer at the tests who had to report to Lieutenant Stapp—who had nearly died on one test—that, in fact, the sensors had been put in backwards. Ironically, a more recent disaster of the space program—the crash-landing of the interplanetary probe *Genesis* at full tilt into the Utah desert in late 2004—turned out to have a similar cause: the decelerators had been installed back to front. These two bookends of the space program, half a century apart, stand as a testament to some strange behavior with very high monetary costs.

The first disaster cost the United States an enormous amount of money and nearly brought an early end to the whole American program of space exploration. The *Mariner 1* space probe was brought down—by a missing hyphen.

When the "space race" between the United States and the Soviet Union began in the late 1950s, NASA's Jet Propulsion Lab had come up with grand plans for a series of large, sophisticated interplanetary space probes, to be named *Mariner*. However, the launch of such large space probes was dependent on the development of a new and powerful booster, the Atlas-Centaur, and this development program proved troublesome. JPL finally had to settle on a less-sophisticated design, based on the simpler *Ranger* Moon probes. The stripped-down *Mariner* was originally named *Mariner Ranger* or just *Mariner R,* and would be launched on the available Atlas Agena B booster. Still, the *Mariner* program cost more than US $500 million.

Mariner 1 was supposed to be the first interplanetary spacecraft. It was the first of the *Mariner* series of unmanned probes, which were supposed to explore the nearby planets of Venus, Mercury, and Mars. *Mariner 1* had wings with solar cells to help power its voyage, and it was equipped with instruments for studying Venus, its planned destination. The probe was put on a rocket and launched on July 22, 1962. About four minutes after lift-off, however, the launch vehicle made an unscheduled maneuver and started to veer off course. The NASA official in charge of safety had less than a minute to decide whether to terminate the flight (and destroy millions of dollars' worth of equipment) or let it continue (and risk having the errant space probe crash into a populated area or the shipping lanes). He decided to abort the mission.

BACK-UP FAILURE

The mishap had two causes, according to a subsequent NASA investigation. First, there was a problem with the rocket's radio guidance system. But the mission's planners had prepared for that eventuality and a guidance computer was supposed to take over. Unfortunately, the guidance computer had a tiny programming error. A single character, a hyphen, was missing from the program. As a result of the missing hyphen, possibly a typo or a programmer's mistake, the spacecraft started making unnecessary course changes. The hyphen (indicating smoothing) was omitted from the expression "R-dot-bar sub n" ("n" = smoothed value of derivative of radius). The program should have read "R-dot-bar sub-n." This error led the software to treat normal minor variations of velocity as if they were serious, causing the computer to swing automatically into a series of unnecessary course corrections with erroneous steering commands, which finally threw the spacecraft off course. The programming mistake wasn't caught ahead of time since the radio guidance system had never failed during tests. The report stated, "Somehow a hyphen had been dropped from the guidance program loaded aboard the computer, allowing the flawed signals to command the rocket to veer left and nose down . . . Suffice it to say, the first American attempt at interplanetary flight failed for want of a hyphen." The vehicle cost more than US $80 million, prompting Arthur C. Clarke to refer to the error as "the most expensive hyphen in history."

Fortunately for NASA, there was another similar spacecraft ready to go. It's plausible that had *Mariner 2* not been ready within a month or two, the huge financial loss would have ended the nascent interplanetary program before it had really begun. *Mariner 2* launched successfully and completed the mission.

In between the *Challenger* and *Columbia* space shuttle disasters in 1986 and 2003 respectively, there came, in the late 1990s, a series of less well-known but avoidable and very costly mistakes, though thankfully no human lives were lost. The causes, as we shall see on pages 232–4, are remarkably similar to that of the *Mariner* disaster.

THE VEHICLE COST MORE THAN US $80 MILLION, PROMPTING ARTHUR C. CLARKE TO REFER TO THE ERROR AS "THE MOST EXPENSIVE HYPHEN IN HISTORY."

MOTIVATION
anger
charity
envy
faith
gluttony
greed
hope
lust
pride
sloth

NAURU'S BIRD DROPPINGS

1968–2005

Main Culprit: Hammer DeRoburt (1922–1992) and Bernard Dowiyogo (1946–2003)

Damage Done: Bankruptcy of country

Why: Failing to manage or preserve the country's one real asset

Being very conservative, they've blown between US $1.5 billion and US $2 billion since 1968. And they haven't done it on their own. Every shonky [an Australian colloquialism for "shady"] financier in the world descended on Nauru, and gave them bad advice. I think Australia's responsibility is to sort it out because we don't want a rogue state taken over by the mafia in the Pacific. If they're really short of money they should sell the island . . . sell it to a company that will develop it for tourism, for its fishing resources and for its mineral resources, pay them US $100–200 million for it and give them an annual income.

Helen Hughes, Centre for Independent Studies, Australia

Nauru, which lies between Australia and Hawaii, is the world's smallest republic, covering just over 5,000 acres (20 sq. km). It is also the setting for one of the most flagrant examples of idiocy one can imagine — the bankrupting of one of the world's richest countries (in per capita terms) in a matter of years by sheer greed. The story, remarkably, brings together the Russian mafia, the British West End stage, Collins Street in Melbourne, Afghan refugees, North Korean scientists, and bird droppings — a lot of bird droppings.

Called Pleasant Island by British whaling captain John Fearn in 1798, it did not remain pleasant for very long. By the time the Germans claimed it as a colony 90 years later, the inhabitants had used the guns left by passing whalers to kill each other, and 40 percent of the small population had died. In 1900 Albert Ellis, a prospector with the Pacific Phosphate Company, discovered that the island was covered in guano, dropped by seabirds over the centuries, which, mixed with the decaying microorganisms from the ocean floor and with the natural coral and limestone that formed the

THE LOCATION OF NAURU IN THE SOUTH PACIFIC

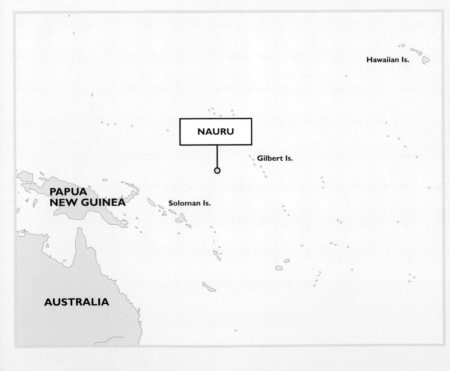

Nauru is a tiny island that covers approximately 5,000 acres (20 sq. km). It lies to the north-east of Australia and is relatively isolated as the nearest inhabited land lies 180 miles (300 km) to the east.

island, made for the richest and purest source of phosphate in the world. Exploitation under an imperial model began in 1907, with Nauru's colonial masters exploiting the wealth that came from the middle of the island. Essentially a littoral beach with a highland in the middle comprising pure phosphate, Nauru had very little natural water of its own and essentially no other resources. It is perhaps the most remote country in the world.

The island was captured by Australian forces during World War I in 1914 and Britain was subsequently granted a mandate, and shared mining rights with Australia and New Zealand under the aegis of the British Phosphate Commission. This arrangement continued until the oppressive Japanese occupation during World War II, when in March 1943 American air raids destroyed the Japanese phosphate facilities, removing Nauru's only source of income. The Australians ended up in charge of Nauru after its liberation, and so run down was the island that they actually offered to move the 600 remaining locals wholesale to Fraser Island off the Queensland coast and abandon Nauru forever. The locals refused and opted instead for a form of independence, and control over the phosphate mining process.

NAURU ACHIEVED, FOR WANT OF A BETTER WORD, INDEPENDENCE IN 1968. BY THE 1970s IT HAD THE GREATEST PER CAPITA INCOME IN THE WORLD.

Nauru achieved, for want of a better word, independence in 1968. By the 1970s it had the greatest per capita income in the world. Newer technology and eager mining companies, no longer held back by colonial administrators, mined the phosphate eagerly and efficiently. Nauru's population swelled to 12,000. Sadly, there really wasn't very much to do with the money. Most of it was held in a trust that made investments across the world—real estate in Australia, including the 50-story Nauru House in Melbourne, an investment in a West End musical based on the life of Leonardo da Vinci that lasted just under three weeks and lost millions, and many other dubious schemes—or was simply spent on jet-set living for government officials. The locals relied on imported food and developed a taste for less-than-healthy Western cuisine, resulting in a 50 percent incidence of diabetes, a huge obesity problem, and a male life expectancy of 55. The only real recreation was drinking beer, then driving around the island's circular road; the road death rate was the highest in the world.

Even this version of the good life had to come to an end. The phosphate began to run out in the early 1990s, the money had pretty much all gone, and the interior of the island, known as "topside," had become an ecological nightmare, a wasteland of jagged coral sticking up as high as 75 ft. (23 m), much like a moonscape. The country's few international assets were seized when GE Capital essentially put the entire island into bankruptcy to recover vast debts. It is estimated that over US $1 billion of cash and assets were squandered by mismanagement and greed, together with the effective destruction not only of the country's only natural resource, but the country itself. Locals in increasingly desperate poverty cling to the coastline and eke out what beer money they can. The phosphate will run out completely any day now.

The world is a strange place, though, and the inhabitants of Nauru are nothing if not resourceful. The mixture of their temporary wealth and independence did give them membership of international organizations including the United Nations, and the ability to act as international agents in ways that most countries choose not to. This type of activity was once limited to issuing attractive stamps with tropical scenes, or even, as with Liberia, acting to license commercial shipping around the world under "flags of convenience." But by the 1990s there were more lucrative alternatives: Nauru established itself online as the freewheeling off-shore banking capital of the world. The Russian mafia, in particular, allegedly used Nauru's "facilities" to launder as much as US $67 billion. Nauru had decreed that it was not necessary to keep records of deposits or withdrawals, in fact, any banking records at all, and that money vanished without a trace. Terrorist organizations also took advantage of Nauru's willingness to issue passports freely, so much so that by 2001 Nauru had ended up on America's list of rogue states.

It would appear then that the Americans made a strange deal with the government of Nauru. They would wipe out all debt and put in money to rebuild the island in exchange for a CIA-sponsored initiative. The Nauru government would formally approach China, abandon its acknowledgment of Taiwan, and open an embassy for the sole purpose of allowing North Korean nuclear scientists to defect. There would be a couple of "listening posts" set up on topside for good measure. Sadly, this all went wrong, as the Chinese had doubts about the supposed trade alliance, not least because Nauru had nothing left to trade and no money to buy anything with, but also because the embassy was staffed

A NEW DEAL

and paid for entirely by Westerners. The Americans pulled out of the deal, though, in another strange twist, the Nauru government took the CIA to the International Court to demand their money anyway, an interesting gambit in what was supposed to be a top-secret deal. Nonetheless, as part of the deal the Nauru government had terminated the offshore banking and passport business and so was again at a loss for income.

Almost immediately, another bizarre income stream turned up in the form of a leaking wooden boat carrying an assortment of refugees from Taliban rule in Afghanistan and from the civil war in Sri Lanka. The refugees' boat was en route to Australia, but was sinking, and they were fortunate to be spotted by a passing Norwegian cargo vessel and rescued. However, Australian Prime Minister John Howard, in the midst of a general election campaign in which immigration and refugees had become major issues, refused the refugees permission to land. Stateless and homeless, they had little choice but to stay on the Norwegian ship for weeks on end. Eventually, what Howard termed the "Pacific Solution" was hit upon. A refugee camp would be set up on Nauru, the nearest landmass to the ship, and the Australian government would pay millions in "aid" to Nauru in return for the refugees being given safe haven. It says much for what has happened to Pleasant Island over the last 200 years that upon seeing their new "home," fighting broke out, with the refugees demanding to stay on-board rather than be off-loaded into the wasteland that Nauru had become.

But who was to blame? Well, two men dominated politics during Nauru's short-lived rise, and subsequent fall: Hammer DeRoburt led the island to independence and served as President for over 20 years in four separate periods, while Bernard Dowiyogo held office in seven separate administrations for a total of 10 years. To the highest office attaches the greatest blame, and as the more illustrious, but far from scandal-free President Harry S. Truman said: "The buck stops here."

DRINKING JIM JONES'S KOOL-AID: THE JONESTOWN SUICIDES

November 18, 1978

MOTIVATION

anger
charity
envy
faith
gluttony
greed
hope
lust
pride
sloth

Main Culprits: Jim Jones (1931–1978) and his 900 followers

Damage Done: Their deaths

Why: Drinking poisoned Kool-Aid before the authorities came to get them

Take our life from us. We laid it down. We got tired. We didn't commit suicide. We committed an act of revolutionary suicide protesting the conditions of an inhumane world.

The last words of Jim Jones, caught on tape

During the fifth century BCE, according to Thucydides, a small group of believers at the Temple of Juno on the island of Corcyra (now known as Corfu) took their own lives when they realized their cause was lost. In the chaos and ruins of the People's Temple in Georgetown, Guyana, in November 1978, charismatic leader Jim Jones persuaded more than 900 of his followers to drink cyanide-laced Kool-Aid.

1970s USA IN MICROCOSM

Jonestown was perhaps a microcosm of 1970s' discontent: the heritage of Black Panther radicalism; the beginnings of televangelism; the lifestyle of the 1960s hippies; and the appearance of strange cults; coupled with the deep violence of the era, and the ease of belief in the coming nuclear apocalypse. The United States was barely out of Vietnam, its cities on fire, its leading politicians and leaders gunned down, its prestige and values in tatters. It is too easy to blame it all on one man, as has popularly been done, or even on the folly of the believers. It was all much more complex than that. Nonetheless, 900 or so people willingly drank poison out of faith in the words of one man. There is little evidence, though, that any of them thought they were going to a better hereafter. Jones did not preach the glories of Heaven. He had a much more apocalyptic and political message. Those who drank the Kool-Aid, with the exception of the unfortunate children whose parents poured it down their throats, believed their act to be one of "revolutionary suicide." Once it was clear their cause was lost, they chose to end their lives. From the few who escaped, there is little evidence of coercion.

Jim Jones was raised in Indianapolis. In the early '60s he became heavily involved in black radical politics and as a white man was subjected to much abuse, especially after attending and being deeply influenced by a Paul Robeson rally in Chicago. He was also heavily influenced by Philadelphia's self-styled black messiah Father Divine, a contemporary of Marcus Garvey and a believer in the black redemptive quest — the notion that there was no future for black people in the United States, that they had to go elsewhere. As early as 1962 Jones spent two years in Brazil looking for a place to colonize. He set up in his hometown the People's Temple, a mixture of radical Pentecostalism with liberal human services, such as food kitchens and the like, together with a political agenda in favor of civil rights and fiercely opposed to segregation. By 1964 Jones had found a property in Mendocino, California, having rejected an offer of land in San Francisco as being too prone to nuclear attack, and a caravan of predominantly black families had followed him there. Slowly they were joined by refugees from the counterculture of California, white middle-class families mixing somewhat uneasily with working-class black refugees from Indiana. It was far from an idyllic community, but it did grow, and by 1970 a centre had been opened on Geary Street in San Francisco where many people heard Jones preach his mixture of radical socialism and apocalyptic vision. Still, Jones sought a way out of the modern-day Babylon that he claimed America to be, and as his fame and notoriety grew in California, he found a potential home for his flock in Guyana, and started clearing land.

California proved fertile not just for the grapes that the People's Temple grew and sold, but for its population's willingness to listen to broadcasts by Jones, and to send in money. Much of the fortune amassed by the Temple came from money willingly sent in by an eager if gullible populace— this was the time of the appearance elsewhere of Jimmy Swaggart and others. But unlike some of the others, Jones does not appear to have engaged in personal accumulation of wealth, nor did he ever preach everlasting salvation in return for the money. It was all about a mixture of revolutionary socialism, black radicalism, and getting away from Babylon and the evils of capitalism. It is perhaps not surprising that this was a heady mix for many in the 1970s, and a peculiarly American mix at that. In fact, during the mid-decade Jones became heavily involved in politics, especially in the election of George Moscone as the mayor of San Francisco. This involvement led to increasing scrutiny of the Temple's finances and lifestyle. Jones had a much more revolutionary end in mind than mere party politics and, as in Indiana before, had a tendency to provoke fervid opposition. Money was filtering out at an increasing rate to the agricultural mission in Guyana, and a series of defections from the Temple aroused publicity. Then there was what looked like the beginnings of a tax investigation. Jones met with Black Panther Huey Newton, in Cuba, but wasn't interested in an armed struggle against the state.

Throughout 1978 the true followers slowly made their way to Guyana.

© Roger Ressmeyer | Corbis

JIM JONES
A shot of Jim Jones taken by photojournalist Roger Ressmeyer in 1978—the same year in which Jones led more than 900 of his followers to mass suicide.

By now a group of relatives had raised serious concerns about the fate of their loved ones, launching a series of legal struggles over the fate of children from estranged families. No matter how far they had gone to found their Zion, the group of Concerned Relatives would now follow them; they themselves were well funded and had an excellent PR machine. There was going to be no Promised Land for the People's Temple. Arriving at the mission, the settlers found privation, as their many predecessors fleeing religious persecution had in the past. The Pilgrim Fathers probably wouldn't have fared too well if at the first Thanksgiving they had also had to contend with the media and the IRS. The Guyanese authorities got caught up in the legal battles over custody. The Concerned Relatives were able to enlist a local congressman and a television crew to head for the People's Temple. California Congressman Leo Ryan and a group of journalists made the trek in November, and arrived at the camp on November 16. Angry negotiations and recriminations followed, but a settlement was reached and a small number of defectors were allowed to leave with Ryan. At the airstrip the group was ambushed by a tractor full of armed men and one of the defectors opened fire on Ryan and the journalists, three of whom died with Ryan and one of the defectors.

The likelihood is that this event was carefully staged by Jones as the instigating act that would anger his followers sufficiently to join him in the revolutionary suicide that he had clearly been planning over the previous month. A 100-pound (45-kg) container of potassium cyanide had been delivered, along with the herbicides and fertilizers being used for agricultural purposes, a week or so earlier. It seems probable that he was terminally ill. He also knew there was no chance that the group would be left in peace or survive out there. A tumultuous meeting took place where Jones persuaded the group that armed forces would descend on the camp and kill or imprison them. He was undoubtedly correct, in that the murder of a congressman would indeed have forced the hand of the authorities. Some remonstrated against the plan, and a few managed to escape. Jones's last words are the epigraph to this chapter.

What is most interesting about the mayhem that followed is the actions of some of the adherents who weren't in the Temple. Some had fled with the Temple's proceeds in an attempt to hand the money over to the

THERE WAS GOING TO BE NO PROMISED LAND FOR THE PEOPLE'S TEMPLE. ARRIVING AT THE MISSION, THE SETTLERS FOUND PRIVATION, AS THEIR MANY PREDECESSORS FLEEING RELIGIOUS PERSECUTION HAD IN THE PAST.

Soviet Union, but they were arrested. One woman who was in a house in Georgetown hiding out from her estranged husband, one of the Concerned Relatives, killed herself and her children with a butcher's knife. The Temple's American PR man called a press conference a few months later in Modesto, California. After trying and failing to defend the Temple against the inevitable cult accusations, he delivered a speech to the assembled journalists saying, "I can't disassociate myself from the people who died, nor do I want to. The people weren't brainwashed fanatics or cultists; the Temple was not a cult." He went into the motel bathroom and shot himself in the head. Gradually, other survivors agreed with the deprogrammers that they had been duped by an evil cult leader. People fought much more readily for the US $10 million in assets that the Temple left behind than for the bodies of the dead. The lawyer appointed to wind up the business affairs awarded himself fees of nearly US $500,000, while more than 200 unclaimed victims were buried two to a coffin in unmarked graves.

Of course, the 900 deserve their place in these pages: drinking cyanide-laced Kool-Aid is a desperate act. But for the most part, they harmed no one except themselves and their immediate families. They faced at best an uncertain future, jail for many, in a society they despised. Given the chance, most of those who had been deemed by their families to be there against their will had not taken the opportunity to go with Congressman Ryan. They weren't drugged, they weren't hypnotized, and while the point they were seeking to make was lost in a welter of media sensationalism and chest beating, the reader will find many more idiotic gestures in this book that caused a great deal more damage and were a lot less explicable than that of the Jonestown 900.

PEOPLE FOUGHT MUCH MORE READILY FOR THE US $10 MILLION IN ASSETS THAT THE TEMPLE LEFT BEHIND THAN FOR THE BODIES OF THE DEAD.

MOTIVATION
anger
charity
envy
faith
gluttony
greed
hope
lust
pride
sloth

UNION CARBIDE'S COST CUTTING: BHOPAL

December 3, 1984

Main Culprit: Union Carbide India

Damage Done: Up to 20,000 dead and horrific after-effects for 150,000 survivors

Why: No care or attention stood in the way of the delights of saving money

The poison cloud was so dense and searing that people were reduced to near blindness. As they gasped for breath its effects grew ever more suffocating. The gases burned the tissues of their eyes and lungs and attacked their nervous systems. People lost control of their bodies. Urine and faeces ran down their legs. Women lost their unborn children as they ran, their wombs spontaneously opening in bloody abortion.

Anonymous eyewitness account, from a survivor's website

The explosion at the Union Carbide chemical factory in Bhopal, India, claimed many lives and stands as a tribute to the craven indifference of those who ran the plant to the wellbeing of those working there. So poor were the safety measures, so determined was the company to maximize profit, and so slovenly were both the design of the plant and the procedures, that this early experiment in outsourcing and globalization will hopefully serve as a warning to those companies eager to save money in this way. Sloth and greed are the defining motivations.

The aftermath of the incident still rankles with many in India; some 20 years later, many still claim that their suffering has not been properly compensated, and blame is still disputed. The chief magistrate of Bhopal issued an indictment for criminal homicide in 1992 for the murder of 20,000 people, which has never been answered in court. Union Carbide, now part of Dow Chemical and long disassociated from the Indian company, claims the disaster was an act of sabotage and that it has amply compensated the victims, and has established the website www.bhopal.com to maintain these claims.

Certain facts are beyond dispute. Union Carbide established its Indian operation in the 1930s. The Bhopal factory was built in 1969, based on the design of a similar West Virginia plant but without the same standards of construction or materials. The plant was built in a highly populated part of the city. Bhopal is the capital of the Madhya Pradesh province in the center of India. Shortly after midnight on December 3, 1984, methyl isocyanate gas leaked from tank 610 at the Bhopal pesticide plant and the resulting explosion killed at least 3,800 people immediately in a fearsome gas cloud that spread over 12 square miles (20 sq. km) within minutes. Methyl isocyanate (MIC) was used to make the pesticide Sevin. It is a derivative of phosgene—better known as the poison gas used in World War I. Mixed with water, MIC boils and becomes unstable, which is what happened on that night. At least 150,000 people are thought to have been in some way disabled by the blast, and 20,000 is the generally accepted death toll. The city's miscarriage rate remains at seven times the Indian national average, and 4,000 people a day still line up for treatment at 23 special gas-relief

© Bettmann | Corbis

WARREN ANDERSON
Warren Anderson, chairman of Union Carbide, meets with a hostile press on December 10, 1984, following his return from India where he was arrested for his company's role in the Bhopal disaster.

BHOPAL ACTIVISTS
Protesters shout slogans
during a procession in
Bhopal on December 2,
2002 the 18th anniversary
of the 1984 disaster.
Demonstrators demanded
that former Union Carbide
chairman Warren Anderson
be hanged.

hospitals. An eyewitness of that night, Rashida Bi, a survivor who lost five gas-exposed family members to cancers, said those who escaped with their lives "are the unlucky ones; the lucky ones are those who died on that night."

By 1989 a final settlement had been reached with Union Carbide paying US $470 million to families of victims and survivors, against an initial claim of US $3.3 billion. By 1992 Union Carbide had pulled out of its ownership of Union Carbide India and the land itself, supposedly absolving it from all further liability in the case. The average disabled survivor receives just over US $2 a month in compensation. In 1999, when the official lease ran out, the plant was simply abandoned. The Indian government claims it lacks the massive resources necessary to clean up the site. Children play on land suffused with toxic chemicals, perhaps 5,000 tonnes of waste materials. Shareholders of Dow Chemical sued to prevent the purchase of Union Carbide, fearing that liability would not, in fact, go away, especially after Dow agreed to settle outstanding asbestos claims relating to Union Carbide—which may now run to US $2.2 billion. A 2004 European Commission reported that leaking chemicals are still affecting water supplies in the region. A 1999 Greenpeace report claimed mercury levels to be at nearly 6,000,000 times what is considered safe.

The problem lay in the plant's control room. The pressure gauge that would have indicated the build-up of MIC wasn't there at all. Other gauges had malfunctioned so often that even though they showed problems in the hours leading up to the explosion, the operators ignored them. One gauge was showing an empty tank as 22 percent full; others had been poorly calibrated. Before the explosion, MIC gas engulfed the control room. The operators did not have oxygen masks and had to flee for their lives, ending any faint hope that an operator could have saved the day. Not one of the six safety systems was working properly and, sabotage or not, cost-saving measures had clearly led to cuts in safety procedures. The work crew of the MIC unit had been cut from twelve to six; the maintenance crew from six to two. The dangers of mixing water with methyl isocyanate were well known. There had been at least three major incidents in the four years immediately preceding the disaster, killing one worker and seriously injuring 35, all from phosgene. Remedial

NOT ONE OF THE SIX SAFETY SYSTEMS WAS WORKING PROPERLY AND, SABOTAGE OR NOT, COST-SAVING MEASURES HAD CLEARLY LED TO CUTS IN SAFETY PROCEDURES.

measures had been taken at the West Virginia plant—but not at Bhopal. Various safety systems were intended to prevent just such an occurrence. All failed. Flares should have come on to burn off the escaping gas and didn't—a missing piece of pipe had not been replaced. Caustic washes could have neutralized it, but weren't turned on until it was too late. The refrigeration unit that would have kept the gas cool and prevented water entering the tank had been shut off to save money. And finally, the warning sirens had been turned off so as not to cause false alarm within the local community. Other investigations showed more problems that had led to these maintenance disasters; personnel problems and weak training plans meant most operators had little idea of the materials they were dealing with, much less their dangers. Instructions were written in English but many operators spoke only Hindi. Organizational rigidity led to no action being taken after the three earlier incidents involving MIC. Many of these issues had come up in a Union Carbide safety audit of 1982, but nothing had been done.

COST CUTTING

Though controversy reigns, it seems likely the plant had been losing money and that cuts had been ordered. Demand had gone down because of a prevailing drought, and there is clear evidence of deliberate cost cutting. Regardless of whether water was deliberately introduced into the tanks or not (commissions found that it was) no motive appears to have been found for the act of sabotage itself. The company claimed its safety systems were in place to prevent water from leaking in, rendering the other safety mechanisms less necessary, since what did happen couldn't happen. The absolute failure of safety precautions, which no one really denies, in a plant using what amounted to poison gas points to a level of neglect that chemical companies all agree should never be repeated. In 1991 the local government in Bhopal charged Warren Anderson, Union Carbide's CEO at the time of the disaster, with manslaughter. If tried in India and convicted, he faces a maximum of ten years in prison; but he has never stood trial before an Indian court. He has, instead, evaded an international arrest warrant and a summons to appear before an American court. For years his whereabouts were unknown, and it wasn't until August 2002 that Greenpeace found him, living in luxury in the Hamptons in New York. Neither the American nor the Indian government seems interested in disturbing him with extradition.

ROBERT MAXWELL AND THE *MIRROR* PENSIONERS

1984 – November 5, 1991

Main Culprit: Robert Maxwell (1923–1991)

Damage Done: The destruction of his own company's pension fund

Why: Multimillionaire "borrows" from employees' pension fund, then when he can't repay the money he goes missing from his yacht before his body is found floating in the Atlantic.

He left me reeling from his charm . . . his amazing panache and the sheer speed at which his brain worked. He was my inspiration and my hero.

Anne Robinson, former Maxwell journalist and now famous television presenter

Like a woolly mammoth stomping through a primeval forest, not immoral so much as pre-moral. You could at moments feel something bordering on pity and affection for him.

Peter Jay, former British ambassador to the United States

Jan Ludwig Hoch—also known as Cap'n Bob, the Bouncing Czech, and the man who revolutionized academic journal publishing—owned one of Britain's most famous tabloids. He twice led the corporate world into new methods of scandal now commonplace. He had to resign his position as a member of parliament, was alleged to be a Mossad spy, died under mysterious circumstances falling off his yacht, and was buried with honors on the Mount of Olives. There need be no one in the cast of this drama other than the man himself—Robert Maxwell.

Under enormous pressure from banks and the media, and based on his inability to accept the imminent failure of his business empire, Robert Maxwell helped himself to the entire proceeds of the pension funds of his many employees across the world, to save the flagging fortunes of his company, and lost them, ruining tens of thousands of families, from print workers at the London *Daily Mirror* to New York publishing executives at Macmillan. After Maxwell's mysterious death, with no one to prosecute but his hapless sons, and no money left after the corporate banks had been paid off, these pensions were never recovered. At the time, this wasn't even illegal. It had never occurred to the authorities that an owner would do anything so stupid and so heinous. They underestimated Robert Maxwell, as many others had in the past.

Jan Ludwig Hoch was born in a tiny village in the Carpathian mountains in what was then Czechoslovakia in 1923. His parents were Orthodox Jews who apparently died at the hands of the Nazis. He claimed never to have had a pair of shoes until he was seven. He fled to England at the age of 17, lied about his age, changed his name to Ian Robert Maxwell, joined the army, and fought with great distinction during World War II, as his early employees had daily cause to remember. When he came into work they had to rise and say, "Good Morning, Captain Maxwell." His war career, at least, seemed genuine enough. He was in the second wave of the Normandy landings and won the Military Cross for bravery under German fire in Holland. Maxwell stayed in Germany as part of the Information Division of the victorious Allies, restructuring the German newspaper industry. Soon after, he saw a gap in the scientific publishing world that had previously been largely conducted in German, and started his own company, Pergamon Press. Relocating to England, he found himself in the company of many Central European refugees,

**CAPTAIN
MAXWELL**

who revolutionized book publishing in this period. Always keen to embrace his new homeland, Maxwell entered politics, and, somewhat incongruously, given his rapidly growing wealth, he became a strongly left-wing member of the Labour party in 1964. In 1968 he tried and failed to buy BPCC, the leading British printer. The following year a planned sale of Pergamon to raise money for another shot at BPCC came to disaster. Serious questions were raised about accounting practices, mostly connected to dubious profits reported from transactions with other Maxwell companies. Interestingly, in the light of subsequent events, Maxwell was accused of buying up Pergamon shares with money from one of his own private companies in Switzerland to inflate the Pergamon share price and make the company appear more profitable and valuable than it was. So serious were the charges that he lost control of Pergamon and was forced to resign from parliament. A Department of Trade and Industry tribunal reached, after a three-year inquiry, what at that time was an almost unprecedented conclusion: "We regret having to conclude that, notwithstanding Mr. Maxwell's acknowledged abilities and energy, he is in our opinion not a person who can be relied on to exercise proper stewardship of a publicly quoted company." This conclusion only makes the willingness of investors and banks to allow Maxwell to create the subsequent catastrophe even more extraordinary.

THE COMEBACK

For ten years Maxwell regrouped. He was horrified by what had happened to him as owner of a public company, and determined that the disgrace should never happen again. He did not appreciate others meddling in his control over his empire, and determined not only that "nobody could tell me how to run my companies," but that no one, not even his family, would fully understand how he was running them. He set up a private trust in the principality of Liechtenstein and set out to buy back all he had lost—and more. No criminal charges were ever brought against him, and only a few years later he was allowed to buy a public company again. First he bought back Pergamon, but this time privately, and made it more profitable than ever. Then he finally bought BPCC, and by 1984 fulfilled one of his deepest ambitions by buying the *Daily Mirror*, Britain's most left-wing tabloid newspaper, where he frequently graced the front page with his gargantuan presence himself, often in support of charitable or patriotic causes. BPCC became Maxwell

Communications Corporation. In 1987 he returned to the business of book publishing and attempted to buy Harcourt Brace Jovanovich in the United States. So horrified was Jovanovich, himself born not 20 miles (33 km) away from Maxwell, and the son of a Polish miner, that he bankrupted himself and his company buying back shares so that the hated Maxwell could never take control. Undeterred and increasingly out of control, Maxwell bought and invested in a number of different interests, including cable TV, more printers, publishers in the United Kingdom and United States, banks and security companies, as well as the fashion house Christian Dior.

In 1988 Maxwell purchased the mighty American publisher Macmillan, which became Maxwell Macmillan, with himself as chairman and chief executive. It is still unclear whether by now any of this mélange of companies was actually making any money. Certainly there was little holding it together other than the mighty ego of the owner and the continued willingness of banks to fund the spree. A number of books attempting to expose some of Maxwell's practices were written, and Maxwell hired libel lawyer Anthony Julius (later to become Princess Diana's divorce lawyer) to use whatever means possible to stop the books from appearing. This even included buying out the paperback publisher of one of the books.

ROBERT MAXWELL
Born Jan Ludvík Hoch in Czechoslovakia on June 10, 1923, Robert Maxwell arrived in Britain as a refugee in 1940 and rose to prominence in the worlds of publishing and politics. This photograph was taken in 1984, the year in which Maxwell acquired Mirror Group Newspapers and Macmillan Publishing.

By 1990, though, even the banks were nervous. The American journalist Seymour Hersh published allegations about Maxwell's potential links with the Israeli Secret Service, the Mossad. The editor of the *Daily Mirror* was fired for merely mentioning another allegation about the connections between Maxwell's private life and his serious connections with international intelligence agencies. Some of the companies were sold off for immediate cash, including Pergamon. Famously, Maxwell sold Berlitz language schools to a Japanese publisher, only for lawyers to discover, after the money had been exchanged, that the company's ownership deeds were missing. Maxwell had already mortgaged Berlitz to a bank and not told anyone. His new daily newspaper, *The European*, was losing money at a fantastic rate. In the middle of all this, Maxwell bought New York's *Daily News*. But a few months later he disappeared from his yacht off the Canary Islands. His bloated body, identifiable by its considerable bulk, washed up a day or so later, and after no apparent autopsy, was flown to Israel where, to the astonishment of all in the United Kingdom, he was given an immediate and most formal state burial and interred on the sacred Mount of Olives.

IT WAS IN ROBERT MAXWELL'S NATURE TO LEAVE BEHIND A SCANDAL MUCH GREATER THAN ANYTHING EVEN HE HAD CONCOCTED IN HIS LIFETIME. IN THIS CASE, HE MANAGED TWO.

It was in Robert Maxwell's nature to leave behind a scandal much greater than anything even he had concocted in his lifetime. In this case, he managed two. The first being the mystery of his death—he had talked to his wife, his sons, his business associates, his libel lawyers, hours before his death and given no hint of being depressed or suicidal. It is not even easy to envisage a man of his bulk lifting himself over the side of a substantial luxury yacht. To this day, conspiracy theories reign, the most recent that he had been spying for the Mossad for decades, publishing the works of famous international celebrities being a wonderful cover for undercover work. Running desperately short of cash, he had approached the Israeli government for financial help, then threatened to uncover all of the Mossad's activities when none was forthcoming, which led to an assassination plot. Then, as the theory goes, the assassination was covered up by the funeral in which Maxwell was buried next to Israel's most revered heroes.

But for his almost 35,000 employees worldwide, things were much worse than anyone had imagined. He had learned rather more from the mistakes he made in 1969 than the regulators ever had, and had done a substantially better job of covering his tracks. And it has to be said that he laid the ground for similar corporate offenses against employees in the United States some 20 years later.

By the time the investigations (contained in a 500-page Department of Trade and Industry report) were completed, it emerged that Maxwell had siphoned close to US $1 billion from his own employees' pension plans. This seems to have started around 1985, when he borrowed money from one of the plans but paid it back the same year and didn't show the transaction on the books. No one noticed or cared, and as anyone who worked for Maxwell would attest, no one involved was going to say anything. Emboldened by this, the borrowing became more and more endemic and complicated. As 16 years previously, Maxwell boosted his company's share price by buying his own shares from off-shore private companies he also owned, except this time with his employees' money rather than his. No one ever really suggested that he didn't intend to repay as he did before; after all, from Maxwell's point of view, his companies were expanding, and were better every day. What safer way to take care of his employees' futures than by investing their money in his company for them? So complex were the ownership schemes that the fund managers for the plans, let alone the pensioners themselves, were not aware that their investments were all being earmarked for Maxwell companies. Decades later, employees in major American companies were at least told their salaries were invested in their own companies, even if they were given little choice. In 1988 Maxwell Communications borrowed around US $3 billion to finance the purchase of Macmillan and Official Airline Guides. He used the pension funds as collateral on the loans. In 1990 he was forced to repay some of this money and had to empty the pension fund to do so. No institution, none of his accountants or legal staff, appeared able or willing to stop him. And no auditor or financial regulator seemed to notice. But only the pension moneys were now holding the whole edifice together. Still he bought companies; after all, the more employees he had, the more pension money he had to spend. Not satisfied with the 20,000 or so employees of the Mirror Group, he now had substantial numbers of American employees as well. Finally, in late 1990 an astute financial journalist noted that the Maxwell pension plans were not invested in any of the FTSE 100 blue chip companies, save one, Maxwell Communications Corporation. Questions were asked, and there is no doubt that they were on Maxwell's mind that fateful night on his yacht.

Shortly after Maxwell's death it came to light that just less than £500 million (US $1 billion) was missing from the pension funds of the employees of Maxwell's various companies. An enormous media outcry led to a number of parliamentary review committees that took many years to report, and attempts were made to introduce more regulation to protect employees.

On December 3, 1991 Maxwell's sons and heirs Kevin and Ian resigned from their respective positions following the media revelations. And in 1992 Maxwell's companies filed for bankruptcy protection, while

Kevin was declared bankrupt with debts of over £400 million (US $800 million). In 1995 the Serious Fraud Office brought a prosecution against Kevin and Ian Maxwell for their part in the scandal, but both were acquitted in 1996. Although a 2001 Department of Trade and Industry report stated that the while the "prime responsibility" for the disaster lay with his father, "Kevin Maxwell's conduct was inexcusable."

A 2001 DEPARTMENT OF TRADE AND INDUSTRY REPORT STATED THAT THE WHILE THE "PRIME RESPONSIBILITY" FOR THE DISASTER LAY WITH HIS FATHER, "KEVIN MAXWELL'S CONDUCT WAS INEXCUSABLE."

Following a campaign by the pensioners who were set to suffer for Maxwell's misdeeds, the funds were partly restored by a £100 million (US $200 million) relief package from the British government and an out-of-court settlement in 1995, known as the "Major Settlement," which distributed £276 million (US $552 million) between four Maxwell pensions. But as late as 2002 the British government wrote to the pensioners telling them that their pensions would be half of what had been promised to them when the trust was closed.

Yet many who worked for Maxwell continued to defend, or at least attempt to explain, his actions as more than sheer greed. Robert Maxwell really believed in himself and that he could do no wrong.

"The most important lesson from all the events is that high ethical and professional standards must always be put before commercial advantage. The reputation of the financial markets depends on it," read the conclusion of the final Department of Trade and Industry report on the Maxwell case. No one was ever successfully prosecuted for their role in the case. As an article in *The Independent* pointed out, many senior employees of the Maxwell group at the time now occupy high positions in the media and government circles. Although "to do a Maxwell" became a byword for corporate greed and idiotic business decisions, recent events have shown all too clearly that the paltry £3 million (US $6 million) fine levied on Coopers Lybrand, Maxwell Communications' auditors, for their failures in the case, did little to stop it all from happening again.

THE SOVIET NUCLEAR LEGACY: CHERNOBYL

April 25, 1986

MOTIVATION

anger

charity

envy

faith

gluttony

greed

hope

lust

pride

sloth

Main Culprits: Soviet management culture

Damage Done: Perhaps 100,000 slow deaths from thyroid cancer

Why: Complete mismanagement of nuclear power plant test procedure results in massive meltdown

I can still picture the bright raspberry glow; the reactor radiated light from within somehow. I had never seen anything like it, even in the movies. Or read about it. When it got dark the whole town piled out onto their balconies, and people who didn't have one went to friends and neighbors who did. We were on the ninth floor, with great visibility. People took their small children outside, lifted them up and said, "Look, how beautiful! Don't forget this!" And these were people who worked at the reactor—engineers, laborers. And teachers. Physics teachers. We stood in the horrible black dust... talking... breathing... admiring. We did not know—that death could be so beautiful.

Unidentified eyewitness

On the night of April 25–26, 1986, an incident occurred in the Russian — now Ukrainian — town of Chernobyl, a name now synonymous with nuclear mishap. One moment led within 45 seconds to a nuclear explosion a hundred times larger than that of Hiroshima. One could argue that the world's entire nuclear power program is potentially more deadly than any folly outlined in these pages, of course, but the immediate impact was actually substantially less than that of countless other accidents. Only 31 people were killed by the explosion and another 50 or so rescue workers and firefighters in the immediate aftermath. However, the extent of the effects of the radiation remain unknown to this day.

Chernobyl lies 62 miles (100 km) north of Kiev, just south of the border with Belarus. It was a massive nuclear complex with four reactors, now closed down — only since 2000 — and is now the site of what is believed to be the largest movable structure ever built, a vast shell that encloses Reactor Number Four and allows machines and workers to continue remove the debris.

CAUSE FOR CONCERN

Two events in 1979 might have given cause for concern to the operators and workers at the complex. On February 21, 1979, future Soviet Premier Yuri Andropov, then chairman of the Ukrainian KGB, wrote a secret memorandum to the USSR Committee for State Security:

> According to data in the possession of the KGB of the USSR, design deviations and violations are occurring at various places at Chernobyl, and these could lead to mishaps and accidents . . . the leadership of the Directorate is not devoting proper attention.

One month later a partial meltdown occurred at Three Mile Island, an American nuclear facility at Harrisburg, Pennsylvania, which had been open for only a year. The reports into this incident over the years bear striking parallels with Chernobyl: poor design, inadequate training, weak systems, bad construction. Much has been made of Chernobyl as an emblem of the general malaise of the Soviet system, an allegory for the fall of the regime itself. But it is reasonably clear that the Three Mile Island incident was just one step away from a tragedy of equal proportions, and that one misstep, as happened in the Ukraine, could have had a similarly devastating effect on the entire eastern seaboard of the United States. Crucially, the chain of events leading to Three Mile Island began with the failure of a pressure valve. Operators believed incorrectly that safety systems would kick into place. By the time they realized what was happening, half the core had melted down and a major accident was only narrowly averted. Thousands had fled, a Roman Catholic priest had offered general absolution, and hysteria had prevailed for four to five days. The unfortunate residents of the town of Chernobyl didn't even get that warning.

On April 25, prior to a routine shutdown, the crew at Chernobyl-4 began preparing for a test to determine how long turbines would spin and supply power following a loss of the main electrical power supply. Similar tests had already been carried out at Chernobyl and other plants, despite the fact that these reactors were known to be very unstable at low power settings. The test was supposed to take place during the day shift when better-trained and more experienced workers were available. However, at 14:00, as power was being reduced, an emergency call from Kiev for more power led to a nine-hour delay in the procedure. Power reduction restarted only 50 minutes before midnight, and was still in progress as the night shift came on. Within half an hour a mistake on shifting the process to manual control had resulted in a dangerous lowering of coolant water. At 01:15 the automatic shutdown system was immobilized so that the test could continue. This test was not essential, but could be done only while the

THE TEST BEGINS

reactor was on its semi-annual shutdown, and great pressure was put on the operators to complete it. The night-shift operators were apparently unaware that the test posed any particular danger, let alone what that might be or how to prevent it. Despite a variety of warnings, insufficient cooling water, and abnormal indicators, the test began at 01:23:04 on the morning of April 26. Up to now, even beyond this point, no accident had occurred, the entire disaster stemmed from a series of errors in every facet of the process, but still would never have happened had one last error not occurred.

© Igor Kostin | Sygma | Corbis

EXCLUSION ZONE
A militia member affixes a forbidden area sign onto a fence situated within the off-limit radius of Chernobyl in October, 1989.

As the flow of coolant water diminished, power output increased. When the operator moved to shut down the reactor from its unstable condition arising from previous errors, a peculiarity of the design caused a power surge. The fuel elements ruptured and the explosive force of steam lifted the cover plate off the reactor, releasing fission products into the atmosphere. A second explosion threw out fuel and graphite from the core and allowed air to rush in, causing the graphite moderator to burst into flames. The reactor exploded just 56 seconds after the test began.

Within days, yellow rain was dropping across the region. More than 131,000 local inhabitants were evacuated immediately, followed within a week by a quarter of a million more. Thyroid cancer rates have more than doubled and are ultimately expected to cause the deaths of up to 100,000 people. Birth defects remain high across Belarus, which took the brunt of the fallout, and Ukraine. Radioactivity was found at unusually high levels as far away as Wales, and remains significant in the soil across Scandinavia and Germany. One-fifth of the population of Belarus has been relocated, and 2 million acres (8,000 sq. km) of farmland cannot be used. In 2000, 5 percent of Ukraine's GDP was being swallowed up by disaster mitigation efforts. The total cost is anticipated worldwide to be US $360 billion and take a total of 200 years to rectify.

AREAS AFFECTED BY FALLOUT FROM CHERNOBYL

This map shows the areas most affected by radioactive fallout throughout Europe, following the Chernobyl catastrophe on the night of April 25–26, 1986.

AHMED BADEEB, AFGHANISTAN, OSAMA BIN LADEN, AND THE CIA

January 1989 – September 11, 2001

MOTIVATION
anger
charity
envy
faith
gluttony
greed
hope
lust
pride
sloth

Main Culprits: The CIA through Ahmed Badeeb

Damage Done: Direct link to September 11, 2001

Why: Arming one potential enemy to fight another, then losing interest

For us, the idea was not to get involved more than necessary in the fight against the Russians, which was the business of the Americans, but rather to show our solidarity with our Islamist brothers. I discovered that it was not enough to fight in Afghanistan, but that we had to fight on all fronts against communist or Western oppression. The urgent thing was communism, but the next target was America ... This is an open war up to the end, until victory.

Osama bin Laden, April 1995

Afghanistan has been the end of many an imperial dream, dating back many centuries. No more formidable empire found its nemesis in Afghanistan, however, than the Soviet Union, which got bogged down in an Afghan adventure in the 1980s that left its army and its finances demoralized and bedraggled. The CIA and the Americans correctly saw the Soviet incursion into Afghanistan as a blunder that they could take full advantage of. As is the way of diplomacy, former enemies became friends, including some particularly unsavory elements. Unfortunately, the fall of the Soviet Union found the Americans believing too much of their own rhetoric and, with extraordinary sloth, they allowed the anticommunist elements they had themselves armed to become an enemy, not only ideologically antagonistic but extraordinarily well armed. Aiding and abetting the arming of a future enemy on such an alarming scale led directly to a series of anti-American terrorist attacks across the world, peaking in the events of September 11, 2001.

At the crossroads of Central Asia, Afghanistan has had a turbulent history. In 328 BCE, Alexander the Great entered the territory of present-day Afghanistan, then part of the Persian Empire, to capture Bactria (present-day Balkh). Invasions by the Scythians, White Huns, and Turks followed in succeeding centuries. In 642 CE, Arabs invaded the entire region and introduced Islam.

A REBEL BREEDING GROUND

Arab rule gave way to the Persians, who controlled the area until conquered by the Turkic Ghaznavids in 998. Mahmud of Ghazni (998–1030) consolidated the conquests of his predecessors and turned Ghazni into a great cultural center as well as a base for frequent forays into India. Following Mahmud's short-lived dynasty, various princes attempted to rule parts of the country until the Mongol invasion of 1219. The Mongol invasion, led by Genghis Khan, resulted in massive slaughter of the population, destruction of many cities, including Herat, Ghazni, and Balkh, and the despoliation of fertile agricultural areas.

Following Genghis Khan's death in 1227, a succession of petty chiefs and princes struggled for supremacy until late in the fourteenth century, when one of his descendants, Tamerlane, incorporated Afghanistan into his own vast Asian empire. Babur, a descendant of Tamerlane and the founder of India's Moghul dynasty at the beginning of the sixteenth century, made Kabul the capital of an Afghan principality.

In 1747 Ahmad Shah Durrani, the founder of what is known today as Afghanistan, established his rule. A Pashtun, Durrani was elected king by a tribal council after the assassination of the Persian ruler Nadir Shah at Khabushan in the same year. Throughout his reign, Durrani consolidated chieftainships, petty principalities, and fragmented provinces into one country. His rule extended from Mashad in the west to Kashmir and Delhi in the east, and from the Amu Darya (Oxus) River in the north to the Arabian Sea in the south. With the exception of a nine-month period in 1929, all of Afghanistan's rulers until the 1978 Marxist coup were from Durrani's Pashtun tribal confederation, and all were members of that tribe's Mohammadzai clan after 1818.

During the nineteenth century, collision between the expanding British Empire in the subcontinent and tsarist Russia significantly influenced Afghanistan in what was termed "The Great Game." British concern over Russian advances in Central Asia and growing influence in Persia culminated in two Anglo–Afghan wars over the Afghan throne. During the reign of Amir Abdur Rahman (1880–1901), the British and Russians officially established the boundaries of what would become modern Afghanistan. The British retained effective control over Kabul's foreign affairs, until the partition of India brought an end to their influence. American influence had never been that great in the region. The first American contact was made by Josiah Harlan, an adventurer from Pennsylvania, who was an advisor in Afghan politics in the 1830s, and the inspiration for Rudyard Kipling's story *The Man Who Would be King*. Diplomatic relations were established in 1934, and thereafter America made modest aid grants and the Peace Corps was active.

© Roger Ressmeyer | Corbis

CIA HEADQUARTERS
The Central Intelligence Agency's headquarters in Langley, Virginia. Photographed on June 14, 1990.

Muslim-governed Pakistan became a very different neighbor from British India, and when Iran, Afghanistan's neighbor to the south and east, came under the rule of the ayatollahs, there were radical Islamist states on both sides. The disasters of the Arab–Israeli wars had led to great disillusionment among many intellectuals in the Arab world. And the oil crisis of the 1970s had put untold billions into the hands of many sheikhs across the Arab world, especially in Saudi Arabia. Strong radical elements saw the reigning monarchs and presidents of Egypt, Syria and Saudi Arabia as dangerously Westernized.

SPHERE OF INFLUENCE

Historically, the Russians saw Afghanistan as part of their sphere of influence. They were also nervous about the increase of Islamic extremism spreading into some of the southern Soviet republics with large Muslim populations. An extremist regime in Kabul was seen as a significant threat to the security of the Soviet Union, so a coup was engineered and a puppet government installed.

Of course, the Americans didn't see things in the same light. The year 1979 was perhaps no longer the height of the Cold War, but the thoughts of the State Department were still dominated by the threat of communism, and this consideration overrode all others. In February 1979 the United States ambassador to Afghanistan Adolph Dubs, a noted expert on the Soviet Union, was kidnapped by Islamists demanding the release of two of their fellow militants. Negotiations between the kidnappers and the authorities stalled, and Dubs died in the ensuing hail of gunfire.

While America's diplomatic protest was relatively mild, this turning point saw the start of a program to undermine Soviet influence in Afghanistan. Initially this meant the withdrawal of any remaining aid to the Soviet-influenced regime; however, as is so often the case when foreign policy is simplified to a case of "my enemy's enemy is my friend," the CIA soon began to back the same Islamist elements that had wrested control of Iran from the shah and were taking American hostages in Tehran. The militants who had been decried as terrorists during the Iranian Hostage Crisis were now vaunted as freedom fighters.

The irony of America's support of the Mujaheddin in Afghanistan was that it was, in fact, very successful. The Soviet invasion of Afghanistan became its own version of Vietnam. Supported by American money, rebels armed with Stinger missiles wreaked havoc, and the Soviets, unable to control the country any more than their colonial predecessors had, withdrew in shame in 1989.

However, with the communist threat gone, the Americans simply lost interest. The State Department and the CIA, still reeling from the mistakes of Vietnam, had no desire to try and control the political process during the anti-Soviet jihad, and no interest at all in further involvement in Afghan affairs after the Soviets had gone. The policy was to focus on supplying arms to anyone who wanted to oppose the Soviets, regardless of their motivation. They left Pakistani and Saudi intelligence to sort out who was who among the rebels. Congress appropriated covert funds; the money would be flown to Riyadh where Ahmed Badeeb, chief of staff to Prince Turki al-Faisal, chief of Saudi intelligence, had almost free reign to distribute it.

Badeeb had been a schoolteacher, and one of his students in Jeddah had been Osama bin Laden, who was a peripheral agent of Saudi intelligence during the anti-Soviet insurgency. Bin Laden used his own personal fortune as well as Saudi and CIA money to establish the infrastructure, not only of the anti-Soviet jihad, but also his own ongoing network—al-Qaeda, meaning "the Base."

Founded in the late 1980s al-Qaeda's first headquarters were in Afghanistan and Pakistan, before being moved to Sudan around 1992. In the meantime the like-minded Islamist fundamentalist group the Taliban was gaining the upper hand in the bitter civil war that followed the Soviet withdrawal and captured Kabul in 1996—where bin Laden and al-Qaeda received a warm welcome that same year, when they were thrown out of Sudan.

Thus, American policy in general—although the United States Department of State hotly disputes this—and Ahmed Badeeb in particular were instrumental in arming the man who would become the FBI's "most wanted terrorist." And also in allowing a vacuum to develop following the Soviet exit from Afghanistan, which was soon to be filled by the unholy alliance of al-Qaeda and the Taliban. Regardless of the initial rights and wrongs of America's involvement in the anti-Soviet campaign, the cost of the subsequent ignorance, inattention, and disinterest in what might follow a Soviet withdrawal is still being counted today.

BADEEB HAD BEEN A SCHOOLTEACHER. ONE OF HIS STUDENTS IN JEDDAH HAD BEEN OSAMA BIN LADEN, WHO WAS A PERIPHERAL AGENT OF SAUDI INTELLIGENCE AT THE TIME.

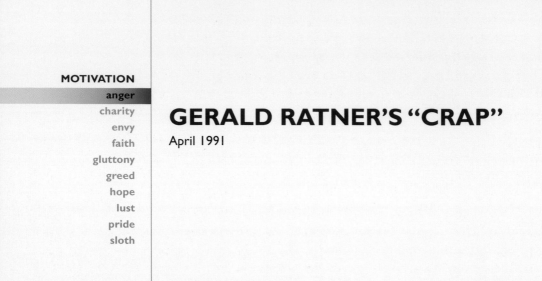

MOTIVATION

anger
charity
envy
faith
gluttony
greed
hope
lust
pride
sloth

GERALD RATNER'S "CRAP"

April 1991

Main Culprit: Gerald Ratner (b.1950)

Damage Done: Destruction of his own company

Why: Deriding his own product in public

It was a total nightmare. One day I was on top of the world, Mr. Big Shot flying on the Concorde . . . the next, I was a complete laughing stock. It was such a seismic event. It's like BC—before crap and afterwards.

Gerald Ratner, 2004

On April 27, 2005, Gerald Ratner took the stage at the annual convention of the United Kingdom Institute of Directors. Hardly remarkable in itself—a remade millionaire and Internet entrepreneur speaking to his peers at their annual shindig. But Ratner was returning to the stage where he had become infamous as the man who broke his own company in ten seconds.

SHEER IDIOCY

In this book there are many complex examples of idiocy, cases where blame could be spread across a number of people, or where many different types of foolishness and stupidity came into play. This is not one of those. Rarely has one man destroyed his own life's work so dramatically and so straightforwardly as Ratner. Rarely has an adage, in this case, "no publicity is bad publicity," been disproved so assuredly. And rarely has a mild obscenity become so rapidly associated, in the minds, at least, of the British, with one event. The only issue is why he did it; without an analyst at hand, the only plausible answer seems to be anger—not, as might normally be the case, at the world, or against a specific individual, but against himself and his own company and his own work.

Gerald Ratner inherited his father's jewelry business in 1984. Within six years he had turned a small retailer into a multimillion-dollar empire. Every British high street had a Ratner's store or one of the associated companies he had bought up. Similar in many ways to the Martha Stewart saga, Ratner was one of those businessmen in the public eye who was associated with his own product. Ratner's was where, to be blunt, working-class boys bought rings for working-class girls. The jewelry business remains a mystery to many observers, as it appears to be able to offer 70 percent discounts forever and still be highly profitable. It is a business that to a large extent depends not on designer labels, but on the name and reliability of the retailer whose box you present the product in. Television advertising stresses the moment rather than the product, the handing over of the box and the joy of acceptance. When it comes to what's inside most of us are unable to tell fake from real, or to identify the number of carats in the ring, so it's left to the plush lining of the box, and the name embossed upon it to set the tone. In other words, it's an industry based in large part on reputation

GERALD RATNER
A publicity shot of Gerald Ratner taken in 1990, a year before his infamous outburst.

and image, rather than the individual products. In fact, the editor of a leading jewelry magazine once reported that it was not uncommon for men to go into Fifth Avenue jewelers in New York with their girlfriends, buy very expensive jewelry on their credit cards, then call an hour later to replace the real diamonds with zirconium at a fraction of the cost, safe in the knowledge that they would never realize.

It is not uncommon for successful entrepreneurs to be asked to speak to "wannabees" about their success and how to emulate it. And Gerald Ratner personified that success. He had a chauffer-driven Bentley, helicopter, boat, luxury homes in London and its suburbs, and a reserved suite at Sandy Lane, the celebrity-favored resort in Barbados. He rubbed shoulders with Margaret Thatcher at 10 Downing Street, and was known in London, not unreasonably, as the man with the Midas touch. So it was that Gerald Ratner was asked to speak at a conference luncheon for the Institute of Directors in London in April 1991, before an audience of 6,000 businesspeople and journalists. In questions after the luncheon, he was asked how it was possible for his company to be selling a sherry decanter for the extraordinary price of £4.95 (about US $10). In one stunning moment of stupidity, he answered: "Because it's total crap."

ASKED HOW IT WAS POSSIBLE FOR HIS COMPANY TO BE SELLING A SHERRY DECANTER FOR THE EXTRAORDINARY PRICE OF £4.95 (ABOUT US $10). HE ANSWERED: "BECAUSE IT'S TOTAL CRAP."

He wasn't finished, though. Warming to the task of self-immolation, he then proclaimed that his company "sold a pair of earrings for under a pound, which is cheaper than a shrimp sandwich from Marks and Spencer, but probably wouldn't last as long."

To this day no one really knows what he was thinking, how anyone could so misunderstand the nature of their own business, or whether, as sometimes is the case, he had misunderstood the dangers of speaking in an offhand manner in a supposedly private place. Whatever the case, the impact was immediate and devastating. The media jumped on the remarks, which became instant front-page news. It no longer became remotely possible for a ring to be presented in a Ratner's box, the word "crap" becoming the *mot du jour* throughout the country. The company's shares dropped £500 million (about US $1 billion) in a matter of days. Ratner was thrown out of the company, lost his entire fortune, and the company was forced to change its name and rebrand completely to stave off bankruptcy. Ratner lost everything.

Ratner stayed quiet on the issue until recently. He shut himself away, became obsessed with getting fit, and then rather typically, bought the gym he went to and sold it for much more money. In an interview early in 2005 with the *Sunday Times*, he explained what happened:

> When I took over my father's jewelry business it was in trouble. The Ratners group that made £150 million [US $300 million] a year bore no resemblance to what I inherited. Then, in that 35-minute speech I referred to a sherry decanter we'd discontinued as "crap." I wasn't a polished businessman who put a spin on everything. But the publicity went on and on and share prices dropped to the point where I had to resign. There was no positive aspect to what happened to me. I loved what I did . . . everything in my life was wonderful and it was all taken away. It was a complete and utter disaster, and it still hurts.

It's a strange trait of those who suffer from their own idiocy that many years of reflection often do little for their understanding of self. A man who in half an hour destroyed his own livelihood and wiped out both his own wealth and that of his investors, still acts as if something was done *to* him not *by* him — presumably by the press.

THE COMEBACK?

There is a rather strange twist at the end of this story. Ratner in early 2003 decided to try to re-enter his favorite industry, this time setting up an online business to undercut the very type of store he himself had owned. Of all things, he attempted to buy his own name, long unused by the company that had once borne it. Strangely, they claimed it was a valuable asset and wouldn't sell it to him, forcing him instead to use his own first name. Now Gerald Online claims to be the UK's largest online jeweler. By all accounts, the online store is a great success, partly because of his own notoriety — which proves perhaps that all publicity is good publicity. Or that there's one born every minute. Ratner's comment on market research showing that consumers related well to his reappearance? "It's perverse, isn't it?"

MOTIVATION
anger
charity
envy
faith
gluttony
greed
hope
lust
pride
sloth

THE BANGLADESH FLOODS AND THE DESTRUCTION OF THE HIMALAYAN RAINFOREST

1998

Main Culprits: The British East India Company and its corporate successors

Damage Done: More than 1,000 dead and 70 percent of the country flooded

Why: Persistent deforestation of the lower Himalayas destroyed the natural order and flooded the low-lying regions

My friend came to me,
With sadness in his eyes,
He told me that he wanted help,
Before his country died,
Although I couldn't feel the pain,
I knew I'd have to try,
Now I'm asking all of you,
To help us save some lives.

George Harrison on Ravi Shankar, *Bangla Desh*
(Concert for Bangladesh, Madison Square Garden, 1971)

There is little doubt nowadays of the fine ecological balance in place across the planet. Fragile ecosystems depend on each other, and on the interaction between flora and fauna in order to remain in equilibrium; as we saw previously when alien species were introduced to devastating effect (see pages 83–7).

These delicate relationships mean that messing with one part of an ecosystem can have far-reaching consequences, stretching for thousands of miles. Waterways, for example, do not like to be changed. In the 1990s parts of the Mississippi in the spring floods angrily reasserted their original routes through the center of America despite the decades of efforts by the Army Corps of Engineers to alter their course. Miles of the Murray-Darling River system in Australia are dead salt-mired dry lands — the after-effects of well-meaning irrigation plans that stopped the natural salts from flowing out to sea. Even one of man's more spectacular successes in watercourse management, the turning of the Chicago River, went strangely adrift in 1992, when a worker drilled a hole into one of the underground cattle tunnels and the river simply drained away. Earthquake, volcano, fire, tsunami, and flood are part of nature's irresistible dynamic equilibrium and cannot be made to end by technology. And if the warnings of environmental lobbyists are correct then this book will need a new chapter (or perhaps volume) to deal with the catastrophic effects of global warming. But, putting what might happen to one side, more than enough damage has already taken place to justify the inclusion of this example of the folly of toying with ecosystems.

BANGLADESH

Bangladesh is the eighth most populous country in the world, with just the 91st largest area in the world. A low-lying delta region in the north-east of the Indian subcontinent, much of the country lies below sea level. More than 200 rivers pass through the country and most of its 134 million people live on the lower reaches of the River Ganges, where it meets the Brahmaputra and Meghna rivers and flows into the Bay of Bengal. It is the most densely populated area in the world, with high agricultural yields but great dangers from flood or famine. According to the United Nation's Human Development Report — 1999, an average of 10,928 are killed each year in Bangladesh by so-called natural disasters.

According to some scientists floods on such a scale are not natural but caused by deforestation and mountainside cultivation in the Himalayas, increasing the amount of sediment carried by rivers massively, raising the riverbeds and with it the likelihood of flooding.

But who is responsible for this deforestation? Blame is often levelled at individual farmers, and their necessarily short-term approach to cultivation; however, this is not the whole story. While further deforestation due to population increases has certainly taken place, it has its genesis (as do so many of the chapters in this book) with the earlier imperial era. In the nineteenth century, having lost its monopoly on trading tea from China, the British East India Company began

AREAS AFFECTED BY THE 1998 FLOODS

Bangladesh is crossed by hundreds of rivers on their way to the Ganges delta and the Bay of Bengal. Much of the country consists of low-lying floodplains. Deforestation of the southern foothills of the Himalayas, started by the British East India Company in order to create tea plantations in areas such as Assam and Darjeeling to the north, has been blamed for the build up of silt, reducing rivers' maximum capacity and increasing the likelihood of severe flooding. This map shows those areas affected by the 1998 floods.

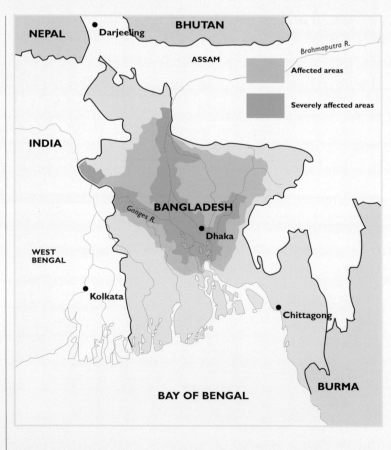

clearing large areas of land in north-east India for tea production. The venture proved a success and names such as Assam, a province on the Brahmaputra River, and Darjeeling, a northern town and district, are now synonymous with the teas that they produce—but at what cost for those further downstream?

The 1998 monsoon season produced the worst flooding in Bangladesh's history, with 70 percent of the country submerged, and 2.5 million acres (10,000 sq. km) of cropland destroyed. Between 30 and 40 million of the population of 126 million were affected. Floodwaters inundated most of the country for more than two months, destroying schools, government offices, and countless homes, and bringing diseases such as diarrhea and hepatitis. More than a thousand people were killed and millions left without food or shelter.

Every year, flooding particularly affects the poor in Bangladesh. According to the United Nations' *Human Development Report – 1999*, 51.1 percent of rural Bangladesh is poor and 26.3 percent in urban areas. The report reveals that since 1985, "the absolute number of poor rose by 1.2 percent annually . . . faster than any historically observed rate."

Little has been done to prevent the annual flooding. In 1989 a Flood Action Plan was formulated at a cost of US $170 million, which aimed to construct 2,174 miles (3,500 km) of embankments, some as high as 24.6 feet (7.5 m), for an estimated US $8 billion to US $12 billion. But major donors scaled down the project to US $4 billion before abandoning it altogether, citing various engineering, ecological, and social complexities. No alternative plan to control floods has been developed by the government or aid agencies since, and the problem still remains.

THE 1998 MONSOON SEASON PRODUCED THE WORST FLOODING IN BANGLADESH'S HISTORY, WITH 70 PERCENT OF THE COUNTRY SUBMERGED, AND 2.5 MILLION ACRES (10,000 SQ. KM) OF CROPLAND DESTROYED.

MOTIVATION

anger
charity
envy
faith
gluttony
greed
hope
lust
pride
sloth

LOCKHEED MARTIN, COLUMBINE, AND THE METRIC SYSTEM

April 30, 1999

Main Culprit: Lockheed Martin

Damage Done: A couple of billion dollars of taxpayers' money disintegrated in space

Why: No quality control

The software was verified at Lockheed Martin Astronautics in Littleton, Colo. The workforce there already had been stung by 900 impending job cuts and the murder of 12 students and a teacher at nearby Columbine High School.

Todd Halvorson, *Florida Today,* **May 8, 1999**

However, it is important to remember that space missions are a "one strike and you're out" activity... If not ready, do not launch.

Mars Program Independent Assessment Team report, 2000

Milstar—Military Strategic and Tactical Radar—was a program as important to United States defense needs as its name suggests. The first Milstars had gone up in 1994 and 1995, and with four near-geosynchronous satellites in space, were supposed to provide enduring, essential communications for the command and control of strategic and tactical forces through all levels of conflict. The missions were deemed crucially important and were monumentally expensive. The first Milstar 2 satellite had upgraded equipment, improved satellite-to-satellite communications, and devices to prevent jamming. It was the 27th launch carried by a Titan 4 Centaur rocket. But all three planned burns at the Centaur stage went off during the first orbit, within 89 seconds of liftoff, instead of over a six-hour period, putting the rocket hopelessly off course, and, like *Mariner* so many years before it, had to be blown up to avoid a potential crash. The reason finally given was that a decimal point was in the wrong place in the rocket's software (specifically, an engineer modified a file to recreate data but entered one parameter as -0.1992476 instead of the correct -1.992476). The mistake was caused, it was claimed in a crude PR effort, by software engineers being upset and angry about the Columbine school shooting. However, an inquiry pointed out that the company had no back-up safety checks of software engineers' work.

The launchers for this type of mission cost US $400 million. The top-secret satellite was estimated to cost over US $750 million. The cost of the faulty software loaded into the rocket to the American taxpayer was therefore immense. Perhaps more significantly in the long run, one of the surveillance targets of the satellite was post-Gulf War Iraq's missile program; estimates of which, it later transpired, Western intelligence services got seriously wrong.

Though Milstar 2 was blown to pieces over Cape Canaveral, NASA's reputation rested on its new missions to Mars, the success of which would undoubtedly wipe out memories of the unfortunate Milstar incident. The launches at the end of 1998 and early 1999 had gone well, and although Mars landings were prone to danger and failure, Mars missions had restarted in earnest in 1994, and the safe arrival and extraordinary discoveries of *Pathfinder* in 1996 and 1997 had stimulated public excitement about the red planet. The Mars Climate Orbiter was the next big mission, intended to orbit the planet for an extended period

ALL THREE PLANNED BURNS AT THE CENTAUR STAGE WENT OFF DURING THE FIRST ORBIT, WITHIN 89 SECONDS OF LIFTOFF, INSTEAD OF OVER A SIX-HOUR PERIOD, PUTTING THE ROCKET HOPELESSLY OFF COURSE.

to investigate the climate, and was launched in late 1998. On arrival on 23 September, 1999, MCO plunged straight into Mars's atmosphere instead of finding orbit. The commission report concluded that the data provided for getting into orbit supplied by contractor Lockheed Martin had been supplied in imperial units, but had been ordered in metric units. Annoying enough if you're on a long drive, but a fairly large problem half a billion miles (or should that be kilometers?) from home.

MARS

A rendered image of the sun rising over Mars, the destination for the Mars Climate Orbiter, which instead of finding orbit as intended, plunged through the atmosphere to impact on the surface on September 23, 1999.

While the MCO was in flight, the next mission was on the way, predestined also to an ignominious failure. The twin Mars Expedition Rovers, *Spirit* and *Opportunity*, failed to function once they landed because simple commands could not be understood. There is less certainty about the cause of these failures, since no contact was ever made, but it appeared to the commission that false signals had been sent out. These gave the impression that the Mars Polar Lander had reached the surface safely when it was still some way off the ground; the engines promptly shut down and the unfortunate craft plunged to its destruction. The reason, familiar to many a frustrated computer user, was that the file directory was full and could not accept commands. No provision had been made to delete the various files that had automatically been created as the craft made its way to Mars on autopilot.

THE Y2K THAT NEVER CAME

December 31, 1999

MOTIVATION

anger

charity

envy

faith

gluttony

greed

hope

lust

pride

sloth

Main Culprits: Much of the Western world

Damage Done: Hundreds of billions of dollars of wasted effort and stress

Why: Mass panic

We may not have got everything right, but at least we knew the century was going to end.

Douglas Adams

American (Airlines) has been a leading airline in addressing the year 2000 challenges . . . American has dedicated significant personnel and resources, including a budget of US $130 million, to address year 2000 compliance.

American Airline press release, December 1, 1999

One thousand years to the day after St. Peter's in Rome was filled with worshippers anxiously waiting for Pope Sylvester to grow horns and for the gates of Hell to open (see pages 41–4), a million or so people gathered in Times Square waiting for the ball to drop, planes to fall from the sky, lifts to crash to the ground, and their bank accounts to empty. While only a few around the world actually expected the physical world to come to an end, there were many more who expected their technologically sophisticated world to come crashing down around them, in perhaps the single greatest display of mass silliness ever experienced on earth.

As far back as 1958, a computer programmer drew attention to a potential problem in some early punch cards used for programming. To save money, the first two digits of the year were often eliminated. This meant that in 2000 all such programs would revert to 1900. No one took a great deal of notice, correctly surmising that neither the companies nor the hardware and software involved would still be around 40 years down the road. By the 1980s and 1990s, most potential problems had been identified and solved. But a series of doom-mongering books, the modern equivalents of the traveling monks predicting the end of the world in 999, managed to whip up storms of concern among an astonishingly credulous population.

You can buy *Time Bomb 2000! What the Year 2000 Computer Crisis Means to You!* by Edward and Jennifer Yourdon for one penny from the online book retailer Amazon. Back in 1997, it was a different story, as the book's blurb proudly indicated:

Time Bomb 2000! has become a worldwide bestseller because it doesn't just tell that there's a Y2K crisis on the way; it spells out how to evaluate your personal risks, and what you can do about them. As the crunch draws closer, this new edition, completely updated to reflect Y2K news in every key area of the economy, is essential reading for everyone who wants to survive Y2K! As more than 140,000 readers can already attest, *Time Bomb 2000* is the most practical guide to the Y2K crisis. Based on the newest information available, you'll learn what problems are likely to occur, how they will impact individuals and society, and what you can do to prepare. This edition contains updated coverage

© Reuters | Corbis

Y2K CONVERSION
John Koskinen, chair of The President's Council on Y2K conversion said the problem of changing "99" and "00" to 1999 and 2000 "affects virtually everything in the world."

of every major aspect of society, including communications, power distribution, transportation, finance, travel, medicine, social services, education, and employment. You'll find the latest expert assessments of the relative probabilities—and consequences—of failure. Best of all, the book presents practical contingency plans and fallback positions in the event the worst happens, for anyone worried about the Y2K problem, in other words, just about everyone.

Each chapter investigates a different area of computing and the possible effects of this disaster on each. From home PCs to world financial networks, the Yourdons explore a variety of "domino effects" that January 1, 2000, could trigger and the necessary time, effort, and cost to fix the aftermath. The impacts on real life could be anywhere between annoying and catastrophic, and the authors examine each extreme.

DÉJÀ VU

The role of the priests who were supposed to save the world's inhabitants of 999 from impending apocalypse was now played by the computer consultants. The "dot com" boom had so influenced everyone that any blip along the way would spell catastrophe and anyone who purported to be able to solve the issue made a fortune. Rarely can so much money have been made to protect mankind against a problem that didn't actually exist. So dependent had Western civilization become on gadgets and items that people did not realize that they were still willing to believe anything, no matter how outrageous. It is perhaps noteworthy that the Wall Street peak of the '90s boom was actually reached on January 14, 2000. From there the stock market lost over a third of its value in just three years, and the impact on the economy of this boom and subsequent bust has perhaps still to be fully estimated. Since the boom was itself largely predicated on non-existent profits by firms that barely existed (see pages 243–7), perhaps it was fitting that the bubble should peak in fixing a non-existent crisis.

But why did so many of us panic? In the tenth century a variety of phenomena and the general uncertainty and desperation of the times led many to build up a head of steam for the panic. In the twentieth, perhaps it was not so different. The century, after all, had seen two catastrophic world wars and the Holocaust, followed by the nuclear threat that overshadowed the youth of many of those in power and supposedly at the peak of their maturity in 2000. The threat of nuclear annihilation had dropped considerably, but the willingness to accept the likelihood of the end of civilization was present in many minds.

DON'T BELIEVE THE HYPE

While much of the hype was clearly misplaced, it is harder to ascertain an absolute cost of the paranoia that surrounded the advent of the new millennium. Certainly there were financial implications, but perhaps the lesson is not so much that mistakes were made—although they certainly were—but that despite a millennium's learning and all the technological advances that it has brought, the human psyche remains much the same as a thousand years before.

ROBERT MUGABE'S GREAT ZIMBABWE LAND GRAB

2000–2004

MOTIVATION
anger
charity
envy
faith
gluttony
greed
hope
lust
pride
sloth

Main Culprit: Robert Mugabe (b.1924)

Damage Done: Turning the breadbasket of Africa into a charity case

Why: Post-colonial dictator gets tired of waiting for land redistribution

I should make it clear that we do not accept that Britain has a special responsibility to meet the costs of land purchase in Zimbabwe. We are a new Government from diverse backgrounds without links to former colonial interests. My own origins are Irish and as you know we were colonized not colonizers.

Clare Short, British Secretary of State for International Development, 1997

It has been a phenomenal and absolute failure on every level.

Tendai Biti, Movement for Democratic Change

History has a habit of repeating itself, but even within the pages of this book the story of Robert Mugabe's attempts to right a colonial wrong stands out as a particularly sad one. These pages have seen famine visited on populations by their own leaders before, and we have also looked at the suffering of Africa, but Robert Mugabe has managed to combine these elements, making a mockery of the fertile lands of his own country, and abusing and ultimately starving his own people. Through a combination of anger, greed, pride, and envy, a country that even after independence was bountiful in the extreme, a net exporter of food, now receives food aid and massive shortages are reported in many places. The cause was not drought, disease, nor even warfare—the scourges that have led to dreadful famines in Ethiopia and Sudan—nor even the optimistic leap forward of Mao who wreaked havoc on his country while trying to improve its lot, but just the stupidity and impatience of an old man who did not consider his job of nation-building finished.

SHARING THE BLAME

Certainly there are other parties to share the blame, not least the British colonizers. The British South Africa Company grew in the late nineteenth century on the model of the British East India Company as settlers spread northwards from the Cape Colony, especially as the Zulu and Boer Wars began to destabilize the region. Rhodesia, named for Cecil Rhodes, was put together as a colony in the early years of the twentieth century, and was always rich farming land. In 1964 most of the territory was given independence—Nyasaland became Malawi; Northern Rhodesia became Zambia. Southern Rhodesia remained a colony and, in an unprecedented move, a group of militant white farmers, under the leadership of Ian Smith, unilaterally declared independence from England in 1965. For 15 years the white-dominated former colony remained a thorn in the side both of black Africa and of the United Kingdom, surviving sanctions of all sorts, relying to some extent on the white government of South Africa for support, and withstanding a civil war conducted by ZANU and ZAPU, two competing Marxist socialist, nationalist movements seeking majority rule in the country.

After a series of compromises and 15 bloody years of fighting, a major settlement was reached in 1980 at the Lancaster House conference in London. Elections were held, the country became Zimbabwe, and its capital, Salisbury, became Harare. Not without incident and not for the last time, a controversial election was won by ZANU and Robert Mugabe. Among the many reforms promised by the British government and the white settlers was land reform. Less than a percent of the population, all white, owned more than 70 percent of the land and essentially all of the farms, which had been simply appropriated in the early twentieth century as the property of the Crown Colony. The compromise promised "willing buyer, willing seller." The British would supply money to help pay for land only when white farmers were ready to sell. To the credit of the Mugabe regime the transition to black rule was so peaceful, for the most part, that the majority decided to stay. Those who did go back to what they fondly remembered as "the mother country" found the land of the Sex Pistols and the Brixton Riots not to their liking. Gradually, through the 1990s, as Mugabe's hold on power became absolute and he moved from being prime minister to president. With the government becoming less democratic and more autocratic, the emphasis moved away from voluntary exchange of land towards compulsory. In the face of an increasingly distasteful regime the British simply started to withdraw their aid, so compulsory purchase, even when the land was voluntarily ceded, became of no use to the reform movement.

By 2000 Mugabe had lost patience. He held a referendum—which he lost—on compulsory purchase without compensation. Within two weeks a shadowy group, the War Veterans Association, launched a violent and vicious campaign of seizing farms from their owners. They murdered both them and their black workers, and no effort was made to stop them, indeed, there was even encouragement from the government. If this was intended as a type of "ethnic cleansing," it worked.

ROBERT MUGABE
President Robert Mugabe of Zimbabwe delivers a speech on Armed Forces Day in Harare on August 15, 2006.

Of the 4,000 white farmers, only 300 or so now remain on the land. Most fled to neighboring African countries, to England, or to Iraq as security consultants. Unfortunately, neither money nor planning had gone into effective land transfer or into providing information on how to actually plant and grow the crops. Most of these farms were not smallholdings but major agribusiness enterprises, and without machinery or even money for fuel or seeds, the black farmers who did move onto the land had little hope of growing very much. Some farms can now be seen being ploughed by horse, the heavy machinery having been stripped along with the contents of the farmhouses.

Moreover, much of the land simply seems to have ended up in the hands of the ZANU faithful and their cronies, rather than anyone with the ability to farm it. Crop production has sunk to around one-third of 2001 levels in just a few years, with almost no hope of improvement. Recently even Mugabe has conceded that more than half the land seized now lies fallow. Many of the black urban middle classes have left the country because of food shortages and the country now suffers from stagflation—an economic term for the twin evils of high unemployment and hyperinflation. Maize production fell from a point where it could be exported to its current state where it is insufficient to meet domestic demand; while tobacco production fell 70 percent, exports falling 80 percent. This economic instability and lack of exports is a major source of further economic difficulties, as the lack of foreign currency that it engenders means that imported goods, including vital ones such as fuel, are increasingly hard to come by.

As is so often the case the tragedy is that these problems could have been avoided. Yes, colonial wrongs certainly existed, and reform was undoubtedly required. However, it seems that Mugabe's increasing hubris cost his country the stable and productive transition that was within its grasp, and instead plunged it into a chaotic state of misrule, from which it has yet to emerge.

CROP PRODUCTION HAS SUNK TO AROUND ONE-THIRD OF 2001 LEVELS IN JUST A FEW YEARS, WITH ALMOST NO HOPE OF IMPROVEMENT. RECENTLY EVEN MUGABE HAS CONCEDED THAT MORE THAN HALF THE LAND SEIZED NOW LIES FALLOW.

WALL STREET, ENRON, AND THOSE WHO BELIEVED

2001

MOTIVATION
anger
charity
envy
faith
gluttony
greed
hope
lust
pride
sloth

Main Culprits: Enron Corporation, accountants, brokers, and stock tipsters

Damage Done: Millions of dollars in lost investment and pension funds

Why: Everyone wanted to believe in the success of a business that didn't really exist

Williams: Ah, we want you guys to get a little creative.

Rich: OK.

Williams: And come up with a reason to go down.

Rich: OK.

Williams: Anything you want to do over there? Any ...

Rich: Ah ...

Williams: ...cleaning, anything like that?

Rich: Yeah. Yeah. There's some stuff we could be doin' tonight.

Bill: That's good.

Taped conversation between an Enron executive and an employee of a Nevada power plant, January 16, 2001

A fool and his money are easily parted. Over the centuries the greedy have gambled and lost their fortunes on foolish ventures and non-existent investment opportunities. They have readily fallen prey, from the South Sea Bubble to the "dot com" era, to the fabulous stories of railways that could never be built, riches that were not there, schemes that only needed a little capital to make millions in return—and then a little bit more. To some, the stock market has never seemed to be far removed from the racetrack. Both the inveterate horse gambler and the stock-market trader listen intently to the analysis and tips of journalists and pundits whose only real unifying feature is that, if they really did have all the answers, they wouldn't still be writing for newspapers and magazines. And the money in each case is put in the hands of a middleman. This could be a bookmaker, or a fancy-sounding investment bank with a good Manhattan address. Both types of institution are sometimes only too happy to give away a "hot tip" to ensnare you. And both, as recent years have demonstrated, are sometimes not averse to ensuring that the deck is stacked in their favor and proving the old saying, "There's a sucker born every minute."

MONEY FOR NOTHING

For every shady track-side shark with a sure-fire tip for the 4:30 race, there's a stock-market pundit with his or her hands firmly in the till ready to pump up a company's shares. The massive frauds perpetrated at Enron were not unique, although their scale and arrogance were breathtaking. Often the damage done in scams of this sort is generally the transfer of large sums of money from the rich to the cunning, but the story of Enron and the State of California transcends this.

Enron transformed itself from a fairly run-of-the-mill local energy company to a multimillion-dollar conglomerate through the cynical and extraordinary manipulation of many of the facets of modern technology and communication. Fired with the success of their Internet global energy trading scheme, they committed the fatal flaw shared by so many criminals before and since: they got too clever for their own good.

The company was formed in July 1985 as a result of the merger of Houston Natural Gas and InterNorth of Omaha, Nebraska. At the time it was hoped to become one of the leading interstate natural gas pipeline companies. By 1995 its executives had determined that Enron would become the world's leading energy company.

Staggeringly, at the time of writing, the Enron website still allows a rare glimpse into the workings of idiocy in real time. Although the main site is essentially a listing of current bankruptcy proceedings and asset sales, lovers of the bizarre can still go to the Press Room section and find the following:

> Enron Broadband Services is a leading provider of high quality, high bandwidth delivery and application services. The company's business model combines the power of the Enron Intelligent Network, Enron's Broadband Operating System, bandwidth trading and intermediation services, and high-bandwidth applications.

> Enron is one of the world's leading electricity, natural gas, and communications companies. The company, with revenues of US $101 billion in 2000, markets electricity and natural gas, delivers physical commodities and financial and risk management services to customers around the world, and has developed an intelligent network platform to facilitate online business. *Fortune Magazine* has named Enron "America's Most Innovative Company" for six consecutive years.

JEFFREY SKILLING
Former Enron CEO Jeffrey Skilling talks to reporters on October 23, 2006 outside the federal courthouse in Houston, having been sentenced to 24 years and four months in prison.

The story of Enron charts the growth from a small provincial pipeline company to a massive conglomerate that claimed to be operating in 30 countries and have sales of US $101 billion, and to be the sixth largest energy company in the world. Yet it accomplished all this, according to the website, with a growth in staff numbers from 15,075 in 1985 to just 18,000 in 2000. No wonder everyone was so impressed and investment banks marched to the Enron tune. No wonder Chief Executive Davis hobnobbed with his good friend the governor of Texas on his way to the White House, and *Fortune Magazine* worshipped at the Enron shrine. A rudimentary knowledge of business would suggest something was very wrong with so much growth and so few new employees. But apparently not. Enron claimed to be on the cusp of a revolutionary age—a traditional provider of services (energy), switching to become a provider of information, using the Internet pipeline rather than a natural-gas pipeline. It turned out, of course, to be all smoke-and-mirrors accounting and wishful-thinking press releases. Rather more sinister was the pressure exerted on financial analysts and journalists to keep pumping up the stock while CEO Jeffrey Skilling, among others, was rapidly selling his.

THE TOLL But what damage was done, other than to the unfortunate staff members and thousands of investors? It is worth remembering that much of the appeal of Enron to investors was that it was still an energy company—the combination of a successful traditional business, assets and actual products with the fly-by-nights of the "dot com" boomers gave a false sense of security. And it was the new arrogance of the Enron management coupled with their pure greed that led to a story that even now is only slowly becoming clear: the California energy crisis of 2001.

Oddly enough, it was old-fashioned price gouging and blatant profiteering that led to the crisis. Enron's executives realized in 2000 that they needed actual profits from somewhere and that the fake companies and partnerships and online scams could not go on forever. They realized that they had a stranglehold on the energy supply to California—and by restricting supply they could raise prices to a phenomenal level and profit accordingly. Enron controlled 3,500 megawatts of supply, enough for two million homes. As early as 1998, Operation Silver Peak was created at Enron to learn how to manipulate the system to their advantage, and internal memos urged: "California gaming—we always say that we need to increase this activity yet we never do. Need to work more closely with cash, scheduling, and real time to maximize opportunities." By 2000 Operation Death Star was in place, with the monopoly and the political backing to make it work.

Having created the shortage, Enron offered to sell power to Western states' desperate utility companies at wildly inflated prices. The conversation that serves as the epigraph to this article has been provided as evidence that Enron was deliberately closing down power plants at the height of the shortage. The next day, as rolling blackouts caused havoc across California, the Nevada plant in question had 52 potential megawatts of energy offline. At its peak, energy that usually cost US $36 a megawatt-hour was being sold for US $1,000 a megawatt-hour. There's more than circumstantial evidence that senior executives used the power that their political contributions, both in California and in Washington, had given them to ensure that suggested caps to energy prices did not take place.

In 2001 the bubble burst as Enron's procedural misconduct began to come to light, and its share price collapsed. When Enron went into Chapter 11 bankruptcy in December 2001, many of the companies involved took the opportunity to break their contracts. Enron promptly sued, and during the course of these lawsuits the truth of Enron's energy dealings began to emerge. One could argue that a company with as much to hide as Enron would do better to keep out of the courts, but there is more than enough idiocy to go around in this story. Estimates from utility companies are that Enron took them, and by extension their customers, for US $1 billion in "unjust profits." The repercussions were huge, the Californian economy was drained of US $10 billion in keeping utility companies from bankruptcy, and it was a major factor in the downfall of the state's governor, and the dramatic cuts in government services that followed. Enron also took Arthur Anderson, its auditor and previously one of the "big five" American accountancy firms, down with it. The spotlight then turned on Anderson's clients and a glut of high-profile business scandals followed. Enron's unwanted status as the largest bankruptcy ever was quickly usurped when WorldCom, another Anderson client, went bankrupt in the middle of 2002.

Ironically, if Enron could have just hung in there, its legitimate profits from the energy price spike caused by September 11, 2001 could have been astronomical without resorting to anything other than normal business practices. BP announced profits of US $2 billion in 2004 just from trading energy globally, much of its growth coming from the gaps in the market left by Enron's collapse. The distance between illegality and brilliance in the corporate world can be, to return to the analogy of the racetrack, little more than a short head.

THE BUBBLE BURSTS

MOTIVATION
anger
charity
envy
faith
gluttony
greed
hope
lust
pride
sloth

WHY A TEN-YEAR-OLD BRITISH GIRL KNEW MORE THAN THE THAI GOVERNMENT: THE BOXING DAY TSUNAMI

December 26, 2004

Main Culprits: South Asian governments

Damage Done: 230,000 dead, as many as 62,000 of whom could have been warned

Why: Governments decided nuclear weapons were more important than undersea ocean sensors

I didn't know what a tsunami was, but seeing your daughter so frightened makes you think something serious must be going on.

Penny Smith

All of a sudden the birds starting flying off in a great commotion . . . I looked up towards the sea and saw water coming at great speed. I knew I had to run. I ran out of the hotel and kept on running and never looked back.

Uditha Hettige, Sri Lankan naturalist

"It won't happen to me." It is the cry of the unprepared everywhere. But in the case of earthquakes and volcanoes, it will. It's the way the earth is. There will be another San Francisco earthquake. Mount St. Helen's will erupt again. It's simply a matter of when. The Ring of Fire is the name given to an extensive underwater fault stretching from Japan as far as Indonesia, responsible for many earthquakes and volcanoes including Krakatoa. Straddling the Pacific and Indian Oceans, the fault has frequently caused eruptions across the region.

When a fault occurs at a spot where the water is shallow enough, and the seabed shifts, the resulting disruption causes a tsunami, a wall of water that tends to flow undetected over wide ocean, but builds to a terrifying height as it approaches land. The majority of these take place in the Pacific Ocean, but the Indian Ocean has also seen many tsunamis, especially during the nineteenth century. In the same area as 2004, tsunamis were reported in 1797, 1833, 1843, and 1861, while the Krakatoa tsunami in 1883 killed 40,000. After the Chilean earthquake and tsunami in 1960, which killed 6,000, a comprehensive Pacific Ocean sensor array was established, but there was nothing similar in the Indian Ocean. Given that a complete deep-water early sensor system would cost only about US $30 million and the December 2004 tsunami caused billions of dollars of damage and claimed probably in excess of 200,000

AREAS AFFECTED BY THE 2004 TSUNAMI

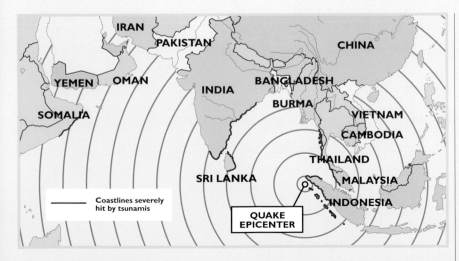

The map shows the epicenter of the quake and the coastlines that the resulting tsunamis hit on December 26, 2004. Indonesia bore the brunt of the catastrophe, with estimated fatalities of nearly 170,000. Further afield the people of Sri Lanka, India, and Thailand suffered heavy casualties, and as many as 62,000 who could have been warned, had a suitable system been in place, died needlessly.

lives, perhaps those governments that decided against the system out of sheer sloth might rethink before the next time. Beyond Indonesia, where victims would have had horrifyingly little time to escape because of their proximity, 35,000 died in Sri Lanka, between 12,000 and 18,000 in India, as many as 8,000 in Thailand and around 1,000 further afield. That's around 62,000 people who could have been warned.

THE AFTERMATH
A train near the southwest Sri Lankan resort of Hikkaduwa, destroyed by the tsunami on December 26, 2004.

A few years before the tragedy, a senior Thai meteorologist warned that the massive resort complex building at Phuket could be exceptionally vulnerable if—when—another tsunami struck. He demanded that sirens and alarms be installed at all hotels, and recommended that new buildings themselves be placed some way back from the beaches. For his trouble he was moved to another department and none of his suggestions were followed—the very suggestion of a tsunami might put tourists off, according to the government. So, little wonder that the Thai weatherman who saw the early reports and realized what was happening on December 26, 2004 decided to keep quiet.

Fortunately, the same reservations did not occur to Tilly Smith, on Mai Khao Beach in northern Phuket, Thailand that morning. While the great seismic detectors of the world's powers—not to mention the non-existent deep-ocean sensors of the South Asian countries—slumbered, Tilly, a ten-year-old English girl, was enjoying a Christmas holiday on the beach with her family when she saw the tide doing strange things.

A LESSON LEARNED

A few months before, at her school, her geography teacher had played videos of a 1980s tsunami disaster and explained what happened. Her mother described what happened next: "Tilly said she'd studied this at school. She talked about tectonic plates and an earthquake under the sea. She got more and more hysterical. In the end she was screaming at us to get off the beach."

There were other means of finding out what was happening and getting out of the way, none of which required especially modern technology. The inhabitants of Simulue, an island in Indonesia, had strong folk memories of a similar event in 1906, and several thousand fled to safety in the islands. Moreover, any islanders or beach dwellers who happened to observe the behavior of birds and other wildlife in the minutes leading up to the event were also able to escape. Interestingly, those coastal areas not remade by man survived comparatively well.

The offices in Vienna of the Comprehensive Nuclear Test Ban Treaty had machines that picked up the activity, but they were unmanned for the Christmas holidays. Messages were relayed to the United States base at Diego Garcia, which is right in the middle of the Indian Ocean, but apparently its staff had no idea who they should call and didn't have any appropriate phone numbers in their system. Australian embassies were informed and appear not to have passed this information on to anybody. A lot of excuses were made, particularly about time frames. But it took almost two hours from the time of the earthquake for the waves to reach Phuket, longer still to reach Sri Lanka. It takes ten minutes to clear a beach. The Japanese, who have been hit by more tsunamis than any other nation in the Pacific, have a three-minute alert system in place and reckon on being able to evacuate appropriate coastal areas within ten minutes of an earthquake. Although there was still the tragic loss of 239 lives when a huge wave hit Hokkaido in 1993, this relatively small number illustrates just how effective such a system can be.

So, a ten-year-old girl saved more than 100 people, and birds and animals, a few thousand more, while the pride of our modern technology saved none. Somehow it makes you think this final entry won't be the last manifestation of such human folly.

THE JAPANESE, WHO HAVE BEEN HIT BY MORE TSUNAMIS THAN ANY OTHER NATION IN THE PACIFIC, HAVE A THREE-MINUTE ALERT SYSTEM IN PLACE AND RECKON ON BEING ABLE TO EVACUATE APPROPRIATE COASTAL AREAS WITHIN TEN MINUTES OF AN EARTHQUAKE.

FURTHER READING

In general the most useful single book for any earnest student of history is a good historical atlas, of which *The Times Atlas of World History* is the best in my opinion. For general reference and fact-checking without expense or inconvenience the Internet is a remarkable resource, and in particular Wikipedia (www.wikipedia.org) is a great starting point, although its nature as an open-source encyclopedia to which almost anyone can contribute means that you should pay close attention to the references and footnotes if you want to make the most of it. You will also find some excellent links and information on www.bbc.co.uk.

Please note that, rather than being sources, the listings below for specific chapters are intended to add to your understanding.

This resource includes web addresses that may change due to the constantly evolving environment of the Internet. If you find a website address that does not work, please try a key-word search, because the information will often still be available online, but have moved to a different page.

In the Beginning: Adam and Eve

Anderson, Gary, and Michael Stone. *An Electronic Edition of "The Life of Adam and Eve."* 1995. 23 May 2005 http://jefferson.village. virginia.edu/anderson/iath.report.html

Milton, John. *Paradise Lost*. Edited by John Leonard. Penguin Classics. London: Penguin Books, 2000.

The Bible: Authorized King James Version. Edited by Stephen Prickett. Oxford World's Classics. Oxford: Oxford University Press, 1997.

Menelaus and His Lost Wife

Herodotus. *Histories*. Translated by Aubrey de Sélincourt. Penguin Classics. London: Penguin Books, 2003.

Homer. *Iliad*. 2nd ed. Translated by A. T. Murray, revised by William F. Wyatt. 2 vols. Loeb Classical Library. Cambridge Massachusetts: Harvard University Press, 1999.

Homer. *Odyssey*. 2nd ed. Translated by A. T. Murray, revised George E. Dimock. 2 vols. Loeb Classical Library. Cambridge Massachusetts: Harvard University Press, 1995.

Virgil. *The Aeneid*. Translated by David West. Penguin Classics. London: Penguin Books, 2003.

Wood, Michael. *In Search of the Trojan War*. Berkeley: University of California Press, 1998.

Hannibal and the Avalanche

Livy. *The War with Hannibal: Books XXI–XXX of the History of Rome from its Foundation*. Translated by Aubrey de Sélincourt, edited by Betty Radice. Penguin Classics. London: Penguin Books, 1972.

Polybius, *Histories. Vol. II*. Translated by W.R. Paton. Loeb Classical Library. Cambridge: Harvard University Press, 1923.

Prevas, John. *Hannibal Crosses the Alps: The Invasion of Italy and the Punic Wars*. Cambridge Massachusetts: Da Capo, 2001.

Cleopatra's Men

Shakespeare, William. *Antony and Cleopatra*. Edited by Barbara A. Mowat and Paul Werstine. Folger Shakespeare Library. New York: Washington Square Press, 2005.

Walker, Susan, and Peter Higgs, eds. *Cleopatra of Egypt: From History to Myth*. London: The British Museum Press, 2001.

Nero and the Burning of Rome

Cassius Dio Cocceianus. *Roman History. Vol VIII*. Translated by Earnest Cary and Herbert Baldwin Foster. Loeb Classical Library. Cambridge Massachusetts: Harvard University Press, 1925.

Griffin, Miriam. *Nero: The End of a Dynasty*. London/New York: Routledge, 2000.

Suetonius. *The Twelve Caesars*. Translated by Robert Graves. Penguin Classics. London: Penguin, 2000.

Tacitus, Cornelius. *Annals of Imperial Rome*. Rev. ed. Translated by Michael Grant. Penguin Classics. New York: Penguin Books, 1989.

Erik the Red's Dream Island: The First Real-Estate Scam

Brown, Dale Mackenzie. "The Fate of Greenland's Vikings." *Archaeological Institute of America*. [online feature] www.archaeology.org/online/features/greenland

Fitzhugh, William W., and Elisabeth I. Ward, eds. *Vikings: The North Atlantic Saga*. Washington, D.C.: Smithsonian Institution Press with the National Museum of Natural History, 2000.

National Museum of Natural History, Smithsonian Institute. "What Happened to the Greenland Norse?" *Vikings: The North Atlantic Saga*. Viking Voyage [virtual exhibition] www.mnh.si.edu/vikings/voyage/htmlonly/greenland.html

Jones, Gwyn, ed. *Erik the Red and Other Icelandic Sagas*. Oxford World's Classics. Oxford: Oxford University Press, 1999.

Pope Sylvester and the End of the World

Lacey, Robert, and Danny Danziger. *The Year 1000: What Life Was Like at the Turn of the First Millennium: an Englishman's World*. Boston: Back Bay/Little Brown, 2000.

Pope Alexander and the Search for Prester John

Mandeville, John. *The Travels of Sir John Mandeville*. Translated by C. W. R .D. Moseley. Penguin Classics. London: Penguin, 2005.

Silverberg, Robert. *The Realm of Prester John*. Athens, Ohio: Ohio University Press, 1996.

George Podiebrad, The Last Bohemian, and World Peace

Fudge, Thomas A. *The Crusade Against Heretics in Bohemia, 1418–1437: Sources and Documents for the Hussite Crusades*. London: Ashgate, 2002.

Moctezuma and the Returning God

Carrasco, David, and Moctezuma, Eduardo Matos. *Moctezuma's Mexico: Visions of the Aztec World*. 2nd ed. Boulder: University Press of Colorado, 2003.

Thomas, Hugh. *Conquest: Montezuma, Cortés and the Fall of Old Mexico*. New York: Simon and Schuster, 1995.

Johan de Witt, New Amsterdam, and Pulau Run: The Worst Deal Ever Made

Audus, L.J. *Spice Island Slaves: History of Japanese Prisoner-of-war Camps in Eastern Indonesia May 1943 – August 1945*. Richmond: Alma Publishers, 1996.

Milton, Giles. *Nathaniel's Nutmeg, or the True and Incredible Adventures of the Spice Trader Who Changed the Course of History*. New York: Penguin, 2000.

Lord North and King George III's Tea Party

Thomas, Peter David Garner. *Tea Party to Independence: The Third Phase of the American Revolution, 1773–1776*. Oxford: Clarendon Press/New York: Oxford University Press, 1991.

Whitely, Peter. *Lord North: The Prime Minister Who Lost America*. London: Hambledon Continuum, 2007.

Napoleon, the March to Russia, and Frankenstein

Seymour, Miranda. *Mary Shelley*. New York: Grove Press, 2000.

Wolfsehr, Thomas. *The Vitebsk Story & Advertisements Connecting Mary Shelley's Frankenstein to a Candid World*. www.hailmaryshelley.com/tcw.html

Zamoyski, Adam. *Moscow 1812: Napoleon's Fatal March*. New York: HarperCollins, 2004.

The War Office Versus the Lady with the Lamp: Disease in the Crimea

Baly, Monica. *Florence Nightingale and the Nursing Legacy*. 2nd ed. Chichester: John Wiley & Sons, 1997.

Smith, F. B. *Florence Nightingale: Reputation and Power*. New York: St Martin's Press, 1982.

The War Office Versus the Indian Army: Mutiny and Beef Fat

Stokes, Eric. *The Peasant Armed: The Indian Revolt of 1857*. Edited by C. A. Bayly. Oxford: Clarendon Press/New York: Oxford University Press, 1986.

Ward, Andrew. *Our Bones Are Scattered: The Cawnpore Massacres and the Indian Mutiny of 1857*. New York: Henry Holt, 1996.

Thomas Austin's Rabbits

Rabbit Free Australia. www.rabbitfreeaustralia.org.au

Rolla, Eric C. *They All Ran Wild: The Animals and Plants that Plague Australia*. London: Angus and Robertson, 1984.

General Custer and Little Bighorn

Custer, Elizabeth Bacon. *"Boots and Saddles", or Life in Dakota with General Custer*. Western Frontier Library, vol. 17. Norman: University of Oklahoma Press, 1961.

Custer, Elizabeth Bacon. *Following the Guidon*. Western Frontier Library, vol. 33. Norman: University of Oklahoma Press, 1994.

Custer, George Armstrong. *My Life on the Plains, or Personal Experiences with Indians*. Western Frontier Library, vol. 52. Norman: University of Oklahoma Press, 1977.

Wert, Jeffry D. *Custer: The Controversial Life of George Armstrong Custer*. New York: Simon and Schuster, 1996.

King Leopold and the Scramble for Africa

Hochschild, Adam. *King Leopold's Ghost: A Story of Greed, Terror, and Heroism in Colonial Africa*. Boston: Houghton Mifflin, 1999.

Pakenham, Thomas. *The Scramble for Africa*. New York: Perennial, 2003.

Nicholas, Alexandra, and the Mad Monk

Figes, Orlando. *A People's Tragedy: The Russian Revolution, 1891–1924*. New York: Penguin Books, 1998.

Moynahan, Brian. *Rasputin: The Saint Who Sinned*. New York: Da Capo, 1999.

Ismay's Lifeboats

Eaton, John P. and Charles A. Haas. *Titanic: Triumph and Tragedy*. 2nd ed. New York: Norton, 1995.

Quinn, Paul J. *Titanic at Two a.m.: Final Events Surrounding the Doomed Liner: An Illustrated Narrative with Survivor Accounts*. Saco, Maine: Fantail, 1997.

Gavrilo Princip's Deli Sandwich: The Assassination of Franz Ferdinand

Bell, J. Bowyer. *Assassin!* New York: St. Martin's Press, 1979.

Keegan, John. *The First World War*. New York: Vintage, 2000.

Winston Churchill and the Disaster at Gallipoli

Visiting Gallipoli and the Anzac Commemorative Site. Australia, Department of Veterans' Affairs. www.anzacsite.gov.au

Facey, A. B. *A Fortunate Life*. Camberwell: Penguin Books, 1985.

Winter, Denis. *25 April, 1915: The Inevitable Tragedy*. St. Lucia, Queensland: University of Queensland Press, 1994.

Trench Warfare, General Haig, and the Battle of the Somme

Coppard, George. *With a Machine Gun to Cambrai*. Cassell Military Paperbacks. London: Cassell, 1999.

Keegan, John. *The First World War*. New York: Vintage, 2000.

Maginot's Line

Allcorn, William, Jeff Vanelle, and Vincent Boulanger. *The Maginot Line, 1928–1945*. Oxford: Osprey, 2003.

Churchill, Winston S. *The Second World War*. London: Pimlico, 2002.

Kemp, Anthony. *The Maginot Line: Myth and Reality*. New York: Stein and Day, 1982.

Winston Churchill Strikes Again: The Map of Iraq

Simons, G. L. *Iraq: From Sumer to Post Suddam*. 3rd ed. New York: Palgrave MacMillan, 2004.

Stalin and the Great Purge

Conquest, Robert. *The Great Terror: A Reassessment*. New York: Oxford University Press, 1991.

Koestler, Arthur. *Darkness at Noon*. New York: Bantam, 1986.

Shenton Thomas's Little Men and the Fall of Singapore

Churchill, Winston S. *The Second World War*. London: Pimlico, 2002.

Swinson, Arthur. *Defeat in Malaya: The Fall of Singapore*. London: Macdonald, 1970.

Suhrawardy, Partition, and the Bengal Rice Famine

Asani Sanket (Distant Thunder). Dir. Satayjit Ray. Perfs. Soumitra Chatterjee, Babita. Balaka Movies, 1973.

Sen, Amartya. *Poverty and Famines: An Essay on Entitlement and Deprivation*. Oxford: Clarendon Press/New York: Oxford University Press, 1992.

Wakefield's Nuts

Watkins, Thayer. *The Tanganyikan Groundnut Affair*. Based on *The Groundnut Affair* by Alan Wood. www2.sjsu.edu/faculty/watkins/groundnt.htm

Wood, Alan. *The Groundnut Affair*. London: Bodley Head, 1950.

Mohammed Mossadegh, *Time's* Man of the Year, and Democracy in Iran

Gasiorowski, Mark J. *U.S. Foreign Policy and the Shah: Building a Client State in Iran*. Ithaca, New York: Cornell University Press, 1991.

Heiss, Mary Ann. *Empire and Nationhood: The United States, Great Britain and Iranian Oil, 1950–1954*. New York: Columbia University Press, 1997.

Risen, James. "Secrets of History: The CIA in Iran." *New York Times*, 16 April 2000, late edition—final.

The British Nuclear Legacy: The Black Mist of Maralinga

BBC Radio 4. *Fallout at Maralinga*. Documentary 29 April 2003, 8pm. www.bbc.co.uk/radio4/factual/falloutatmaralinga.shtml

Tame, Adrian and F. P. Robotham. *Maralinga: British A-Bomb Australian Legacy*. Melbourne: Fontana, 1982.

Sir Anthony Eden, Suez, and Speed

Tuner, Barry. *Suez 1956: The Inside Story of the First Oil War*. London: Hodder & Stoughton, 2007.

Yergin, Daniel. *The Prize: The Epic Quest for Oil, Money and Power*. New York: Simon and Schuster, 1991.

Grünenthal's Outstandingly Safe Drug: Thalidomide

Knightley, Phillip, Harold Evans, Elaine Potter and Marjorie Wallace. *Suffer The Children: The Story of Thalidomide*. New York: The Viking Press, 1979.

Stephens, Trent and Rock Brynner. *Dark Remedy: The Impact of Thalidomide and its Revival as a Vital Medicine*. Cambridge, Massachusets: Perseus Pub., 2001.

Thalidomide UK
www.thalidomideuk.com

Vaccines, Aids, and the Chimps of the Congo

Hooper, Edward. *The River: A Journey to the Source of HIV and AIDS*. New York: Back Bay/Little Brown, 2000.

Porter, Roy. "Tissue Wars." *London Review of Books* 22:5 2 March 2000. http://lrb.veriovps.co.uk/v22/n05/port02_.html

Mao and the Great Leap Forward

Becker, Jasper. *Hungry Ghosts: Mao's Secret Famine*. New York: Henry Holt, 1998.

Chang, Jung. *Wild Swans: Three Daughters of China*. London: Flamingo, 1993.

Robert McNamara's Terrible Wrong: Agent Orange

The Fog of War: Eleven Lessons from the Life of Robert S. McNamara. Dir. Errol Morris. Perf. Robert S. McNamara. Sony Picture Classics, 2003.

McNamara, Robert S. *In Retrospect*. New York: Random House, 1996.

Murphy's Law and the Missing Hyphen

National Aeronautics and Space Administration. www.nasa.gov

Vaughan, Diane. *The Challenger Launch Decision: Risky Technology, Culture and Deviance at NASA*. Chicago: University of Chicago Press, 1997.

Nauru's Bird Droppings

"The Middle of Nowhere." *This American Life*, Episode 253. Interview and documentary by Ira Glass. NPR, 3 Dec. 2003. www.thislife.org/pages/descriptions/03/253

McDaniel, Carl N. and John M. Gowdy. *Paradise for Sale: A Parable of Nature*. Berkeley: University of California Press, 2000.

Drinking Jim Jones's Kool-Aid: The Jonestown Suicides

Hall, John R. *Gone from the Promised Land: Jonestown in American Cultural History*. New Brunswick: Transaction, 1987.

Layton, Deborah. *Seductive Poison: A Jonestown Survivor's Story of Life and Death in the People's Temple*. New York: Anchor, 1999.

Union Carbide's Cost Cutting: Bhopal

Lapierre, Dominique and Javier Moro. *Five Past Midnight in Bhopal: The Epic Story of the World's Deadliest Industrial Disaster*. New York: Warner, 2002.

Union Carbide's Bhopal website
www.bhopal.com

Robert Maxwell and the *Mirror* Pensioners

Bower, Tom. *Maxwell: The Outsider*. New York: Viking, 1992.

Thomas, Gordon and Martin Dillon. *Robert Maxwell, Israel's Superspy: The Life and Murder of a Media Mogul*. New York: Carroll and Graf, 2003.

The Soviet Nuclear Legacy: Chernobyl

Chernobyl.info: The International Communications Platform on the Longterm Consequences of the Chernobyl Disaster. Swiss Agency for Development and Cooperation. 2002. www.chernobyl.info

Read, Piers Paul. *Ablaze: The Story of the Heroes and Victims of Chernobyl*. New York: Random House, 1993.

Ahmed Badeeb, Afghanistan, Osama bin Laden, and the CIA

Coll, Steve. *Ghost Wars: The Secret History of the CIA, Afghanistan and bin Laden, from the Soviet Invasion to September 10, 2001*. New York: Penguin Press, 2004.

Zegart, Amy B. *Spying Blind: The CIA, the FBI, and the Origins of 9/11*. Princeton: Princeton University Press, 2007.

Gerald Ratner's "Crap"

Ratner, Gerald. *Gerald Ratner: The Rise and Fall . . . and Rise Again*. Chichester: Wiley, 2007.

The Bangladesh Floods and the Destruction of the Himalayan Rainforest

Hofer, Thomas, and Bruno Messerli. *Floods in Bangladesh: History, Dynamics and Rethinking the Role of the Himalayas*. Tokyo: United Nations University, 2006.

Lockheed Martin, Columbine, and the Metric System

NASA's Mars Climate Orbiter website http://mars.jpl.nasa.gov/msp98/orbiter

The Y2K that Never Came

Yourdon, Edward and Jennifer Yourdon. *Time Bomb 2000: What the Year 2000 Computer Crisis Means to You!* Upper Saddle River, New Jersey: Prentice Hall PTR, 1998.

Robert Mugabe's Great Zimbabwe Land Grab

Blair, David. *Degrees in Violence: Robert Mugabe and the Struggle for Power in Zimbabwe*. New ed. London/New York: Continuum, 2003.

Wall Street, Enron, and Those Who Believed

McLean, Bethany and Peter Elkind. *The Smartest Guys in the Room: The Amazing Rise and Scandalous Fall of Enron*. New York: Portfolio, 2004.

Why a Ten-Year-Old British Girl Knew More than the Thai Government: The Boxing Day Tsunami

Tibballs, Geoff. *Tsunami: The World's Most Terrifying Natural Disaster*. London: Carlton Books, 2005.